Horace's

OXFORD APPROACHES TO
CLASSICAL LITERATURE

SERIES EDITORS
Kathleen Coleman and Richard Rutherford

OVID'S *Metamorphoses*
ELAINE FANTHAM

PLATO'S *Symposium*
RICHARD HUNTER

CAESAR'S *CivilWar*
WILLIAM W. BATSTONE
CYNTHIA DAMON

POLYBIUS' *Histories*
BRIAN C. McGING

TACITUS' *Annals*
RONALD MELLOR

XENOPHON'S *Anabasis*, OR *The Expedition of Cyrus*
MICHAEL A. FLOWER

ARISTOPHANES' *Frogs*
MARK GRIFFITH

CICERO'S *Catilinarians*
D.H. BERRY

HORACE'S *Odes*
RICHARD TARRANT

Horace's
Odes

Richard Tarrant

OXFORD
UNIVERSITY PRESS

OXFORD
UNIVERSITY PRESS

Oxford University Press is a department of the University of Oxford. It furthers the University's objective of excellence in research, scholarship, and education by publishing worldwide. Oxford is a registered trade mark of Oxford University Press in the UK and certain other countries.

Published in the United States of America by Oxford University Press
198 Madison Avenue, New York, NY 10016, United States of America.

© Oxford University Press 2020

All rights reserved. No part of this publication may be reproduced, stored in a retrieval system, or transmitted, in any form or by any means, without the prior permission in writing of Oxford University Press, or as expressly permitted by law, by license, or under terms agreed with the appropriate reproduction rights organization. Inquiries concerning reproduction outside the scope of the above should be sent to the Rights Department, Oxford University Press, at the address above.

You must not circulate this work in any other form and you must impose this same condition on any acquirer.

Library of Congress Cataloging-in-Publication Data
Names: Tarrant, Richard, 1945- author.
Title: Horace's odes / Richard Tarrant.
Other titles: Oxford approaches to classical literature.
Description: New York : Oxford University Press, 2020. |
Series: Oxford approaches to classical literature |
Includes bibliographical references and index.
Identifiers: LCCN 2019051772 (print) | LCCN 2019051773 (ebook) |
ISBN 9780195156751 (hardback) | ISBN 9780195156768 (paperback) |
ISBN 9780197515167 (epub) | ISBN 9780197515174 (online)
Subjects: LCSH: Horace. Carmina.
Classification: LCC PA6411 .T37 2020 (print) | LCC PA6411 (ebook) | DDC 874/.01—dc23
LC record available at https://lccn.loc.gov/2019051772
LC ebook record available at https://lccn.loc.gov/2019051773

1 3 5 7 9 8 6 4 2

Printed by LSC Communications, United States of America
Hardback printed by Bridgeport National Bindery, Inc., United States of America

To the memory of
ROBIN NISBET

Contents

Editors' Foreword *ix*

Preface and Acknowledgments *xiii*

Introduction: Reading the *Odes* Today *xvii*

1
Horace's Life *1*

2
Before the *Odes* *6*

3
To the Cool Grove: The Ascent to Lyric *25*

4
Odes 1–3: The Collection *35*

5
Three Odes *47*

6

Friendship and Advice   66

7

Amatory Poems   90

8

Political Poems   117

9

After the *Odes* 1: The Book of *Epistles*   141

10

Lyric Revisited: The *Carmen saeculare* and the Fourth Book of *Odes*   150

11

After the *Odes* 2: The Literary Epistles   183

12

Reception of the *Odes*: From Propertius to Seamus Heaney   190

Further Reading   219

Works Cited   223

General Index   229

Index of Passages   235

Editors' Foreword

The late twentieth and early twenty-first centuries have seen a massive expansion in courses dealing with ancient civilization and, in particular, the culture and literature of the Greek and Roman world. Never has there been such a flood of good translations available: Oxford's own World Classics, the Penguin Classics, the Hackett Library, and other series offer the English-speaking reader access to the masterpieces of classical literature from Homer to Augustine. The reader may, however, need more guidance in the interpretation and understanding of these works than can usually be provided in the relatively short introduction that prefaces a work in translation. There is a need for studies of individual works that will provide a clear, lively, and reliable account based on the most up-to-date scholarship without dwelling on the minutiae that are likely to distract or confuse the reader.

It is to meet this need that the present series has been devised. The title Oxford Approaches to Classical Literature deliberately puts the emphasis on the literary works themselves. The volumes in this series will each be concerned with a single work (with the exception of cases where a "book" or larger collection of poems is treated as one work). These are neither biographies nor accounts of literary movements or schools. Nor are they books devoted to the total oeuvre of one author: our first volumes consider Ovid's *Metamorphoses* and Plato's *Symposium*, not the works of Ovid or Plato as a whole. This is, however, a question of emphasis, and not a straitjacket: biographical issues, literary and cultural background, and related works by the same author are discussed where they are obviously relevant. Series authors have also been encouraged to consider the influence and legacy of the works in question. As the editors of this series, we intend these volumes to be accessible to the reader who is encountering the relevant work for the first time; but we also intend that each volume should do more than simply provide the basic facts, dates, and summaries that handbooks generally supply. We would like these books to be essays in criticism and interpretation that will do justice to the subtlety and complexity of the works under discussion. With this in mind, we have invited leading scholars to offer personal assessments and appreciations of their chosen works, anchored within the mainstream of classical scholarship. We have thought it particularly important that our authors be allowed to set their own agendas and to speak in their own voices rather than repeating the *idées reçues* of conventional wisdom in neutral tones.

    The title *Oxford Approaches to Classical Literature* has been chosen simply because the series is published by Oxford University Press, USA; it in no way implies a party line, either Oxonian or any other. We believe that different approaches are suited to different texts, and we expect each volume to have its own distinctive character. Advanced critical theory is neither compulsory nor excluded; what matters is whether it can be made to illuminate the text in question. The authors have been encouraged to avoid obscurity and jargon, bearing in mind the needs of the general reader; but, when important critical or narratological issues arise, they are presented to the reader as lucidly as possible.

    This series was originally conceived by Professor Charles Segal, an inspiring scholar and teacher whose intellectual energy and range of interests were matched by a humility and generosity of spirit. Although he was involved in the commissioning of a number of volumes, he did not—alas—live to see any of them published. The series is intended to convey something of the excitement and pleasure to be derived from reading the extraordinarily rich and varied literature of Greco-Roman antiquity. We hope that these volumes will form a worthy monument to a dedicated classical scholar who was committed to enabling the ancient texts to speak to the widest possible audience in the contemporary world.

Kathleen Coleman, Harvard University
Richard Rutherford, Christ Church, Oxford

Preface and Acknowledgments

When Kathleen Coleman and the late Charles Segal suggested that I write a book on Horace's *Odes* for the Oxford Approaches series, I was enormously flattered but also somewhat surprised, since I had not devoted much attention to Horace in my scholarly work and had published only one article on the *Odes*. That initial reaction was soon succeeded by recollections of my earliest encounters with Horace, and the realization that I had been living with his work for most of my adult life.

Horace was the first Latin author whom I read with an aim that went beyond producing an accurate translation. Reading the *Odes* as a student at Fordham College, in the idyllic surroundings of the New York Botanical Garden, was a transformative experience: I began to see, however dimly, what Latin poetry could be. Reading them alongside Steele Commager's recently published book was also a revelation, offering a glimpse of what appreciating and writing about poetry might be.

David Armstrong has offered what may be the best one-line description of Horace's poetry ever written: "In Horace even the simplest lines have so much going on" (Armstrong 1989: 44). One way of describing my aim in this book is to show readers at least some of what is going on, and to do so for readers who may not have access to Horace in Latin. To that end I have quoted Horace's own words more often than is usual in this series, always accompanied by a translation or explanation. Where possible I cite what I consider the most successful modern English version; when I have not found a version that conveys the aspects I regard as important, I have provided my own translation.

My primary audience is readers of poetry who are encountering Horace for the first time, but I hope that the book will also interest classicists and other readers who have some familiarity with his work. I have had to be selective, and in choosing topics for discussion I have given preference to those that put readers in contact with a variety of individual poems. I have tried to give my readers a sense of Horace's range of subjects, but I have also felt free to highlight what I consider his most successful poems.

The introduction and opening chapters provide background and orientation for reading the *Odes*. Readers who would like to get an immediate sense of how Horace's poetry works and why it is so enjoyable may wish to start with chapter 5, "Three Odes."

I often cite other critics and commentators, in both agreement and dissent, as a reminder that the criticism of poetry is a collaborative process; with Horace in particular, any reader who attempts to understand an ode steps into a river of interpretation that has been flowing for centuries. I have cited other views more generously when the interpretation of an ode or a passage is disputed, but I have not attempted a comprehensive coverage of critical opinion.

Noël Coward is supposed to have said that having to read a footnote was like having to go downstairs to answer the door while in the midst of making love. I have tried to minimize this form of readerly coitus interruptus by making most footnotes simple citations. A reader who prefers to ignore or defer reading them will lose nothing essential for following my argument.

One of the most pleasant results of finishing a book is the opportunity to thank the people who have helped bring it into being. My greatest debt of thanks is to the series editors, Kathleen Coleman and Richard Rutherford, both for many acute comments and for their unwavering support and encouragement during a long process of writing and revision. My wife, Jacqueline Brown, read and improved drafts of each chapter with her keen editorial eye and fine sense of style. I have also greatly benefited from comments by Cynthia Damon, who very kindly read the entire manuscript at a late stage. Audiences at Bryn Mawr College and Washington and Lee University offered helpful responses to earlier forms of chapters 7 and 12, respectively. Discussions with students in my 2016 class on the *Odes* helped me to clarify my thoughts on several poems. For advice and information on a variety of topics I am grateful to Rebecca Benefiel, Kevin Crotty, Lauren Curtis, Julia Gaisser, Tom Jenkins, John Morgan, Ellen Oliensis, Hope Patterson, Lee Pearcy, Ariane Schwartz, James Taylor, and Elliott Wilson. Special thanks to Jeanne Neumann for many stimulating conversations about Horace over the past three decades.

The book is dedicated to a great Horatian scholar and a beloved teacher.

Cambridge, Massachusetts
April 2019

Introduction

Reading the Odes *Today*

O 'tis a verse in Horace; I know it well.
I read it in the grammar long ago.

(*Titus Andronicus* 4.2.22–23)

The subject of this book is a body of lyric poetry by Quintus Horatius Flaccus ("Horace" in English), one of the leading writers of the Augustan Age of Latin literature. The *Odes* comprise 103 poems, which appeared in two distinct collections, the first in three books, containing eighty-eight poems published in 23 BCE, and the second, a single book of fifteen poems, which came out approximately ten years later.[1] The poems range in length from eight to eighty lines, but the majority are not longer than thirty lines. Their subject matter includes comments on the current state of Rome and on a variety of private themes, such as advice to friends, erotic relationships, and reflections on time and mortality.

That description hardly suggests the enormous impact the *Odes* have had and continue to have. Among poets Horace is acknowledged as a master of the craft, "adroitest of makers" in W. H. Auden's description. Some years ago J. D. McClatchy was able to enlist thirty-five British and American poets to contribute translations

---

[1] Henceforth, unless otherwise specified, all dates relating to the ancient world are BCE.

Horace's Odes. Richard Tarrant, Oxford University Press (2020). © Oxford University Press.
DOI: 10.1093/oso/9780195156751.001.0001

of individual odes to a collaborative translation.[2] No other classical poet commands that broad respect and affection, and McClatchy suggests a reason for it when he calls Horace "the man who first gave us the lyrics by which we have understood the nature and duty of poetry itself" (2002: 6).

But Horace no longer occupies the privileged position in the wider culture that he held in the eighteenth and nineteenth centuries, when familiarity with his work was a badge of cultural respectability and Horatian quotations—usually in the original Latin—were the common coin of educated discourse. In 1741 Sir Robert Walpole, defending himself in Parliament against an impeachment proceeding brought by William Pulteney, concluded with the thought that he had been guilty of nothing and need grow pale at no wrongdoing: "*Nil conscire sibi nulli pallescere culpae*" (*Epistles* 1.1.61). Pulteney leapt at once to correct Walpole's grammar: "Your Latin is as bad as your logic: *nullA pallescere culpA!*" The matter was appealed to the clerk of Parliament, who correctly rejected Walpole's reading in favor of Pulteney's.[3] Horace is still being quoted in the Houses of Parliament, but now he is being translated, at times incorrectly. According to the Hansard Debates for November 23, 2001, Mr. Edward O'Hara (Labour, member for Knowsley South) delivered a speech in which he said, "Let me quote Horace, who wrote: '*Eheu fugaces, Postume, Postume, Labuntur anni*,' which translates as 'Alas fleeing Postumus, the years glide by'" (or rather "Alas, Postumus, Postumus, the fleeting years glide by").

Horace's poems were long endowed with a sense of comfortable familiarity. The most popular were referred to in shorthand, "the Pyrrha ode" (1.5) or "the Soracte ode" (1.9) or "the Cleopatra ode" (1.37), and sometimes by their opening words in Latin: *Persicos odi* (1.38) or *O fons Bandusiae* (3.13). Now those practices are more or less limited to professional classicists.

---

[2] McClatchy 2002.
[3] Ogilvie 1964: 45.

As recently as 1962, Steele Commager could write that "*carpe diem, aurea mediocritas*, and *simplex munditiis* are practically household terms."[4] Only one of those phrases, *carpe diem* (usually translated "Seize the day"), still has widespread currency, and most of the contexts in which it appears have no relation to Horace: as the name of a guesthouse in Provincetown, Massachusetts; a restaurant in Charlotte, North Carolina; and a bistro in Decatur, Georgia; it is also the name of a thoroughbred racehorse which placed tenth in the 2015 Kentucky Derby. My most memorable sighting of the phrase was on a California vanity license plate, SEEZ2DA; the car was a new-model BMW convertible, so the driver may have taken Horace's injunction to heart. (For *carpe diem* in its original context see 51–52.)

Horace remains a ghostly presence as a source of Latin mottos, especially for educational institutions. The motto of the Massachusetts Institute of Technology, *Mens et Manus* ("Mind and Hand"), may derive from *Ars Poetica* 348, *manus et mens*. The Channing School for Select Young Ladies, a Unitarian establishment in North London, rejoices in the phrase *Cras ingens iterabimus aequor* ("Tomorrow we will recross the huge sea"), taken from *Odes* 1.7.32. The University of Toronto can lay claim to a Horatian trifecta: the motto of the university is *Velut Arbor Aevo* ("As a tree [grows] over time," from *Odes* 1.12.45), University College has *Parum claris lucem dare* ("To shed light on the obscure," *Ars Poetica* 448), and the residents of Massey College are exhorted *Sapere aude* ("Dare to be wise," *Epistles* 1.2.40), also the motto of at least a dozen other schools, among them Manchester Grammar School and the University of Otago in New Zealand.

While in some ways a loss, Horace's changed position can also be liberating: no longer charged with carrying the burden of the Western literary tradition, Horace can be appreciated simply as a master poet. In particular it is probably an advantage for him that he is no longer a standard school author—a fate that he pretended

---

[4] Commager 1962: vii.

to foresee with dread (*Epistles* 1.20.17–18) and one that soon befell him. There is a mini-tradition of British writers who hated being dragged through Horace at school and who only came to appreciate him later in life, if then; it includes Byron (whose recollection of "the drilled dull lesson, forced down word by word" led him to say, "Then farewell Horace, whom I hated so"),[5] Tennyson ("I was so overdosed with Horace that I hardly do him justice even now that I am old"),[6] and Kipling ("C[rofts] taught me to loathe Horace for two years; to forget him for twenty, and to love him for the rest of my days and through many sleepless nights").[7]

As Horace has become less familiar than he was in previous centuries, he has ceased to appear as knowable as he seemed to those earlier times. In an extraordinary reversal, the poet who was once regarded as the most forthcoming of ancient writers is now thought to be one of the most elusive, "this master of deceptive self-revelation" in Jasper Griffin's words.[8]

The earlier sense of knowing Horace was probably connected to the fact that we can visualize him to an extent unique among classical authors. Horace describes himself as short in stature and prematurely gray (*Epist.* 1.20.24–25). The biography by Suetonius more bluntly calls him "short and fat" and quotes from a letter of Augustus twitting him on his physique ("It is height you lack, not girth"). Horace's corpulence is as firmly fixed a part of his image as his mellow wisdom, and the two elements may be connected, as if his shape suggested an absence of sharp edges in his outlook: "a chubby little man with a chubby little philosophy," as he was once described.[9]

---

[5] *Childe Harold's Pilgrimage* 4.77
[6] Recalled by Hallam Tennyson 1899: i.16).
[7] Kipling 1937: 32–33.
[8] Griffin 1997: 67
[9] According to my former Toronto colleague John Rist, that description was offered by a member of the audience after a lecture on Horace by Niall Rudd; what makes the anecdote even more delicious is the fact that Rudd was a person of short stature and a certain rotundity of shape.

Readers who believe that they know the "real" Horace often fashion him in their own image. In nineteenth-century England Horace was often treated as an honorary Victorian, while Robin Nisbet's Horace has more than a touch of the Scottish rationalist, and the "slippery" Horace of much recent criticism has an obvious appeal for critics of a postmodern bent.[10]

Our understanding of Horace has also been affected by a more general change in the way we read classical literature. Instead of imagining a poet communing directly with his readers, we are now much more inclined to place Horace in a long tradition of ancient poetry and to see him in dialogue with his predecessors, both Greek and Latin. (For an example of a poem whose interpretation calls for that style of reading, see 107–08 on *Odes* 1.22.)

The main compensation for sacrificing the knowable Horace is the chance to find what he has to say more interesting. Instead of a purveyor of trite moralizing sentiments, Horace can be seen as a writer who observes the human condition without illusions and with a deep-seated sense of irony. We can also become more aware of his less jovial, more anxiety-laden moods, what in a late ode he called the "black cares" (*atrae curae*, 4.11.35–36), a form of *Angst* that wine, companionship, and poetry could alleviate but not entirely banish.

Because the *Odes* have long been recognized as a classic, they have often been exempted from the kinds of evaluation to which collections of poems are normally subjected, such as questions of quality (are all the poems equally successful?) or range (are there subjects that Horace can't do, or doesn't do well?). The acknowledgment of excellence can be a deterrent to criticism. I have therefore highlighted readings that resist falling under the spell of Horace's verbal mastery or that focus on the strategies by which he achieves his effects.

One of my models has been the late Robin Nisbet. I can still recall the pleasurable shock of reading such tartly phrased judgments

---

[10] Fowler 1993 especially 276.

as "The ode lacks nothing except seriousness and involvement" (on 1.5) or "A masterpiece of compact and tasteless ingenuity" (on 2.5), and the ensuing realization that there was a way of writing about Horace that did not consist of bland paraphrase or unquestioning admiration.[11] The commentary team of Nisbet and Hubbard was similarly ready to issue crisp assessments of individual odes such as "An accomplished piece of versification, but little more" (on 1.3) or "Does not fulfill its considerable pretensions" (on 1.12). Other critics who have expressed themselves with refreshing candor include Kenneth Quinn and David West.

Horace's aphorism *nihil est ab omni parte beatum* ("Nothing is perfect in every part," *Odes* 2.16.27–28) applies to poetry in that it is notoriously difficult to get a whole poem just right. There are numerous odes in which Horace does not put a foot wrong, and almost no duds. There are, though, some curate's eggs, poems in which some sections operate at a higher level of inspiration than others. For example, none of the odes that deal with the theme of luxury versus simplicity seems to me to be among Horace's best, and some of them are among the least well known and appreciated of his works. The theme may have been too trite for Horace to invigorate it, or the motif may have been one he felt obliged to treat rather than one that sparked his imagination. More broadly, the "public" or "state" poems seem to me on the whole less successful than the private poems; each of them contains passages of brilliance or beauty, but none seems to equal the best of the private poems in sustained quality. That is a controversial opinion, which I shall try to justify in the appropriate places.

Given the biases I have identified (and blind spots of which I am unaware), this book is inevitably a description of my Horace; I hope it may offer a stimulating comparison for readers who already have their Horace, and that it may serve as an inducement for readers who have not yet formed their own version of the poet.

---

[11] Nisbet 1962: 183, 184–85.

· 1 ·

Horace's Life

Almost all our information about Horace's life comes from two sources: Horace himself, who speaks of himself more often than any other Latin poet, and a biography that preserves material from the *Lives of the Poets* by Suetonius (early second century CE), better known as the author of *Lives of the Caesars*. Both sources are invaluable—Horace for obvious reasons, Suetonius for his access to otherwise unknown documentary material—but both need to be used with caution: poets are rarely interested in imparting biographical information for its own sake, and much of what Horace tells us about himself is shaped by literary ends; as for Suetonius, he tends to present as facts what are actually inferences from the work of the writer in question. Despite those caveats, enough can be stated with confidence to produce the outline of a biography.

Quintus Horatius Flaccus was born on December 8 in the consulship of L. Aurelius Cotta and L. Manlius Torquatus (= 65), in or near the town of Venosa in Apulia, whose other famous native son is the sixteenth-century madrigalist and murderer Carlo Gesualdo. His father was a freedman (*libertinus*), that is, a former slave who had purchased or been granted his freedom. (It is unclear whether Horace's father was born a slave or suffered enslavement as an adult, perhaps as a result of Venosa's support for the losing side in the Social Wars.) The sons of freedmen were considered freeborn, and so Horace himself had full citizen rights, but his descent from a *libertinus* would expose him to scorn and resentment in later life.

Horace's father figures prominently in the *Satires*; his mother remains in the shadows, and there is no mention of siblings. Horace expresses warm gratitude for the moral instruction he received from his father, but when he describes that instruction in terms that recall a scene in Terence's comedy *The Brothers*,[1] we sense that Horace's father as depicted in his poetry is to an extent a literary creation.

Following his emancipation, Horace senior worked as a middleman at auctions, an inglorious but remunerative occupation. He had the means to give his son a better education than the schools of Venosa could provide. He brought him to Rome and enrolled him with a teacher of literature of some repute, L. Orbilius Pupillus, unfondly recalled by Horace with the nickname *plagosus*, "Whacker" (*Epist.* 2.1.70). He also financed a further period of philosophical study in Athens, which may have lasted for several years. Horace's sojourn "amidst the groves of the Academy" (*Epist.* 2.2.45) was interrupted by the civil war that erupted after the assassination of Julius Caesar in 44. When the principal assassin, Marcus Brutus, came to Athens to rally support for the conspirators' cause, Horace joined his army and received the rank of military tribune, an uncommon distinction for someone of his social background and perhaps the first occasion on which preferment for Horace rankled with others (*Sat.* 1.6.45–48). His brief military career ended at the battle of Philippi in 42, where the forces of Brutus and Cassius were routed by Antony and Octavian (the future Augustus).

The years following the debacle at Philippi are the least documented of Horace's adult life. It is usually thought that he returned to Italy under an amnesty declared by Octavian. Horace himself says only that his wings were clipped and that, having lost his paternal resources and land, poverty drove him to write poetry (*Epist.* 2.2.49–52); Suetonius supplies the further detail that he obtained a position as a clerk in the quaestor's office—the Roman equivalent of the Treasury—presumably through connections or by using what remained of his inheritance. Given Horace's gentleman's

---

[1] *Sat.* 1.4.105–15; cf. Ter. *Ad.* 413–20.

education, he is more likely to have been a supervisor than a mere copyist, with enough leisure to begin writing poetry. His statement that poverty was the motive may contain a grain of truth—not that he could expect to earn a living from his poetry, but he might have hoped that it would help him to secure patronage. Before long he had attracted the notice of two leading poets of the day: Virgil, whose recently published *Eclogues* had established him as a major talent, and L. Varius Rufus, a respected writer of epic and tragedy whom posterity has to thank for editing the *Aeneid* for publication after Virgil's death.

In 38 Virgil and Varius introduced Horace to the man who would turn his career around once and for all, Gaius Cilnius Maecenas, a wealthy descendant of Etruscan nobility and a trusted advisor of Octavian. Maecenas had literary interests of his own, but in his dealings with writers he functioned as a go-between for Octavian, enlisting talents who might side with him in the propaganda war then being waged against Mark Antony and who might voice support for his rule once he had prevailed. Following an interview of which Horace gives a carefully edited account (*Sat.* 1.6.56–62) and a waiting period of eight months, he was admitted to Maecenas's circle of friends.

Horace's association with Maecenas yielded benefits of several kinds. The most tangible came in the form of property, an estate in the Sabine hill country near Rome (sometimes referred to, in misleadingly modest terms, as the "Sabine farm"), which provided Horace with financial independence and a retreat from the city during the warmer months of the year. Maecenas also afforded him entrée to Rome's political and literary elite, an opportunity that must have dazzled this freedman's son, but one that he was quick to exploit. His earliest published collection of poems, the first book of *Satires*, from about 35, ends with a passage in which Horace advises aspiring poets not to court success with the crowd but to be content with few readers (*Sat.* 1.10.73–74); he then describes his own target audience, naming fifteen members of Rome's cultural establishment (81–90). He would hardly have dared to invoke those eminences if he had not been confident of having already gained their favor. Finally, Maecenas supplied Horace with a rich vein of poetic material. A number of poems in the *Epodes, Satires, Odes* 1–3, and *Epistles* 1 depict their relationship as a genuine friendship between persons of unequal status, rather than the transactional connection implied by the terms "patron" and "client."

Horace repaid Maecenas's benefactions by leaving behind a highly flattering image of him as a hard-working public servant, who needs to be persuaded at times to take the day off (as in *Odes* 3.29). Augustan sources do not dispute Horace's characterization, but the Younger Seneca, writing under Nero, presents in his *Epistles* (114.4–8) a wickedly amusing portrait of Maecenas as a notoriously dissolute figure, equally lax in his dress, morals, and prose style.

The prominent place Maecenas occupies in so much of Horace's poetry makes his near disappearance in the last collections especially striking. The fourth book of *Odes* contains no poem addressed to him, only a mention of his birthday, which Horace proposes to celebrate in the company of a woman named Phyllis (4.11.13–20). The three long literary letters make no mention whatever of Maecenas. This diminished position is often explained as the consequence of Maecenas's having lost favor with Augustus, and his fall is in turn accounted for by his having divulged confidential information, but the facts are murky, and much tells against any such hypothesis. The reference to Maecenas's birthday in *Odes* 4.11 has all the warmth of earlier times: Horace regards the day as almost more sacred than his own *dies natalis* (17–18). Furthermore, Maecenas's request to Augustus in his will, "Remember Horatius Flaccus as you would me," does not sound like the appeal of a man who has fallen from grace.

Rather than inferring coolness toward Maecenas, it is more plausible to think of Horace as growing closer to Augustus. When, perhaps in the mid-20s, Augustus wished to invite Horace to become his secretary and assist him with his correspondence, he did so in a letter to Maecenas (cited by Suetonius), playfully suggesting that Horace would "leave that parasitical table of yours and come to my royal one." But as Horace's prestige increased following the appearance of *Odes* 1–3 in 23, and after the death of Virgil in 19 left him Rome's greatest living poet, Augustus no longer found it necessary to use Maecenas as an intermediary. The commission to compose the hymn for the Secular Games of 17 (the *Carmen saeculare*) almost certainly came from Augustus himself, and he also had a role in encouraging Horace to celebrate the victories of his stepsons Tiberius and Drusus in poems that became *Odes* 4.4 and 4.14. Finally, Horace's *Letter to Augustus*, written soon after the publication of *Odes* 4, may have been his response to a complaint from the *princeps* that he had not addressed him in his previous writing. In a letter to Horace (quoted by Suetonius) Augustus asked, with remarkable foresight, "Are you afraid that being seen as a friend of mine will harm your reputation with posterity?" Augustus insisted on being written about only by authors of the first rank (Suet. *Aug.* 89.3); his courting of Horace shows that he agreed with the poet's own high opinion of his work.

Horace died on November 27 in the consulship of C. Marcius Censorinus and C. Asinius Gallus (= 8), just two months after the death of Maecenas, near whose tomb on the Esquiline he was buried. He is not known to have married, and no descendants are on record.

·2·

Before the *Odes*

Modern editions of Horace's works place the *Odes* first, reflecting an ancient view that they constitute his crowning achievement. But by the time *Odes* 1–3 appeared, Horace had published three collections of poems, two books of satires (in the original entitled *Sermones*, or "conversations") and one book of epodes (called *Iambi*). A brief look at those early works will help to place the *Odes* in context, but first it is necessary to sketch the literary background.

In 62 Cicero, at the height of his fame following his momentous year as consul, delivered a speech in defense of a Greek poet named Archias, whose standing as an alien resident in Rome had been challenged. The speech contains an eloquent defense of the utility of poetry, designed to appeal to the presuppositions of Cicero's audience. The strongest claim that Archias has on the goodwill of Romans, according to Cicero, is that his poetry celebrates the achievements of individual Romans and of the Roman people, and thereby confers on them the lasting renown they deserve.

Cicero also makes this remarkable statement: "If anyone thinks that there is less glory to be gained from Greek verses than from Latin ones, he is greatly mistaken, because Greek poetry is read among all nations, while Latin is confined to its own natural limits, which are quite narrow" (*In Defense of Archias* 23). The point serves Cicero's aim of promoting the value to Romans of a Greek poet such as Archias, but it is also a useful reminder of the state of Roman poetry at the time. After a period of enormous creativity in the second century BCE that produced the comedies of Plautus and

Terence, the epic and drama of Ennius, and the satires of Lucilius, Roman poetry had entered a phase of near dormancy: during the previous forty years, since the death of Lucilius in c. 102, the only poet of note on record is the tragedian Accius (died c. 86).

Within a decade of Cicero's speech the situation had changed dramatically, and within little more than two decades it had been altered nearly out of recognition. Roman poets began to create works of unprecedented ambition and originality, competing with their Greek predecessors and challenging traditional Roman notions of the role of poetry. In the decade of the 50s two writers stand out: Titus Lucretius Carus, author of *De rerum natura* (*On the Nature of Things*), an exposition of Epicurean philosophy in verse whose language would profoundly influence the next two generations of Latin poets and whose thought would have an even more far-reaching influence, and Gaius Valerius Catullus, Rome's first great writer of personal poetry. Because of the accidents of transmission and survival Catullus is for us an isolated figure, but in his time he was a member of a group of like-minded writers, called by Cicero "new poets" and "moderns," both terms with a slightly mocking edge. Catullus and the other new poets were not foreigners or low-status characters, like Plautus, Terence, and Ennius, but Romans of good or high standing. They were not concerned to win popular favor but wrote to please themselves and a select circle of appreciative readers. They preferred short poems, written with care and intended to last.

Those attitudes had a Greek background, in Hellenistic poetry. (The Hellenistic Era conventionally begins with the death of Alexander the Great in 323 and ends in 31 with the battle of Actium, after which the last of the Hellenistic kingdoms, Ptolemaic Egypt, was absorbed into the Roman empire.) Although several poets of that period exerted significant influence on the new generation of Roman poets, the most influential figure was Callimachus (c. 305–240), a scholar-poet who also served as the head of the Alexandrian Library. Callimachus was remarkable for the variety of genres in which he worked, from epigrams to hymns to iambic and elegiac verse. That multiplicity of form would inspire several of his Roman followers, including Virgil, Horace, and Ovid. Callimachus's scorn for traditional epic was encapsulated in aphorisms such as "A big book is a big nuisance" and "Thundering is Zeus's job, not mine," and his regard for originality and fine craftsmanship was expressed in images of the narrow, untrodden path (to be preferred to the much-traveled highway) and the clear-flowing spring (in contrast to the muddy Euphrates). Like other Hellenistic poets, he cultivated a bookish and allusive style; his work was not directed to a popular audience and presupposed readers almost as learned as the poet himself.

Catullus is best known to modern readers as a love poet, but he also wrote poetry of an erudite character, including a translation of a poem of Callimachus, and all his work is rooted in Callimachean principles. Poem 95 comes close to being a manifesto of those convictions: it celebrates the appearance of his friend Cinna's poem *Smyrna*, a condensed mythological narrative of a type called an epyllion (little epic) by modern scholars.

> At last my Cinna's *Smyrna* has appeared, nine harvests
> and nine winters since it was begun!
> Hortensius meanwhile in just a single [year
> can spew] a half million [lines of trash].
> *Smyrna* will make its way to Satrachus's grooved bed,
> *Smyrna* will long be read through the white-haired
> ages;
> but Volusius's *Annals* will croak at home on the banks
> of the Po
> and often furnish loose coats for mackerel.
> Dear to my heart be [my friend's] small monument;
> let the crowd applaud their bloated Antimachus.[1]

Volusius and Hortensius apparently wrote historical epic of a kind pioneered by Ennius in his *Annales*, a genre that had traditionally enjoyed favor at Rome but one that the new poets regarded with

---

[1] The text of lines 3–4 and 9 is defective, but the general sense is clear, as reflected in the bracketed words.

contempt. Despite its brevity, Catullus's poem exhibits the subtlety that it admires in Cinna's work. Predicting far-reaching fame for *Smyrna*, Catullus singles out the river Satrachus in Cyprus, which probably figured in Cinna's narrative; the obscure foreign locale contrasts with the native Po, the *patria* of Volusius and the final resting place of his poetry, and also suggests an opposition between a small, clear stream and a vast but impure body of water. In the final couplet Catullus hails Cinna's "small monument" and sneers at the popular approval given to Antimachus: not a contemporary but a poet of the fourth century whom Callimachus had attacked for his long-windedness. It is almost as if Catullus were speaking in the persona of Callimachus.

In about 40, when Horace began writing, the Roman literary scene was at a point of transition. The leading figures of the 50s and early 40s were gone: Lucretius and Catullus died before 50, and Catullus's friend Cinna lost his life in the rioting following the assassination of Julius Caesar in 44, when a mob mistook him for a namesake who had been among the assassins; in the following year Cicero perished, the most prominent victim of the proscriptions carried out by Antony and Octavian. A new generation of writers was emerging, and among its leading figures were Virgil and Varius, Horace's friends and early supporters.

Horace drops some hints about the beginnings of his poetic career, but like all his ostensibly revealing remarks, they need to be read with caution. In a passage of the *Satires* he recalls that at one point he began to compose poetry in Greek but was warned off that endeavor by Quirinus (the name given to Romulus after his deification):

> When I set about writing some verses in Greek, though born
> on this side of the water, Quirinus stopped me and
>   spake thus
> (appearing after the midnight hour, when visions are true):
> "It makes as much sense to bring wood into a forest as
>   for you
> to wish to swell the mighty battalions of the Greeks."
>   (*Sat.* 1.10.31–35)

If the statement were true, the most likely time for that experimental phase would be Horace's period of study in Athens, which would make his Greek compositions his first poetic venture. But skepticism is in order. Callimachus had begun his most ambitious work, the *Aetia* (*Causes*), by explaining why he refused to write a continuous long poem; Apollo, he said, had advised him to "feed the sacrificial victim to be as fat as possible, but keep the Muse slender." All good Roman Callimacheans, beginning with Virgil at the opening of *Eclogues* 6, staged a version of that scene, in which they depicted themselves as embarking on a grand poetic enterprise before being steered in another direction by a benevolent deity. As the conventional character of such episodes became more obvious, belief in the reality of the abandoned projects became harder to sustain. Horace's aborted Greek poems probably belong to this genre of fictitious compositions.

Of more interest are Horace's reasons for beginning his career with satire and iambic poetry, both genres that entailed criticism or invective directed at others. It would be too easy to see the choice as dictated by his position as an outsider on his return to Italy after Philippi; whatever influence that may have had at first, once Horace had been taken up by Maecenas, he could hardly continue to write out of a sense of grievance or dispossession. Other factors must be considered, some of which emerge from Horace's own account of his choice of satire (*Sat.* 1.10.40–49):

> You alone among the living, Fundanius, can delight us
>   with comic repartee
> as Davus the slave and a crafty mistress give old man
>   Chremes the slip;
> Pollio sets the deeds of kings to the triple rhythm of
>   tragedy;
> Varius marshals heroic epic with an unequaled spirit;
> to Virgil the Muses who love the countryside have granted
>   wit and charm.
> This form had been tried by Varro of Atax and some others
>   without success, which I might be able to improve on,

though inferior to the founder; nor would I dare to take
   from him
the crown that adorns his head with much praise.

Horace refers to several contemporaries as excelling in their respective genres: Fundanius in comedy and Pollio in tragedy, Varius in epic, and Virgil in pastoral poetry. The implied notion that Horace chose satire as the only genre that did not yet have a modern Roman master is not to be taken literally, but it does point to the intensive cultivation of diverse genres at this moment in Roman literary life.

We may still ask why Horace started with satire rather than embarking on a career in lyric, another genre without a Roman exponent. One possible explanation is that Virgil had set a precedent for beginning with a relatively modest genre (the *Eclogues*) and then progressing to a more ambitious one, in his case didactic poetry in the form of the *Georgics*.

The word *satura* is related to various forms of mixture, several of them involving food (e.g., a combination of items as in a mixed grill). Satire as a literary genre at first similarly denoted writing of a miscellaneous character, both as regards form (prose alternating with verse, different metrical forms, Greek interspersed with Latin) and content. The unifying element was the personal outlook of the writer. Satire had a long history at Rome, going back to Ennius, but its most distinguished exponent before Horace was Gaius Lucilius (180–102/1), whom Horace designates as the founder of the genre.

Lucilius composed thirty books of satires, of which slightly under 1,300 lines (roughly equivalent to two books) survive as fragments, mostly in quotations by grammarians documenting some detail of language. Generalizing on the basis of such a slender body of evidence is hazardous, but some recurrent themes stand out: denunciations of urban luxury, especially in the realm of food and dining; criticism of the loose morals of women; parodies of philosophical doctrines; attacks on public officials for misconduct; polemical statements about bad writing. The high proportion of critical comment seems to bear out the view of later writers that Lucilius made the criticism of individuals or society, originally just one among many topics for satire, the leading element, thereby creating the concept of satire that has endured to the present.

Lucilius was also credited with attacking prominent persons by name, taking advantage of his secure social position and the *libertas* (free speech) that had characterized the Republic. That aspect of his work is difficult to assess from the surviving fragments: a number of known individuals are mentioned in unflattering terms, but most of them seem to have been dead when Lucilius was writing, and other named characters may be fictitious representatives of a type. There are exceptions in the area of literary criticism, where Lucilius names the tragedians Pacuvius and Accius, mocking the overblown style of the former and dissenting from the latter on questions of orthography. In general, though, Lucilius's outspokenness may have been exaggerated by later satirists, in order to contrast his alleged freedom with their own more restricted circumstances.

Horace's satiric corpus comprises two collections published several years apart: Book 1, containing ten poems, appeared in 36 or 35, and Book 2, with eight poems, came out around 30.

The subject matter of the *Satires* displays considerable overlap with topics treated by Lucilius: criticism of vices such as greed (1.1), sexual license (1.2), and extravagance in food (2.4); mockery of philosophical pretensions (2.2, 2.3); recollections of travel (1.5); opposition of urban and country living (2.6); an account of a court case (1.7); anecdotes of everyday experience (1.7, 1.9); and literary-critical opinions (1.4, 1.10).

Strikingly absent are attacks on prominent figures, even deceased ones; the targets of Horace's barbs are shadowy characters, either nonentities or figments. The difference is often interpreted as the consequence of changed political conditions; as Ronald Syme wrote, "Nor would the times now permit political satire or free attack upon the existing order in state and society. Republican *libertas*, denied to the *nobiles* of Rome, could not be conceded to a freedman's son."[2] Temperament probably played a part as well: in a phrase from the first of the *Satires* that is often taken to describe the work as a whole, Horace asks, "What's to stop me from telling the truth with a smile?" (*Sat.* 1.1.23–24).

In his meter and language Horace creates an impression of informality and spontaneity. The opening words of *Satires* 1.1 are "How does it come about, Maecenas . . . ?"; it is as if we had come upon Horace and Maecenas in mid-conversation. The frequent use of direct quotation, often from an imagined interlocutor who questions or objects to Horace's words, produces a feeling of lively dialogue and helps to account for the original title of the collection, *Sermones*, or "Conversations."

Beneath the charming surface, though, lie a number of paradoxes or contradictions that make the poems more complex and more interesting. I will single out three ways in which the *Satires* are not quite what they claim to be.

Horace's attitude toward Lucilius is a mixture of admiration and criticism. He accords him the deference that Greek and Roman poets customarily showed to the inventor of a genre, and in the passage of 1.10 cited earlier he describes himself as "inferior to the founder," adding, "Nor would I dare to take from him the crown that adorns his head with much praise" (48–49). But in the very next line Horace repeats a negative judgment he had made in an earlier satire: "But I have said that he flows muddily, and often carries along with him more that ought to be removed than deserves to remain" (50–51). The Callimachean imagery is unmistakable and raises a central issue. The notion of a Callimachean satirist ought to be a contradiction in terms, since the low language and informal style that had traditionally characterized satire are the antithesis of Callimachus's exquisite and recherché manner. At the level of explicit pronouncement Horace leaves the contradiction unresolved. While faulting Lucilius for hasty composition and lack of polish, he

---

[2] Syme 1939: 254.

affects to regard his own satires as not even meriting the name of poetry, calling them "nearer to everyday speech" (1.4.42).

The preponderance of Horace's statements, though, are clearly on the side of requiring the highest standards of craft even in the satiric mode. After the criticism of Lucilius in *Satires* 1.10, Horace allows that, were the older poet to find himself transported to Horace's more polished age, he would surely expend more effort on his satires: "He would now be smoothing out much in his writing and cutting back anything drawn out beyond its due limit; in shaping his verses he would often scratch his head and bite his nails to the quick" (1.10.67–71). The implied comparison—as Horace himself has done—is easily supplied.

The *Satires* contain numerous allusions to Lucilius, and many more would doubtless be recognizable if Lucilius's works had survived intact. Allusion is a sign of respect, but many of Horace's references have a corrective element, acknowledging the predecessor but also improving on him. Lucilius had devoted an entire book (of perhaps five to six hundred verses) to recounting a trip to Sicily; exemplifying the compression that he found lacking in his predecessor, Horace describes his trip to Brundisium in a poem of just over a hundred lines, the shortest up to that point in the collection. Even so, the closing line announces, "Here is the end of a long journey and a long text" (1.5.104).

The appearance of looseness and informality that the *Satires* present is therefore just that, an appearance. Close attention to Horace's writing shows a level of artistry in no way inferior to that which he lavished on the *Odes*.

A second contradiction relates to the element of criticism in the *Satires*. As previously noted, Horace differs from Lucilius in refraining from criticizing prominent persons by name. At the same time Horace pretends that his satires are capable of giving offense, and in 1.4 he mounts a self-defense that presupposes that his writing had in fact been found excessively harsh. The accusation is so manifestly implausible that its reality cannot be taken seriously.

Finally, according to Horace, the satires of Lucilius were heavily autobiographical: he confided his secrets to his poems as if to trusted friends, with the result that "the old man's whole life lies open, as if painted on a votive tablet" (*Sat.* 2.1.32–34). Horace adds, "I follow him," implying that he follows Lucilius in that regard. It is true that the *Satires* are in relative terms Horace's most autobiographical works: only there do we hear of his devotion to his father and the latter's concern for his son's upbringing, and only there does Horace speak of the backbiting he endured when he, a freedman's son, was raised to the rank of military tribune. By comparison the *Odes* are markedly sparing of biographical detail; if Horace's life had to be reconstructed from them, the story would be brief and uneventful. But even in the *Satires* Horace is hardly prodigal with personal information, and much of what he does offer has a literary pedigree: the most intimate detail he divulges, the wet dream he had after being stood up by a girl on the road to Brundisium (*Sat.* 1.5.82–85), has its counterpart in a fragment of Lucilius.[3]

Those and other contradictions have resulted in a lack of critical agreement on the purpose of the *Satires*. One view sees them as intended to give pleasure while raising moral awareness, essentially taking Horace at his word when he speaks of "telling the truth with a smile." For others, the moral messages are so confused and inconsistent as to undermine the authority of the satirist, who is exposed as a *doctor ineptus* (a description coined by William Anderson).[4]

One theme in *Satires* 1 that unites the spheres of poetry, friendship, and the art of living is the Callimachean ideal of selectivity, which requires knowing what to exclude as superfluous or deficient in quality. Success is described in terms that praise the small and the few. The first appearance of the theme is in the moral sphere:

> Tell me, if a man lives within nature's
> limits, what matter whether he has a hundred or a
>   thousand acres
> of ploughed land? "But it's nice to draw from a big pile!"
> But if you let us draw the same amount from our *little* pile,

---

[3] 1183 Warmington.
[4] Anderson (1982).

> why should your granaries be superior to our bins?
> It's as if you needed only a jug or a glass of water
> and said "I'd sooner draw it from a big river than from this
> piddling stream, although the amount would be just
>   the same."
> That's how people who like more than their fair share
> get swept away, bank and all, by the raging Aufidus,
> while the man who wants only what he needs doesn't
>   draw water
> clouded with mud, nor does he lose his life in the torrent.
>   (*Sat.* 1.1.49–60; trans. Niall Rudd)

The Callimachean opposition of the vast but muddy river and the small, pure stream is neatly transposed to the theme of excessive greed. Other instances of the motif include the reference to Maecenas as "a man of few friends" (1.9.44), Horace's recommendation that an aspiring writer be content with few readers (1.10.74), and this modest self-description:

> The gods did well to give me a feeble and poverty-stricken
>   nature,
> one that speaks rarely and even then in just a few words.
>   (*Sat.* 1.4.17–18)

That looks at first like ironic self-depreciation, but it makes more sense as a pointed contrast to Lucilius. There is no evidence that at the time of *Satires* 1 Horace was looking ahead to another book; for all that we can tell, this single collection, called in its last line a *libellus* (i.e., smaller than a *liber*) was meant to be his counterpart to Lucilius's massive corpus of thirty books.

A second thread in *Satires* 1 is Horace's entry into Maecenas's friendship, not recounted in chronological order—the trip with him to Brundisium in 5 precedes the account of their first meeting in 6—but culminating in 9, where Horace is the insider whose position is envied by an ambitious social climber. Here the two themes merge, since this fellow has exactly the wrong idea both about what sort of literary talents will commend him to Horace and about how he might enter the circle of Maecenas.

> "If I'm any judge
> you'll value my friendship just as highly as that of Viscus
> and Varius. No one can write as many verses as I can—
> and in so short a time. I'm the smoothest dancer in town,
> and even Hermogenes might well envy my singing voice."
> Here was my chance: "Have you a mother or next of kin
> expecting you home?"
> "No, not one. I've buried them all."
> "Lucky for them! That leaves me."
>
> (23–28, trans. Niall Rudd)

> He starts up again: "How are things with you and Maecenas?
> He's choosy about his friends and has a good head:
> no one has made better use of his luck. You would have
> a great supporter who would take your part, if you
> were willing to introduce yours truly. I swear, by now
> you'd have got rid of all your rivals."
> "We don't live there
> as you imagine" I said. "No house is more upright or freer
> of that sort of fault. I'm not bothered if this one is better off
> or better read than I am. Each of us has his own place."
> "What you describe is amazing, I can hardly believe it!"
> "And yet
> it's true."
>
> (44–53)

In *Satires* 1, good taste in poetry, in friendship, and in morals forms a coherent unity.

When a poet's works are collected along generic lines, they tend to be read as units; so the four books of *Odes* are seen as a collectivity, and similarly the two books of *Satires*. But with Horace the discontinuities between installments of the same genre are also significant, and nowhere more so than in the *Satires*. The opening of *Satires* 2, far from building on the achievement that

Horace claims for his work at the end of *Satires* 1, confronts us with the astonishing statement that Horace knows it would be best to follow the candid advice of his friend Trebatius and "shut up" (5), that is, give up writing poetry for good; his lame excuse for not doing so is that writing is his cure for insomnia. Soon afterward the distinction of style that Horace was at pains to draw between himself and Lucilius in *Satires* 1 is casually tossed aside: it pleases him "to enclose words in metrical shape in the manner of Lucilius" (28–29). We have returned, it would seem, to the false modesty that Horace appeared to have set aside at the end of *Satires* 1. But if Horace does not take Trebatius's advice literally, he does the next best thing, yielding the podium to a series of guest lecturers who come close to monopolizing the satiric voice for the remainder of the book. They are not an impressive lot—Ofellus, a farmer down on his luck (2.2), Damasippus the interminable Stoic (2.3), the gourmand Catius (2.4), a seedy version of the famous seer Tiresias (2.5), Horace's own slave Davus—and much of what they say sounds either trite or overblown. One effect of this sequence of surrogate speakers is to call into question the attempt at moral improvement that was alleged to be part of the aim of *Satires* 1, by showing it applied to trivial or shady ends (e.g., gastronomy or legacy hunting). The last of these would-be instructors is the most inept: the imperious host Nasidienus, who manages to drive away a captive audience of dinner guests by lecturing them on the provenance and preparation of the dishes he serves.

Satires 2 also offers a strikingly different perspective on Horace's relations with Maecenas. In 1.9 he characterized the behavior of Maecenas's friends in terms so rosy as to prompt disbelief, but in 2.6, which begins with thanks to Maecenas for the Sabine estate, Horace depicts himself discharging the duties of an ordinary client and spending more time in the city than he would wish. He even imagines someone rebuking him for shoving aside anyone who stands in his way as he hastens to Maecenas (29–32). In 2.7 Davus calls Horace the miserable slave of another, like a puppet that moves when someone else pulls the strings (81–82);

in the context of Davus's sermon this "master" is lust (89–94), but the image also embodies the worst possible reading of Horace's situation. Davus can speak as he does because it is the Saturnalia, when slaves were given license to abuse their masters, but his question "Who then is free?" (83) could have a wider application, suggesting that Saturnalian *libertas* may be the only kind of freedom left in Rome.

At around the same time that *Satires* 2 appeared, in 30, Horace brought out another collection of seventeen poems conventionally known as the *Epodes*. ("Epode" refers to the metrical shape of most of the poems, in which a second line in a different meter follows a first one to produce a distich. Horace refers to the poems only as *iambi*, "iambics.") Although we cannot tell when Horace began to compose these poems, in several ways they mark a transition from the *Satires* in the direction of the *Odes*. The *Epodes* display some of the same metrical virtuosity as the *Odes*, though within a more restricted sphere: after ten poems in the same meter, poems 11–17 are each in a different iamb-based meter. The poems range in length from sixteen to 102 lines, with the majority shorter than thirty lines. That average length is much closer to the size of individual odes than the longer satires. Several of the roles that Horace will assume in the *Odes* make their first appearance here, such as the lover (11, 14, 15), the concerned citizen (1, 7, 9, 16), and the giver of advice (13). The *Epodes* also resemble the *Odes* in engaging with a genre rooted in archaic Greek poetry. That genre was iambic, and its principal exponent was Archilochus, from the island of Paros (seventh century), the earliest Greek poet apart from the writers of epic-style verse, Hesiod and Homer, whose work survives. Iambic poetry is defined primarily by its meters, but as practiced by Archilochus it was also identified in later times with a distinctive ethos, that of stinging invective. A literal reading of references in his poems had produced the story that he was engaged to marry Neobule, the daughter of one Lycambes, when her family broke off the betrothal; to avenge the offense, Archilochus attacked them so bitterly in his iambics that both father and daughter hanged themselves.

A number of Catullus's short poems are in iambic meters, and others can be called iambic in spirit, but Catullus never produced a volume of such poetry, and it is in that sense that Horace could later boast of being the first Roman writer in that genre:

> I was the first to show Latium
> the iambics of Paros, following the meter and spirit
> of Archilochus, but not his themes or the words that
>   hounded Lycambes.
>
> (*Epistles* 1.19.23–25)

From that description, especially the reference to the "spirit" of Archilochus, one would expect the dominant tone of the *Epodes* to be invective. Several poems (2, 4, 6, 8, 10, 12, 15) do consist of attacks on individuals who, like the targets of Horace's criticism in the *Satires*, are either unnamed or fictitious characters. The manner is more aggressive than in the *Satires* and the language sometimes conspicuously coarse, nowhere more so than in two poems (8 and 12) directed at a woman of a certain age whose physical repulsiveness, Horace says, is responsible for his failure to perform sexually with her: "A most fit partner for black elephants" (12.1) is one of the milder taunts.

But personal attack is only one facet of the collection. It also includes a fake invective (3) in which Horace pretends to denounce Maecenas for poisoning him with a dish laced with garlic, two amatory poems (11, 14), four political poems (1, 7, 9, 16), an exhortation to friends to escape cares with wine (13), and two poems devoted to the witch Canidia (5, 17), a figure who had appeared in *Satires* 1.8 but who assumes a more prominent and sinister role here. The overall impression is one of "polymorphous diversity,"[5] or, in less favorable terms, "rather a jumble."[6]

Such heterogeneity was not new in iambic poetry, and may have characterized Archilochus's work; its fragmentary state of

---

[5] Watson (2007), 93
[6] A. Y. Campbell (cited by Shackleton Bailey (1982), 9 n. 26).

preservation makes it hard to tell. Variety of content was certainly a feature of another major body of Greek iambic, Callimachus's *Iambi*. Imitation of Callimachus may also account for a curious feature of the epode collection's shape, the introduction of new metrical forms in poems 11–17. Poem 11 alludes to the change by stating that because of love Horace no longer delights in writing verses "as before." Callimachus's *Iambi* comprised thirteen poems to which were added four more; their relationship to the *Iambi* proper is still debated, but if Horace thought of Callimachus's work as consisting of seventeen poems in two groups, he may have structured his own iambic corpus along similar lines.

The *Epodes* are Horace's least popular body of poetry. In part this is because they have been overshadowed by the *Odes*; even their title conspires against them, suggesting that they are an appendage or adjunct to the *Odes*. It is telling that 13, "the acknowledged gem of the collection,"[7] is often said to be more like an ode than an epode. The acerbic role that Horace is playing in some of the poems is also difficult to reconcile with the genial image of the poet that readers have constructed from his other works. Many have been repelled by the obscenity of 8 and 12, which are often omitted in school editions,[8] although the notion of Horace as a stud is arguably more off-putting than anything in the poems' language. Horace might have derived wry pleasure from the fact that the best-known of the *Epodes* is so appreciated because it is misunderstood: the praises of country life in *Epode* 2 have often been read as expressing Horace's own sentiments, while the point of the poem is that they are clichés mouthed by the hypocritical moneylender Alfius. (Among those naive readers was Thomas Jefferson, who had lines from the poem carved on a fountain in the gardens at Monticello.)

The years in which Horace composed the *Satires* and *Epodes* were an increasingly troubled time for Rome, as the fragile alliance

---

[7] Shackleton Bailey 1982: 8.
[8] A copy of the Loeb edition in the departmental library at Harvard bears the traces of one reader's revulsion: across the translation of 8 is written "Disgusting" and across that of 12 "Rot!".

between Octavian and Antony, held together until 36 by their common enemy Sextus Pompey, unraveled and led to war. Little of this turmoil is visible in Horace's poetry, at least not until after Octavian's decisive victory at Actium in September of 31. It is noteworthy that in *Satires* 2 and the *Epodes*, both published c. 30, Caesar (i.e., Octavian) is prominent in the poems that open the collections. In *Sat.* 2.1 Horace is confident enough of his favor to describe him with a potentially undignified metaphor, as responding to inept approaches by kicking out like an angry horse (18–20). It is unlikely that Octavian had found the time to cultivate a relationship with Horace in the crowded months following Actium; the connection must have existed previously, but it was one that Horace until now had declined to highlight. From Horace's description in *Satires* 1.5 of the trip he took with Maecenas to Brundisium in 37, a reader could not readily infer that the purpose of the mission was to negotiate a treaty with Antony: Horace focuses on the trivial pleasures and irritations of the journey and on his own humdrum experiences. The effect is gently self-mocking, but the approach also insulates Horace from political commentary that he might have found irksome. The fleeting reference to the mission itself is strictly neutral, referring to Octavian and Antony only as "friends who had fallen out" (29). Horace may have been hedging his bets in the unsettled years before the final showdown. A more creditable explanation is that he was reluctant to lend his talent to partisan political poetry. In *Eclogues* 6 Virgil had used Callimachus's hostility to large-scale poetry as an excuse for not praising the exploits of Alfenus Varus, and Horace would later employ a similar tactic in declining to commemorate the victories of Agrippa (*Odes* 1.6). There is a rich irony in Roman poets turning to Callimachus, court poet of the Ptolemies, to authorize their reluctance to write panegyric.

In contrast to the ostensibly apolitical *Satires*, the *Epodes* collection includes four overtly political poems; their presence and placement constitute one of that collection's main points of interest. Two deal with Actium. In *Epodes* 1 Horace professes himself ready to accompany Maecenas to the scene of the conflict, and in 9, set soon after the battle, he longs for the time when he will be able to celebrate Caesar's victory with his friend. In stark counterpoint to those poems are two others, 7 and 16, that express despair at Rome's plight. In both poems Horace assumes the persona of a speaker addressing an assembly. In 7 he rebukes his fellow citizens for succumbing to the Roman original sin of civil war (which Horace traces to Romulus's murder of his brother Remus), while in 16 he urges them to abandon Rome and seek the Golden Age by journeying to the Isles of the Blessed.

The order of poems cannot represent a chronological sequence, since the gloomiest of all, 16, would then refer to a time after Actium; it is hard to believe that Horace would have wished to create that impression. Also, the opening lines of 16 suggest a continuation or fresh outbreak of civil war, which does not fit events after Actium. But it is still remarkable that when assembling the *Epodes* Horace not only included those two pessimistic utterances but assigned to the longer one a prominent position just before the end of the book. The effect may have been inspired by what Virgil had done in the *Eclogues*: two poems in that ten-poem collection, 1 and 9, allude to the confiscations of land that afflicted parts of Italy during the civil war, but while the first poem records the gratitude of a shepherd who had been permitted to remain on his land, the ninth presents a picture of farmers dispossessed with no hope of restitution. In both collections the positive and negative components are left in tension, and in both an optimistic opening is countered by a dark near conclusion.

Both the *Satires* and the *Epodes* pretend to be something they are not—Lucilian-style poetry of criticism and invective in the manner of Archilochus—but they do not pretend very convincingly; indeed, questions about Horace's ability to sustain the generic roles he has assumed are written into the collections themselves. In the *Satires* that ambivalence is expressed by the passivity that Horace as satirist often exhibits, in such episodes in Book 1 as the trip to Brundisium (5) and the encounter with the social climber (9), and throughout *Satires* 2 where other speakers take over the leading role. The epode collection takes that process even further. It is the poetic equivalent of a self-destroying artifact, which progressively plots its own undoing through images and situations of incapacity and impotence: in 11 and 14, where the "softening idleness" (14.1) of love is retarding the completion of the book and the love in question is of the unmanning rather than the aggressive kind; in 8 and 12, where the speaker tries to excuse his failure to perform by attacking the woman; in 15, where the issue of potency is explicitly raised and implicitly answered—"if there is any manhood in Floppy" (= Flaccus, 15.12); in the civic despair of 16 and in the growing control of Canidia, a rival source of power who in the last poem has reduced Horace to a groveling suppliant.

By portraying himself as a passive satirist and an impotent iambist, Horace adopts an ironic stance in relation to both generic roles. To be in an ironic relationship with a poetic genre is a typically Hellenistic attitude, the product of a literary culture that is aware of the artificial nature of all literary genres. In the *Odes* Horace succeeded in transcending that outlook by adopting a genre, and a persona, that he could inhabit with complete conviction.

· 3 ·

To the Cool Grove

The Ascent to Lyric

> Lyric poets
> usually have—as he knew—cold hearts.
> It is like a medical condition. Perfection in art
> is given in exchange for such an affliction.
>   Czeslaw Milosz, "Orpheus and Eurydice"

"Laudatory poem," "words of praise," "stanzaic salute," "work for heroes": those are among the definitions for "ode" found in the *New York Times* crossword puzzle in recent years. Others include "lofty words," "inspired poem," and "uplifting poem." It would seem that the strongest associations of "ode" in modern English are laudatory content and elevation of style. Odes are sometimes defined in relation to individual poets of the past, as in "poem by Sappho," or "Wordsworth composition." Implicit in the latter definitions is the assumption that the ode is no longer a medium of contemporary poetry, which does seem to be the case. Baron Pierre de Coubertin's "Ode to Sport," awarded a gold medal for literature at the Stockholm Olympics in 1912, may mark the last time at which a poem could be entitled an "ode" without an ironic or distancing effect being intended.

Early modern uses of "ode" more relevant to its ancient meaning connect it with music, as in the odes to Saint Cecilia composed in honor of the patron saint of music by Dryden, Addison, and others.

In Greek an "ode" is simply a song, and with reference to poetry the term denotes any composition to be performed to musical accompaniment. The lyre was the instrument most often used for that purpose, whence the name "lyric" as the genre to which odes belong.

Musical performance was a fact for archaic Greek poets, who were thought of as singers and instrumentalists as well as writers. Several Attic vases depict Sappho, Alcaeus, or Anacreon in the act of performance, accompanying themselves on the *barbitos* (a low-pitched lyre), and a bowl for mixing wine now in Munich shows Sappho and Alcaeus, each holding a *barbitos*, with sounds—a string of "o"s—coming from Alcaeus' mouth.[1]

The appearance of musical performance is carefully maintained by Horace, beginning in *Odes* 1.1, which ends with a reference to "tuning the lyre of Lesbos" (34; Horace even uses the Greek term *barbitos*). A later ode in the same book calls upon the *barbitos* to "utter a Latin song," and when in Book 4 Horace describes the standing he has attained as a poet, he calls himself "player of the Roman lyre" (4.3.23). The *Odes* teem with the language of song and musical instruments;[2] some scholars have taken that language literally, but most see it as Horace's way of recreating the ethos of archaic lyric in a book-oriented culture.

But even if the *Odes* are songs only in a figurative sense, the musical element is still central to them in the form of meter. The Latin vocabulary of meter overlaps with that of music: *modi* can refer to melodies or to metrical forms, and the verb *modulari* means both "to set to music" and "to put into meter." The meters of archaic lyric were among the most complex in all of Greek poetry, and their adaptation to Latin, a language in many ways unsuited to them, was Horace's main technical challenge. The opening of *Odes* Book 1 declares Horace's metrical mastery in

---

[1] Photograph in Yatromanolakis 2007: 74.
[2] Lowrie 2009b: 73–74 gives full lists.

a spectacular fashion: each of the first nine poems is written in a different meter, a display of virtuosity that would never be repeated, or even approached, in classical Latin. In the conclusion to *Odes* 1–3 Horace sums up his achievement in explicitly metrical terms, describing himself as "the first to bring Aeolian song into Italian measures" (3.30.13–14). Another sense of the verb Horace uses, *deducere*, is "to spin (i.e., thread) finely," which in the context of Callimachean poetics had become a metaphor for producing finely spun verse. That is not the primary sense here, but Horace could be hinting that his adaptation of Greek lyric also possessed refinement and delicacy.

Lyric held a relatively high place in the Hellenistic Greek scheme of poetry, partly because of its performative aspect and partly because of the prestige of its most eminent exponents, such as Sappho, called "the tenth Muse" by no less a figure than Plato. Another aspect of the codification of literary genres by Alexandrian scholars was the formation of a "canon" of the best writers in each genre. The canon of Greek lyric poets formulated by Aristarchus in the third century comprised nine writers: Alcman, Stesichorus, Alcaeus, Sappho, Ibycus, Anacreon, Simonides, Pindar, and Bacchylides.

In the Roman context the standing of lyric poetry was more equivocal. Seneca quotes Cicero (in a lost dialogue) to the effect that even if his lifespan were doubled, he would not have the time to read the lyric poets. To a Roman of a certain type there was nothing socially beneficial to be gained from lyric poetry, as there was from tragedy or even satire.

In choosing lyric, therefore, Horace was both raising his sights, generically speaking, after the *Satires* and *Epodes* and also attempting to confer on lyric a prestige that it had not traditionally enjoyed at Rome. In that enterprise he had virtually no Roman predecessors; the only known exception is Catullus, whose collected works contain three poems in lyric meters, one a free translation of an ode of Sappho, another in the same "Sapphic" stanza, and a third in a metrical form used in three odes of Horace. Against that background the eighty-eight poems of *Odes* 1–3 constitute a staggering achievement. The forty-eight preludes and fugues of

Bach's *Well-Tempered Clavier* are sometimes cited in comparison, but Bach came at the end of a long line of composers in that medium; Horace could justly say, "Beholden to no one I blazed a trail over virgin country; / nobody had trodden that ground" (*Epistles* 1.19.21–22, trans. Niall Rudd).

The ambitions Horace entertained for his lyric poetry are stated in the final lines of the first ode, addressed to Maecenas (1.1.29–36):

> As for me, the ivy crown, prize of learned brows,
> makes me one with the gods; as for me, the cool grove
> and the light-stepping dances of nymphs and satyrs
> set me apart from the crowd, if Euterpe does not withhold
> her flute, and Polyhymnia does not refuse
> to tune for me the lyre of Lesbos.
> But if you should rank my songs with the masters',
> I shall soar with pride, my head will touch the stars.

Horace's aim is nothing less than to join the lyric canon and to be recognized as the first Roman member of that group. For poets of Horace's generation the concept of canonicity had been given a tangible form by Augustus: the buildings connected to the Temple of Apollo on the Palatine, dedicated in 28, included libraries of Greek and Latin writers. Horace's language suggests that he was thinking of his work's future in such physical terms: a literal translation of line 35 would read "but if you place my poems among those of the lyric masters." Even as Horace evokes the performance-based ethos of archaic lyric with references to the flute and the lyre, he conceives of his Greek predecessors in Hellenistic terms, as poets whose canonical status is manifested by their presence in a library. The statement that poetry offers Horace seclusion from the crowd is also closer to a Callimachean disdain for popular taste than to anything Sappho or Alcaeus is likely to have said or thought.

In taking up lyric Horace was engaging with a genre that had a well-defined set of traditional characteristics, but he also shaped it to suit his own artistic tastes and preferences. In the next few pages I will discuss some of Horatian lyric's inherited and individual features.

One requirement of lyric was verbal decorum; the freedom of language that marks Catullus's short poems was not appropriate for the *Odes*, nor could Horace have begun an ode with the Latin equivalent of Philip Larkin's "They fuck you up, your mum and dad." Not that Horace is likely to have chafed much under that restriction; the obscenities sprinkled through the *Satires* and *Epodes* have a dutiful feel to them, as if Horace felt obliged to use such language to establish credibility in those genres.

The elevation of language that characterizes Horatian lyric is visible in the opening words of *Odes* 1.1: a grand apostrophe to Maecenas is enhanced first by an adjectival phrase, "descended from ancestral kings," and is then elaborated by an exclamation: "O my protection and my pride and delight." The exalted language expresses Horace's respect for and gratitude to his friend, but it also establishes immediately the verbal register that the *Odes* will largely occupy. It is instructive to contrast that opening with the informal beginning of *Satires* 1.1 (13), especially since the two poems have a common theme, the various forms of life that people pursue.

Another traditional feature of lyric was its flexibility, its capacity to encompass a wide range of themes and tones with the person of the writer as the principal unifying element. In that respect lyric contrasts both with epic, in that lyric allows for lighter material, and also with satire and iambic, which have very limited scope for elevated language or subjects. Lyric also offers the poet a variety of roles: praise poet, love poet, political poet, and so on. For Horace that multiplicity is further increased because at any given moment he can adopt any of the nine canonical lyric poets as his model.

A corollary of the previous point is that praise poetry was only one of many modes of lyric discourse available to Horace; nevertheless, the connection between "ode" and praise is so firmly established in modern usage that it comes as something of a shock to find that only a handful of poems in *Odes* 1–3 are praise poems in the full sense. A number of odes contain flattering remarks about their addressees as part of a larger rhetorical strategy; but on my reckoning only three are predominantly laudatory, and none of those is addressed to a contemporary: 1.12, an explicitly Pindaric ode most of which celebrates a parade of past Roman heroes; 1.32, to the poet's lyre; and 3.13, to the Bandusian spring. Borderline cases include 1.6, which pays tribute to Agrippa in the form of a polite refusal to commemorate his achievements in an epic, and 1.26, which honors Aelius Lamia but gives more prominence to Horace's Muse and the power of poetry. (I have excluded hymns, which are a form of laudation but which constitute a distinct generic subcategory.) It seems that the aversion to panegyric that was noted in the *Satires* and *Epodes* (22–23) was still present in *Odes* 1–3. In *Odes* 4, by contrast, more than half the poems are partially or wholly panegyrical; the eulogistic character of the later collection is one of the most striking differences between it and *Odes* 1–3.

Odes 1.1 is programmatic in this respect as well, revealing that the kind of lyric Horace aspires to write is not the poetry of praise associated primarily with Pindar. The first "other" way of life that is mentioned and rejected is that of the Olympic victor, the honorand of Pindar's Olympian odes. The rhetorical form the ode takes, listing a series of alternatives before ending with "as for me," has a distinguished exemplar in an ode of Sappho, which begins "Some say that an army of horsemen is the fairest thing on the black earth, some of foot soldiers, some of ships; but I say that it is whatever one loves." Horace surely knew Sappho's poem, and his appropriation of its structure is a first indication of his engagement with her form of lyric. One might further suggest that Horace, in replacing "whatever one loves" with poetry, is implying where his own heart lies.

Lyric as Horace defined it did not have room for literary polemic; that was appropriate to satire and poetic epistles, but it would apparently have lowered the tone Horace was aiming to set. So his statements of poetic allegiance are either positive (e.g., affirming his devotion to lyric) or are subsumed under the heading of friendly advice, as in the disparagement of elegiac weepiness in 1.33 and 2.9.

It is not uncommon for poets to express reservations about their work or to admit defects in their writing. W. H. Auden offered this (doubtless overstated) assessment: "In the eyes of every author,

I fancy, his own past work falls into four classes. First the pure rubbish which he regrets ever having conceived; second—for him the most painful—the good ideas which his incompetence or impatience prevented from coming to much . . . ; third, the pieces he has nothing against except their lack of importance; these must inevitably form the bulk of any collection since, were he to limit it to the fourth class alone, to those poems for which he is honestly grateful, his volume would be too depressingly slim."[3] The epigrammatist Martial made an equally blunt admission: "Avitus, some of what you read here is good, some is so-so, more is bad; it's the only way to make up a book" (1.16).

Ancient and modern poets are also eloquent about the difficulty of getting a poem right. T. S. Eliot in *East Coker* wrote of "the intolerable wrestle / with words and meanings" and "a raid on the inarticulate / with shabby equipment always deteriorating / in the general mess of imprecision of feeling, / undisciplined squads of emotion." Horace in the *Satires* speaks of the head-scratching and fingernail-biting that attends any serious poetic enterprise (see oo), and in *Epode* 14 he makes a poem out of his supposed inability, because of love, to bring his iambic collection to an end.

But the *Odes* attest to no such effort or incapacity, and they do not question their success; instead they radiate confidence in their own excellence. That apparent assurance is probably the consequence of Horace's high aspirations: an artist engaged in constructing a monument cannot be seen to doubt the quality of the building materials.

A related question is whether the *Odes* are Horace's *Collected Lyrics* or a selection of those he thought the best. The sheer volume of *Odes* 1–3 makes it unlikely that Horace composed many more poems than appear in that collection, but it seems equally unlikely that he was satisfied with every lyric he wrote, and the poems' generally high quality and consistency of finish argue for either some culling of inferior efforts or a rigorous process of polishing.

---

[3] Auden 1945: vii.

Finally, within *Odes* 1–3 Horace never portrays himself as hankering to write in another form, unlike the elegists Propertius and Ovid, who profess to feel drawn to a higher genre, epic and tragedy, respectively. It is impossible to say whether Horace felt no such attraction or whether the absence of gestures toward other genres results from a wish to inhabit the role of the lyric poet as completely as possible. But a tentative suggestion can be offered to explain why he may have found lyric a uniquely satisfying medium of expression.

Each of Horace's choices of genre can be seen as an attempt to create a voice that is at once personal and authoritative; only lyric, though, provided a framework and a set of conventions that fully met those requirements. The iambist, satirist, lyric poet, and writer of admonitory/hortatory/instructive letters are all engaged in exercises of verbal power. The satirist and the iambist derive their authority from a primarily personal source, a sense of grievance or an awareness of the faults of others; the writer of philosophical letters must rely on his superior wisdom and access to accepted dogma to give weight to his advice and instruction. The authority of the lyric voice, by contrast, is grounded in the concept of divine inspiration, given form in the persons of the Muses, daughters of Zeus and Memory. The lyric poet, like the writer of epic, can invoke the aid of the Muses, but without sacrificing his or her individual persona and perspective.

References to the Muses, and to Horace's relationship with them, act as a framing motif for *Odes* 1–3. At the end of 1.1 the cooperation of Euterpe and Polyhymnia in Horace's lyric enterprise is sought, but not assumed:

> if Euterpe does not withhold
> her flute, and Polyhymnia does not refuse
> to tune for me the lyre of Lesbos.

The first poem of Book 2 ends with an address to Horace's "impudent Muse" (2.1.37), urging her not to treat the tragic subject of the civil war but to seek out lighter themes. Book 3 opens in a more solemn vein, with Horace proclaiming himself "priest of the Muses" (3.1.3). It ends with a final address to a Muse:

> take the proud honor
> well-deserved, Melpomene, and be pleased
> to circle my hair with the laurel of Delphi.
>
> (Trans. David West)

Horace's language here is more confident and assertive than in 1.1: his success is no longer conditional, and he can address Melpomene with imperatives ("take," "be pleased to circle"). His boldness may be more than syntactical. West's translation "Take the proud honor / well-deserved" preserves an ambiguity present in *sume superbiam / quaesitam meritis*: this is usually understood to mean "accept the honor" (literally "pride") "that you have won by your merits," but the Latin also admits the meaning "accept the honor won by my merits," which I believe coheres better with the tone of the poem. Horace has made good use of the Muses' favor, and he can even enhance their eminence through his achievement.

Invocations of the Muses could be written off as expressions of poetic convention, but Horace's statements have a warmth that is not so easily discounted. His words suggest that he saw his poetic talent, and in particular his talent for lyric, as a gift that set him apart from others and that was responsible for his rise from humble origins. Horace's sense of being under the Muses' protection takes its most remarkable form in the myth he creates in 3.4 about his infancy: he writes of having fallen asleep while wandering in the countryside and of doves weaving for him a blanket of myrtle and bay leaves, a story that closely resembles one told about Pindar. He describes himself as "a fearless child, not without divine help" (3.4.20), and the following line, addressed to the Muses in their Italian incarnation, the Camenae, makes it clear where that divine assistance lay.

Perhaps Horace's most affecting address to a Muse comes from his second collection of lyrics, when his status as Rome's writer of lyric was assured. In it a frank expression of pride is subordinated to a sense of gratitude, and lightened by a disarming irony (4.3.17–24):

> O goddess of Pieria, who temper
> to sweetness the sound of the golden lyre,
>   o you who could, if you so willed,
> grant even to dumb fish the song of the swan,
>
>   this is all your gift, that men
> as they pass on their way point a finger at me,
>   the player of the Roman lyre;
> that I live and please, if I do please, is from you.

·4·

Odes 1–3

The Collection

> Do you take great care in ordering the poems in a collection?
> Yes, great care. I treat them like a music-hall bill: you know, contrast, difference in length, the comic, the Irish tenor, bring on the girls.
>
> Philip Larkin, *Further Requirements*

It is natural to assume that in planning his lyric monument Horace devoted considerable attention to the order in which the poems appear, and that assumption is amply borne out by the collection itself. This chapter will explore some of the principles Horace used in arranging the contents of his collection, and some of the consequences of that arrangement for the reader. Before I can embark on that discussion, however, a fundamental question about *Odes* 1–3 must be addressed.

Scholars have traditionally held that Horace published *Odes* 1–3 as a unit in 23. In 2002 that belief was challenged by Gregory Hutchinson, who argued for separate publication of the books, perhaps in 26, 24, and 23, respectively.[1] His strongest evidence was an evolution in Horace's metrical practice, which would support the more limited conclusion that the poems of Book 1 are on the

---

[1] Reprinted with revisions in Hutchinson 2008.

whole earlier than those of Book 2, and those of Book 2 earlier than those of Book 3, but the hypothesis of separate publication runs into difficulties of various kinds. One is the prominent place of L. Sestius, the addressee of *Odes* 1.4, after poems addressed to Maecenas, Augustus, and Virgil and preceding poems addressed to Agrippa and Munatius Plancus. Sestius's place in such a carefully plotted sequence makes it almost certain that at the time of publication he was one of the leading men in Rome; that was the case in the second half of 23, when Augustus named him to fill out the consulship he had relinquished, but it would not have been so at any previous time. An argument of a different sort also points away from an earlier date of publication for some of the *Odes*. Horace's younger contemporary the elegist Propertius was a highly reactive writer; each of the books that followed his initial collection shows him responding to a fresh poetic stimulus, his fellow elegist Tibullus in Book 2, Horace's *Odes* in Book 3, and Virgil's *Aeneid* in Book 4. If the *Odes* had begun to appear by 26, one would expect to see signs of Propertius's response to them in his second book, published in about 25–24, rather than his third, from about 20. (This argument retains its force even if the collection transmitted as Propertius Book 2 is a conflation of two originally separate books, as some scholars believe.) Furthermore, Propertius's allusions include echoes of *Odes* 1.1, 3.1, and 3.30, suggesting that he is responding to *Odes* 1–3 as a totality. (On Propertius's response to Horace see 191.)

Odes 1–3 also exhibit a number of structural features characteristic of a unified collection. The opening and closing poems (1.1 and 3.30) respond to one another in subject and in meter, a form used only in those poems. Poem 1.5 corresponds to 3.26 in position and content: in each poem Horace's retirement from love is signaled by a votive offering displayed on a temple wall (1.5.14, 3.26.4). Halfway through the middle book stands a poem that commends moderation (*mediocritas*), the virtue of "being in the middle" (2.10.5). It is not impossible that Horace could have published three separate collections of poems that, when read together, create the impression of a unified whole, but that is not the most economical hypothesis.

Finally, Horace's aspiration to become a canonical lyric poet required him to produce a corpus of work in that genre, comparable to the multi-book Alexandrian editions of Sappho, Alcaeus, Pindar, and the other canonical poets. No single book of lyric, even one as large and impressive as *Odes* 1, would have been sufficient to achieve that ambition.

For those reasons I will proceed on the assumption that *Odes* 1–3 are a unified collection.

The signs of careful ordering range from the large-scale architecture of the collection just mentioned to the placement of many of its individual poems. The first half of Book 1 displays the greatest concentration of organizing principles, probably intended to make a powerful first impression on the reader. I have already noted the opening sequence of nine poems each in a different meter with which Horace establishes his command of Greek lyric form (above, 27). The reader who then finds that 1.10 repeats the Sapphic meter of 1.2 and who concludes that Horace has exhausted his metrical repertory is in for a surprise, since the next poem, 1.11, introduces yet another new form. (Horace may be doing more here than toying with his readers' expectations; Oliver Lyne has noted that the metrical sequence of *Odes* 1.9–11 corresponds to that of the first three poems of the first book of Alcaeus's odes as established in the Alexandrian edition of Aristarchus.)[2] It has become traditional to refer to this opening sequence as the "Parade Odes," a term apparently coined by Karl Christ in 1868. Other patterns have only recently come to light. In 1995 Michèle Lowrie drew attention to a second sequence of poems, spanning 1.12 through 1.18, each of which alludes to a different Greek predecessor.[3] (The order is Pindar, Sappho, Alcaeus, Bacchylides, Stesichorus, Anacreon, and Alcaeus.) Then in 2008 Andrew Fenton pointed out that twelve varieties of trees are mentioned in the first fourteen poems, with none being repeated—a pattern not likely to be coincidental.[4] As

---

[2] Lyne 2005.
[3] Lowrie 1995, reprinted in Lowrie 2009a.
[4] Fenton 2008; quotation is from 563.

he remarks, "The overall effect . . . is the creation of a literary grove," a tangible counterpart to the metaphorical grove (*nemus*) to which Horace claimed entrance in the opening poem (1.1.30; see 28).

The midpoint of Book 1 is strongly marked, dividing the book into two equal halves: poem 20, the start of the second half, is the first poem addressed to Maecenas after 1. It is followed by an appeal to Diana and Apollo, paralleling the appeal to several gods in 1.2. A poem to Virgil soon follows (24), balancing 3—these are the only poems addressed to Virgil in *Odes* 1–3.

In the first half of *Odes* 1 Horace is primarily concerned to display his connections to the Greek lyric tradition; following the start of the second half come two poems (21 and 22) that pay tribute to his only Roman predecessor by referring to all three of Catullus's poems in lyric form. *Odes* 1.22 quotes a phrase from Catullus 51, also in Sapphic meter, and alludes to Catullus's other Sapphic poem, 11. (For discussion of 1.22 see 107–08.) The previous ode is Horace's response to the third of Catullus's lyric poems, 34, a hymn to Diana. Again the relationship is signaled by metrical similarity: the third and fourth lines of Horace's stanzas are identical to the meters used by Catullus.

Odes 1 is also remarkable for the number of poems it contains, thirty-eight. Roman poets of this period show a tendency to group poems into books containing multiples of five: ten poems for Virgil's *Eclogues*, Horace's *Satires* 1, and Tibullus Book 1; fifteen, twenty, and fifteen for the three books of Ovid's *Amores*; twenty-five for Propertius Book 3. *Odes* 2 (twenty poems) and 3 (thirty) follow the same pattern. Lyne suggested that the first book of Alcaeus's lyrics in the Alexandrian edition contained thirty-eight poems,[5] but he admitted that this was pure speculation, and other explanations should be considered. Horace may have wanted the first installment of his lyrics to impress by its sheer profusion of content. There is a possible precedent in the problematic Book 2 of Propertius, which

---

[5] Lyne 2005: 557–58.

as transmitted contains thirty-four elegies—some of which need to be subdivided, possibly increasing the total number to thirty-eight!—and which runs to nearly 1,500 lines, compared to 876 in *Odes* 1. If that mammoth body of elegy really is a single book (as I incline to think), it was probably intended to astonish readers by its bulk. It appeared sometime in the mid-20s, when Horace was assembling *Odes* 1–3.

The opening sections of Books 2 and 3 are defined in metrical terms that move progressively away from the virtuoso display of *Odes* 1. The first half of Book 2 comprises ten poems that alternate between Alcaic and Sapphic stanzas, while seven of the latter ten poems are in Alcaics; the dominance of the Alcaic meter is then carried further at the beginning of Book 3, with a unique sequence of six poems in that form. That opening sequence inverts all the markers that distinguished the opening of Book 1: as metrical uniformity replaces a profusion of meters, an absence of individual addressees replaces a parade of distinguished figures, and instead of a combination of personal and public poems there is a much stronger focus on political and social issues.

But while the opening of each book is strongly marked, the placement of poems nearest the book divisions encourages reading across book boundaries. This is clearest in the transition from Book 1 to Book 2, where the penultimate poem of 1 (1.37) and the first poem of 2 are publicly oriented responses to the civil war, separated by a personal envoi (1.38). (On 1.37 and 2.1 see 120–26.) The end of Book 2 and the opening of Book 3 are more subtly connected by similarities linking the Bacchus who appears in 2.19—a teacher of poems and a metamorphic figure, not bound by the underworld and so immortal—and Horace as he is described in 2.20 and 3.1, first as a metamorphic figure, implicitly immortal, and then as a teacher of poems.

In addition to these larger-scale devices of arrangement, individual poems can be linked to their neighbors by shared vocabulary. Some such juxtapositions underscore thematic connections between poems, as when two poems addressed to close friends (2.6 and 2.7) each end with a form of the word for "friend" (*amici, amico*), or when the concept of hope is placed in a questionable light in successive odes (1.4.15, 1.5.11). The significance of other connections is less clear. The word for "cork" (*cortex*) appears only twice in the *Odes*, in 3.8 and 3.9; that is not likely to be a coincidence, but neither does it seem to carry weight beyond the purely formal.[6]

A related technique, in which adjacent poems share themes or situations, allows Horace to modulate his tone. Thus the fanciful description of the underworld in 2.13 is followed by a much grimmer version in 2.14. (On both poems see 00 and 00.) The shift can also go from seriousness to something lighter: in 3.11 Hypermestra stands up to what she foresees as drastic punishment (chains and exile) from her father, while in the next poem Neobule is one of the wretched women who are "scared stiff" (*exanimari*) by the prospect of a tongue-lashing from a stern uncle. The repeated motif of criticism from a family member effects a transition from high drama to near farce.

One such modulation is so extreme as to be unsettling. In 3.6 Horace thunders against marital infidelity with the fervor of a revivalist preacher. The next poem takes up the theme in an almost playful manner. Horace consoles Asterie, who is worried about the fidelity of her lover (or, less probably, her husband) Gyges, stranded by storms on the other side of the Adriatic. He assures her that, though tempted by his hostess Chloe, Gyges remains deaf to her blandishments (at least so far). Asterie herself, however, is being serenaded by a handsome neighbor, Enipeus, and Horace counsels her to show a similar resistance. Horace holds up Gyges as a paragon of constancy to fortify Asterie in the face of a temptation to stray, but the poem has a teasing quality (how can Horace know about Gyges's situation?), and the Greek names of all its characters distance it from the Roman reality of 3.6. The two poems thus adopt a similar attitude, but in radically different modes.

As that example suggests, juxtaposed poems can comment on one another and in so doing reveal the partial character of each. The opening of *Odes* 1 already shows that reading poems in order

---

[6] Renehan 1988: 317–18 lists the places in which a word is used in two successive odes.

complicates the impression that each poem in isolation might make. In 1.1 Horace depicts himself in Callimachean terms as aloof from the common crowd, and by implication unbothered by its concerns. But in the next poem he casts himself as deeply troubled by Rome's current situation. A similar adjustment takes place in literary terms: 1.2, an appeal to the gods with connections to Pindar's paeans, revises the impression created by 1.1 that Horace will not imitate Pindaric lyric but rather that of Sappho and Alcaeus. When read together 1.1 and 1.2 serve as an introduction to *Odes* 1–3, presenting two aspects of Horace that will be developed in subsequent poems, the detached private poet and the engaged citizen.[7]

The patterns of arrangement I have been describing are either static or limited in their movement, but *Odes* 1–3 also traces progress of several kinds, an evolution that reveals itself to a reader over the course of its eighty-eight poems. Here again the closest precedent is in Propertius: in his first collection of elegies, which appeared a few years before *Odes* 1–3, the emotional arc of the elegies featuring the poet's mistress, Cynthia, describes a clear movement toward separation and ultimately toward death.

In speaking of progress or evolution, I do not mean to suggest that *Odes* 1–3 constructs a continuous narrative; each poem creates its own reality, and even a sequential reading needs to respect the independence of the individual poem. In the amatory poems, for example, when, two poems after 1.11, a poem of seduction addressed to Leuconoe, we find Horace experiencing jealousy when Lydia praises her boyfriend Telephus, we are probably not meant to think "Whatever became of Leuconoe? I guess things didn't work out there." On this point Steele Commager strikes a reasonable balance: "Each of the Odes is, to be sure, a whole, and it may be that we violate its integrity even by regarding it in conjunction with any other. Yet each is also an integer in Horace's total output, and the temptation to add them together is almost irresistible."[8]

---

[7] Oliensis 1998: 127–28, with different emphasis.
[8] Commager 1962: viii.

With what I hope is due caution, I would propose to see development across *Odes* 1–3 in three areas: the realization of Horace's poetic ambitions, the treatment of the civil war and its sequel, and the depiction of the poet's relationship to Maecenas. As we shall see, the first and third of these overlap to a considerable extent.

The evolution of Horace's poetic ambitions can be most readily traced through the opening and closing poems of each book. *Odes* 1.1 sets out his aspiration to join the canonical lyric poets, while 1.38, pointedly modest and small-scale, refrains from making any claims of success. *Odes* 2.1 begins in a more ambitious vein but pulls back at the end, professing to return to "trifles" (*ioci*). In 2.20 Horace predicts his immortality, but immediately undercuts it with a grotesque description of physical metamorphosis:

> Already, even now, rough skin is forming
> on my legs, my upper part is changing
>   into a white swan and smooth feathers
>   are sprouting along my fingers and shoulders.
>   (Trans. David West)

The notion of a poet as a swan works as a metaphor, as when Horace salutes Varius as "the swan of Homeric song" in 1.6.2, or when Ben Jonson calls Shakespeare "sweet swan of Avon"; the picture of Horace actually turning into a swan can only be ludicrous. In 3.1 Horace claims for himself a more exalted status (priest of the Muses, teacher of the youth), and in 3.30 he triumphantly proclaims the success of his lyric project.

Once we reach Book 3, there is no more hesitation or display of false modesty. When at the end of 3.3 Horace rebukes himself for relating the speeches of the gods, it is for transgressing the bounds of lyric and trespassing on the terrain of epic. In this connection 3.13 deserves particular notice. The poem has the character of a hymn addressed to the *fons Bandusiae*, a relatively obscure local spring. (The poem was long a favorite, and its familiarity probably gave the *fons Bandusiae* a fame it did not possess until Horace celebrated it.) After describing the offerings the spring will receive on the following day, the poem concludes with a confident prediction (13–16):

> You too will become one of the famous springs,
>   once I tell of the scarlet oak placed above
>   the fluted rocks where your
>   speaking waters come leaping down.
>   (Trans. Stanley Lombardo)

The "famous springs" are those celebrated in Greek poetry as sources of poetic inspiration, like Hippocrene. The Bandusian spring will join this aquatic canon once it is immortalized by a canonical poet. From here it is a small step to the odes of Book 4 that promise immortality to Horace's addressees.

We cannot date the composition of *Odes* 1–3 with precision, but it seems likely that Horace turned to lyric soon after the appearance of *Satires* Book 2 and the *Epodes* in about 30. The period from 30 to 23, the likely year of publication of *Odes* 1–3, marked an epoch in Rome's political history, the transition from a generation of civil war to a new political system under Augustus. That development finds its reflection in the course of *Odes* 1–3.

Poems relating to the civil war frame Book 1 and open Book 2. The first of these poems, *Odes* 1.2, is the darkest. The legacy of civil war is treated as a crime (*scelus*, 29) that has provoked divine disfavor and that requires divine aid for its expiation. Horace canvasses several potential saviors before settling on Octavian (referred to by his preferred name "Caesar"), who is mysteriously amalgamated with Mercury. The poem captures the mood of Rome in the years just after Actium, when Octavian had crushed all opposition but had not yet revealed how he would use his dominant position, leaving poets unsure of the terms in which to address him. *Odes* 1.37 and 2.1 adopt contrasting perspectives on the civil war, 1.37 celebrating the victory at Actium as the triumph of Rome over Egypt and 2.1 lamenting the earlier phases of the war as a tragic conflict of citizens. (Both poems are more fully treated at 000.) But the opening poems of Book 2 also begin to move past the civil wars. The addressees of the first three odes—Asinius Pollio,

Sallustius Crispus, and Quintus Dellius—are all former opponents of Octavian who were soon reconciled to him. The process of reconciliation is completed a few poems later, in 2.7, when Horace welcomes back to Italy an old friend, Pompeius, who had fought with him at Philippi and had afterward held out against Octavian until the bitter end. (For discussion of this poem see 53–58.) To celebrate Pompeius's return Horace calls for Massic wine, which has the power to induce forgetfulness (*oblivioso*, 2.7.21); the wine produces its intended effect on the collection as well, consigning the painful past to a welcome oblivion. When in the first six poems of Book 3 Horace offers a sustained reflection on the state of Rome, he finds much cause for concern, but civil conflict or unrest is not to blame; instead the threats are essentially personal and moral, the consequences of excessive materialism and the loosening of traditional restraints on behavior. Those poems also make clear the extent to which the future of Rome and the safety of its citizens have come to depend on one man: as Horace says in an ode later in Book 3, "I shall have no fear of upheaval or violent death while Caesar is master of the earth" (3.14.14–16).

While Caesar/Augustus is mentioned more often than any other individual in *Odes* 1–3 (in 1.6, 1.12, 1.21, 1.35, 1.37, 2.9, 2.12, 3.3, 3.4, 3.5, 3.14, and 3.25), he is directly addressed in only one poem, 1.2. Maecenas, on the other hand, has the distinction of being the recipient of eight odes, which span the collection from its opening (1.1) to its next-to-last item (3.29). The placement of odes to Maecenas varies from book to book. In Book 1 they open the book and introduce the second half. In Book 2 they are clustered in the second half (12, 17, 20) and end the book. In Book 3 they come shortly after the opening sequence (3.8), immediately after the midpoint (3.16), and in penultimate position. The distribution of poems ensures that Maecenas is never far from Horace's (or our) mind. (*Odes* 1.20, 2.12, and 3.29 are discussed at 81–89.)[9]

---

[9] On the portrayal of Horace's relationship to Maecenas see Santirocco 1986: 153–68.

The odes to Maecenas that bear on Horace's activity as a poet follow a progression that mirrors Horace's own growing confidence. In 1.1 Horace is dependent on Maecenas's opinion for his admission to the canon of lyric poets. In 1.20 he can offer him only a cheap Sabine wine in a Greek jug (suggesting that his poetic progress is still at an early stage), whereas in 2.12 Horace can exercise control over the kind of poetry he will write, declining an implied request from Maecenas to celebrate Augustus's victories. At the end of Book 2, Maecenas is an observer of Horace's curious transformation into a swan. The fact that none of the odes to Maecenas in Book 3 associate him with Horace's poetry is part of the same progression: in 3.30 it is the Muse, not Maecenas, who confirms Horace's success.

The depiction of Horace's relationship to Maecenas in other poems also undergoes development, as Horace evolves from Maecenas's dependent to his mentor. That shift is most evident in the three odes of Book 3 that are addressed to him. In 3.8 Maecenas is invited to leave behind his statesman's worries and join Horace in celebrating the anniversary of his deliverance from a falling tree (recounted in 2.13, on which see 58–65). In 3.16 Horace enlists Maecenas as the audience for a lecture on the dangers of wealth and the joys of a simple life. Both themes then recur in 3.29. In all three poems Horace is implicitly Maecenas's superior in wisdom, and his plain country life is presented as preferable to Maecenas's luxurious but anxiety-ridden existence.

As *Odes* 1 began with a pair of introductory poems, so *Odes* 3 ends with a dual conclusion that highlights two aspects of Horace's self-presentation: 3.29 is the fullest statement of Horace's way of life, and 3.30 is the proudest statement of his identity as a poet. As a man like others (the perspective adopted in 3.29), the most Horace can aspire to is a life lived to the full each day and graced by the pleasures of wine and friendship. But speaking as a poet in 3.30, he can lay claim to something greater, a survival beyond death.

After this overview of *Odes* 1–3, the four chapters that follow will explore some of the contents of this extraordinary collection in more detail. The first offers close readings of three representative poems (1.11, 2.7, and 2.13). Then come three chapters each devoted to a selection of poems on a related theme: poems of friendship and advice, amatory poems, and political or civic poems. By proceeding in this way I hope to illustrate the range of Horace's material and the skill with which he varies the treatment of similar themes in different poems.

· 5 ·

Three Odes

Since I do not have space to analyze many of the *Odes* in detail, I have chosen to present more rounded interpretations of a few poems to illustrate some of Horace's characteristic themes and techniques, and also to suggest strategies of reading that can be more broadly applied. I have selected three odes, 1.11, 2.7, and 2.13. It is a small sample, but one that embraces the quintessential Horatian themes: friendship, politics, nature, love, death, and poetry. I shall discuss them in the order in which they appear in *Odes* 1–3, which happens to be in order of increasing length and complexity.

Every ode of Horace takes the form of an address to a person or, less often, an object. The address is situated in a context that the reader needs to construct from information in the poem. Modern poems usually have titles, and we can often get an initial sense of a poem's content from its title, as with Robert Lowell's "The Quaker Graveyard in Nantucket." Horace's *Odes* as initially published had no titles, which would have made the reader's task more challenging; that is one reason why Horace normally specifies the addressee in the opening lines of a poem. In many odes constructing the situation is straightforward, since the text presents it in explicit terms. In some poems, however, the imagined situation is suggested rather than stated, and in those cases the reader must be attentive to details that will assist in constructing the implied circumstances and the relationship the poem creates between speaker and addressee.

Horace's Odes. Richard Tarrant, Oxford University Press (2020). © Oxford University Press.
DOI: 10.1093/oso/9780195156751.001.0001

I.11

Odes 1.11 is one such poem. Horace addresses a woman named Leuconoe, advising her not to inquire into the future but instead to leave such concerns to the gods and enjoy the present moment.[1] So much is obvious, but if we wish to understand what has prompted this advice and what it means in its context, we need to read more closely. So let us make a first pass through the poem, focusing on its implied situation.

> Don't ask, Leuconoe—we must not know—what end
>   the gods
> have fixed for me, for you, and don't turn to Babylonian
> tables of the stars. Much better by far to endure what comes,
> whether Jupiter grants more winters or whether this is
>   the last,
> which now wears down the Tuscan sea on the opposing
>   pumice   5
> rocks. Be smart, strain the wine, cut back long hopes
> to fit a narrow span. Even as we speak, envious time
> has fled. So pluck this day, putting no trust in the one
>   to come.

It is a natural assumption that what Horace advises Leuconoe against doing in the opening lines corresponds to what she has been doing, namely, attempting to learn what end the gods have in store "for me, for you." Her interest in both their fates is a strong indication that her motive is erotic: she wants to know if their relationship has a future before deciding whether to become or stay involved with him. The poem is therefore a poem of seduction, and Leuconoe is an ancestress of Marvell's "coy mistress."

That initial impression is strengthened by what Horace says about Leuconoe's way of addressing the issue. She is not merely

---

[1] For the sake of simplicity I refer to the "I" of the *Odes* as "Horace," while not assuming that the sentiments expressed by that figure correspond to those of the historical Horace.

wondering what the future may hold but is actively investigating; she has even been consulting experts, adepts in astrology who use "Babylonian tables" to predict what will come. Her motive must therefore be strong and personal. And yet those anxious inquiries also suggest diffidence on her part. Perhaps her uncertainty is a sign of inexperience, or else the reluctance of a young woman to become involved with an older man.

The next indication of the poem's context comes at its midpoint, in Horace's description of the winter that might be their last: this winter, "which now wears down the Tuscan sea on the opposing pumice / rocks." Horace often uses geographical epithets like "Tuscan" for greater vividness, but here the adjective suggests a setting for the poem on the west coast of Italy. The fact that the rocks are specified as pumice, that is, volcanic, allows for further localizing, since the most conspicuous concentration of volcanic material on that coastline is around the Bay of Naples, where many well-to-do Romans had seaside villas. David West concludes that "Horace and Leuconoe are indoors on a wild winter's day in a villa on the shore of the Bay of Naples."[2] If that is right, the image from nature is not a commonplace but a description of what is going on outside the window.

The poem provides at least one further detail that assists in recovering its implied situation. Horace urges Leuconoe to "strain the wine." The significance of straining is not obvious (I will come back to it shortly), but more important is the presence of wine as part of the scene. West interprets the phrase as indicating that Leuconoe is a slave, like Thaliarchus in 1.9, who is similarly bidden to pour out the wine, but that notion makes the situation harder to understand: Why would Horace bother with persuading Leuconoe when he could have exercised a master's prerogative, and why would a slave girl be consulting astrologers about the future of a sexual relationship with her master? But West's reading is useful in making us notice the absence of slaves, since if they were

---

[2] West 1995: 50–51.

on hand, they would be pouring the wine. Horace and Leuconoe are therefore alone, and the drinking that Horace encourages is the prelude to the lovemaking that in this poem is the implied meaning of *carpe diem*.

Leuconoe is typical of the women in the *Odes* in having a Greek name, perhaps to distance her from the possibility of being a real life partner. Her name appears to be derived from the adjective λευκός (literally "white," also "clear") and the noun νοῦς ("mind," "intelligence"). Derogatory meanings such as "empty head" are probably not appropriate, and the name might have been chosen simply for its metrical convenience, but it could also suggest a simplicity bordering on naiveté.

Having established the implied situation of the poem, we can turn our attention to some of its formal elements and see how they work in harmony with the scenario we have sketched.

At eight lines, the poem is conspicuously short; there are a few other odes of the same length (1.30, 1.38, 3.22, and 4.10) but none that are shorter. The poem races by and is over almost before we are aware that it has begun—which is exactly what Horace is saying about the present moment. The feeling of speed is enhanced by Horace's choice of meter. This is one of only three odes written in a form called the Greater Asclepiad (the others are 1.18 and 4.10). Its basic component is a four-syllable metrical unit with the shape ‿‿‿ [long-short-short-long] known as a choriamb, a constituent of many of the Greek lyric meters adapted by Horace. What makes this form distinctive is a series of three successive choriambs, introduced by a spondee (‿ ‿) and followed by an iamb (‿‿). The chains of choriambs create the feel of a galloping pace, and Horace heightens the effect of breathlessness with several enjambed lines, that is, lines in which the sense runs over the line end and is completed at the beginning of the following line (1/2, 2/3, 5/6, 6/7, 7/8); there is no full stop at the end of any line before the last one. Horace also employs the choriamb as the smallest possible building block of sense: several of the poem's key statements are in the form of a two-word choriamb: "we must not know" (*scire nefas*), "strain the wine" (*uina liques*), and, finally, "so pluck this day" (*carpe diem*).

This reduction of thought to its smallest elements is another way in which Horace underscores the urgency of his message.

The urgent tone is set by the poem's first words, *tu ne quaesieris* ("don't ask"). In Latin the person who performs the action of a verb is denoted by the verb's ending, and so personal pronouns such as *ego* (I) and *tu* (you) are added only for emphasis or some other special effect. Meter apart, Horace could have written *ne quaesieris* and the meaning would have been the same, "do not ask." The addition of *tu* begins the poem on a note of "earnest admonition" (Nisbet and Hubbard 1970), as if Horace needed to shake Leuconoe out of her absorption with the future and get her to focus on the moment at hand.

Short as it is, the ode exhibits one of Horace's favorite forms of poetic structure, a tripartite arrangement in which related opening and closing sections are separated by a contrasting middle section. The effect is comparable to a *da capo* aria, and, as in that musical form, when the opening material returns it undergoes development of some sort, creating a pattern that can be represented as ABA'.[3] In 1.11 the opening and closing sections are dominated by exhortations to Leuconoe, and the B element is the glance away to the sea pounding on the rocks, which also varies the syntax with an exclamation ("how much better"). The concluding section (A') responds to the opening in stronger verbal terms: two negative commands ("don't ask," "don't turn to") are countered by three positive injunctions ("be smart," "strain," "cut back"). Horace even exploits a nicety of Latin grammar for greater immediacy at the end: the negative commands use the perfect tense of the subjunctive (*quaesieris, temptaris*), but the positive recommendations are in the more vivid present subjunctive (*sapias, liques, reseces*). For his final piece of advice, Horace shifts to the most direct and peremptory form possible, the present imperative: *carpe*.

I conclude with a look at the imagery of the final lines, working backward from *carpe diem*. The fact that the phrase has

---

[3] See Tarrant 1995 for further discussion and examples.

become a cliché should not obscure how brilliantly it works: although similar in thought to "gather ye rosebuds while ye may," it is stronger and more pregnant in meaning. As Kenneth Quinn notes, the action denoted by *carpere* ("plucking") suggests quick, firm movement, befitting the unhesitating enjoyment of the present that Horace advocates. The verb's sense is matched by its strong consonants. *Carpe* transforms the colorless *dies* ("day") into a metaphorical flower: beautiful but short-lived, literally ephemeral.

The floral imagery in *carpe diem* is prepared for by a previous phrase, "cut back long hopes / to fit a narrow span," where "cut back" evokes pruning, an apt metaphor for keeping hope under control, since hope, like a quickly growing vine, can soon expand beyond its proper limits. Hope tends to have positive associations for moderns, perhaps because of its status along with faith and charity as one of Christianity's theological virtues, but the Greeks and Romans took a dimmer view, aware of its capacity for clouding the vision.

We return to the puzzling injunction "strain the wine." We may sense that something more specific than "drink up" or "pour us some wine, there's a love" is intended, but what exactly is the point? Quinn 1980 comes close in saying that "straining the wine symbolizes the sort of practical, positive step toward limited happiness that is worth taking," but Nisbet and Hubbard 1970 offer an explanation that makes even more of the phrase. They note that sediment could be removed from wine either by pouring it through a strainer or by letting it stand for a period of time; the latter method produced better results but required putting off consumption. With this precise domestic image, Horace advises Leoconoe to accept an immediate form of pleasure rather than putting off enjoyment in the hope of obtaining something finer. Transposed to the erotic situation and spelled out with a crudity that the poem avoids, the implied advice might be something like "Make do with me, since I'm interested and available, and don't hold out for a more promising or younger lover."

2.7

O you who were so often led with me
into danger when Brutus was our army's leader—
    who has given you back as a citizen
        to your country's gods and Italian sky,

Pompeius, first of my companions? With you
   I often broke   5
the resistance of the dragging day with wine,
    my glistening hair crowned
        with the finest Syrian nard.

With you I knew Philippi, the headlong rout,
when to my shame I left behind my shield,   10
    when courage broke and fierce spirits
        fell, chins on the foul ground.

But fleet Mercury lifted me quaking
high through the enemy ranks in a mist,
    while you were sucked down by the wave,   15
        carried back into the surge of war.

So render now the feast you owe to Jove,
let your war-weary body recline and rest
    beneath my bay tree, and show no quarter
        to the wine casks reserved for you.   20

Fill the polished goblets with Massic wine
that helps us forget, pour perfume from shells
    brimming over. Who will make haste
        to weave garlands from fresh-cut parsley

or myrtle? Whom will Venus elect master   25
of the revel? I will rave more wildly
    than a Thracian bacchant. Madness
        is sweet for me when a friend has been regained.

In 2.7 Horace gives the reader more help in reconstructing the occasion of the poem than in 1.11. From the first stanza we can infer that Horace is welcoming Pompeius, a friend of his youth, back to Italy. Like Horace, Pompeius fought in the army of Brutus, and the poem's middle stanzas (9–16) supply the additional information that they were at Philippi together but then parted ways; from lines 15–16 we can infer that Pompeius went on fighting after the destruction of Brutus's army. Pompeius owes his return to the benevolence of an unnamed individual (the referent of "who" in line 3), and the fact that he has been restored "as a citizen," that is, that he has regained citizen status after having lost it, is presumably owing to the same source.

On one scenario that would account for those details, after Philippi Pompeius might have joined the forces of Sextus Pompey (son of Pompey the Great) and continued to oppose Antony and Octavian until Pompey's defeat at the naval battle of Naulochus in 36, after which he might have sided with Antony until Antony was in turn defeated at Actium in 31. Pompeius may have been among the former supporters of Antony then pardoned by Octavian; if so, his return to Italy could be dated to 30 or 29. After Actium there was no longer any organized resistance to Octavian, but a diehard opponent could have remained in the East in self-imposed exile for some time before bowing to the inevitable.

The occasion of Pompeius's homecoming is festive, but it is also delicate. Both he and Horace had fought against Octavian, who is now in power as Augustus. Furthermore, while Horace had long since made his peace with his former adversary, Pompeius held out for some time. As they meet again, he might well be unsure whether his old friend will resent his embrace of Caesar's heir. Horace's control of a situation is usually so complete that moments when it is put under pressure generate particular interest. So one approach to this poem would be to observe Horace's way of dealing with the potential for awkwardness that this meeting entails.

We glimpse one aspect of his strategy in the opening lines. Given how much of the ode centers on the bond between Horace and Pompeius, it is striking that the first stanza gives even greater prominence to a third party, the source of Pompeius's repatriation, who can only be Augustus. Though phrased interrogatively, "Who has given you back . . . ?" is not a request for information but a kind of implied exclamation ("who can have been so good as to return you?"), a tribute to Octavian's vaunted clemency and, perhaps, a gesture of atonement for earlier opposition. The verb that describes Octavian's action, *redonare*, means "to return as a gift"; it is rare and always stresses the free will of the one who acts. It may be in counterpoint with the verb that Horace applies to himself in the last words of the poem: the primary sense is "when a friend has been regained" (*recepto . . . amico*), but *recipere* can also denote receiving something from someone else, and so Octavian's gift of Pompeius can be seen as having Horace as its beneficiary. The first stanza ends with several emotively charged terms relating to Pompeius's return: he has come back "as a citizen," that is, with his citizen rights restored, and he has been restored to his ancestral gods and the sky of Italy. Calling on the powerful attachment that Italians felt to their *patria*, Horace suggests that through the graciousness of Octavian Pompeius is back where he belongs, and that any separation was unfortunate and temporary.

The next lines, describing their activities before Philippi (6–8), depict a scene of hedonistic indulgence, not unlike a party at an upscale fraternity. The exotic-sounding "Syrian nard" contains another of Horace's particularizing geographical terms, here connoting both foreignness and luxury, as one might (if fortunate) recall good times in Paris when the Veuve Clicquot flowed freely. Old political passions are erased; there is no hint of joining the cause of Brutus the Tyrannicide or of fighting for the Republic against the successors of Caesar. There may also be a suggestion that Horace and Pompeius were not the most promising of recruits to Brutus's army.

This poem is one of the clearest examples of da capo (ABA′) structure in the *Odes*; the two stanzas on Philippi (9–16) form the B section. It begins with the two friends united as before ("with you"), but the battle separates them in a way that puts Horace's tact to its stiffest test.

Horace is devastating in his description of the wreck of the Republican forces. "When courage broke" (from *frangere*, "break") bitterly echoes the use of the same verb four lines earlier: "I often broke (*fregi*) the resistance of the dragging day." Horace and Pompeius were good at breaking the resistance of the day, but their courage broke when it faced a real battle. Horace's abandoning his shield is consistent with that indictment, but that object's literary pedigree raises the possibility that he is speaking metaphorically: "The shield that he admits . . . to have left on the field of Philippi . . . had been left in a bush by Archilochus, and before the walls of Sigeum by Alcaeus."[4]

Horace and Pompeius now go their separate ways, and as he recounts his own escape, Horace's tone becomes overtly whimsical. He paradoxically makes himself look unheroic by invoking a heroic convention, the Homeric rescue of an endangered mortal by a divinity; applied to a historical battle and a real-life Horace, the convention becomes ludicrous. In addition, Mercury is not the most imposing of the Olympians, and "quaking" contributes a further deflating touch: Horace quakes as he is lifted in mid-air, like a child on a roller coaster.

The lines recalling Pompeius's fortunes following Philippi are couched in a metaphor that makes him the victim of an undertow too powerful for him, or by implication anyone, to resist ("You were sucked down by the wave, / carried back into the surge of war"). In a later poem (*Epistles* 2.2) Horace applies the same metaphor, and even some of the same vocabulary, to his own involvement in the civil wars, with similar exculpatory intent: "The surge of civil war carried me, a novice, into battle" (46).

Horace was carried upward, high above the battlefield, Pompeius dragged downward into a metaphorical swell. But the common element in their fates is underscored by the close relationship of the verbs used: Mercury lifted Horace clear (*sustulit*), while the undertow of war carried Pompeius back (*tulit*). It is also significant

---

[4] Wilkinson 1945: 60.

that each of them is the object of their respective verb: Horace and Pompeius are recipients of action emanating elsewhere. A similar tactic is at work in the poem's opening lines: "so often led [*deducte*] with me / into danger when Brutus was our army's leader" [*duce*].

The picture of two young men tossed about by forces beyond their control is skillfully drawn, but it remains no less false for that. Horace and Pompeius were not forced to join Brutus's army, and after Philippi Pompeius presumably chose to go on opposing Octavian, just as Horace chose not to do so. Horace develops a fiction of passivity that permits him to construe the past in the most favorable possible light, but the deception involved cannot be entirely concealed—and perhaps Horace wanted it so. Nisbet and Hubbard fault Horace for lack of sensitivity ("It is disconcerting to find him describing so terrible an experience with discreet jokes and elegant allusions"), but it may be preferable to see the patent artifice in his account as inviting disbelief, allowing the reader to see through the comforting lies Horace now tells about his past.

In the final three stanzas, Horace turns with palpable relief from the recollection of past events to the celebration he has prepared for Pompeius. The concluding section represents a return to the *status quo ante*, with the two friends once again drinking together, but now under the proper circumstances: in Italy and in peacetime.

The proceedings begin decorously, with Horace enjoining Pompeius to repay a debt to Jupiter. There may be a hint here of the more immediate source of his return, since the assimilation of Octavian to Jupiter began long before Actium.

Pompeius is then bidden to "show no quarter" to the wine casks reserved for him; military vocabulary again figures in a sympotic context, as earlier with "breaking" the day's resistance. The imagery is part of Horace's attempt to recreate his earlier intimacy with Pompeius while correcting their actions. With no real enemies left, they can return to waging phony wars against wine. The wine is an honest Italian Massic. It brings forgetfulness, a much-desired commodity on this occasion. The wine is poured into "polished goblets" (*ciboria*): no ordinary vessels, but imports from the East, perhaps even souvenirs of those long-ago drinking bouts before Philippi.

The pseudo-question in the opening section (3–4) is matched and expanded by two in lines 23–26. These new questions are effectively commands: "Who will weave the parsley into crowns?" implies "Will someone please get started on those parsley crowns?" Combined with strong enjambment—most remarkably in lines 24–25, across the stanza boundary—they convey a sense of Horace's growing excitement (or is it anxiety?) as the party gets under way.

By the end of the poem Horace has whipped himself into a state of frantic jollity, far removed from his customary self-possession. In fact, so ingrained is his moderation that when he proposes to go wild, he appends a justification for doing so (27–28). Perhaps because it is so uncharacteristic, this manic gaiety seems forced; is he turning up the volume to drown out the discomfort he feels at the sight of his old friend?

Horace is doing here what he does so often, modeling the behavior he regards as appropriate to a particular set of circumstances. He suggests what Pompeius ought to be experiencing: gratitude to Jupiter/Octavian for his restoration, a recognition that his youthful Republicanism was not a cause worth fighting for, and joy at being reunited with his friend. But is Pompeius buying it? The poem does not say. At the end the spotlight lingers on Horace in his self-induced Bacchic frenzy, while Pompeius remains just out of sight, mute and inscrutable, a ghost at the feast.

2.13

Whoever was the first to plant you, tree,
did it on a black day; those impious hands
trained you to massacre posterity
and bring disgrace upon our local lands.

I can imagine him—a homicide   5
who'd strangled his own father, stabbed a guest
at night and smeared the hearth with blood, applied
the Colchic poisons, in a word professed

every abomination that one could
conceive of. Last, he placed you on my farm 10
to topple, miserable lump of wood,
onto a master who deserves no harm.

No man is hourly armed against surprise.
The Carthaginian pilot who takes care
passing the Bosphorus forgets what lies 15
beyond, and runs on hidden dooms elsewhere.

When Parthians flee, the legions are afraid
of arrows; Parthians fear the captor's chain,
the strength of Rome; but death's an ambuscade
that has destroyed the world and shall again. 20

How close the realm of dusky Proserpine
yawned at that instant! I half glimpsed the dire
judge of the dead, the blest in their divine
seclusion, Sappho on the Aeolian lyre

mourning the cold girls of her native isle, 25
and you, Alcaeus, more full-throatedly
singing with your golden quill of ships, exile
and war, hardship on land, hardship at sea.

The admiring shades accord the reverent hush
due to them both; but when the theme is war 30
and tyrants banished, then the elbowing crush
thickens, the ghostly hearers thirst for more.

No wonder, when such music can disarm
the hundred-headed hell-dog till he droops
his dark ears in bewilderment, can charm 35
the snakes that braid the Furies' hair in loops,

yes, even beguile Prometheus and the sire
of Pelops of their torments; while Orion,
leaving the chase to listen to the lyre,
forgets the shy lynx and the ghostly lion. 40
     (Trans. James Michie)

The situation of this poem is set out in full in its opening stanzas. A tree on Horace's estate has come crashing down, nearly killing the poet. Although Horace speculates in lurid terms on the character who could have planted the offending object, the poem does not invite any serious thought about the background to the event; instead, its interest lies in the associations that the incident touches off in the speaker. These begin with furious imprecations on the villain who planted the tree, segue into general reflections on human shortsightedness, and conclude with a description of the underworld that Horace nearly entered before his time.

Whatever basis the poem may have had in Horace's biography, his narrow escape from the falling tree is recalled several times in subsequent odes and is variously credited to the rural deity Faunus in 2.17.27–30, to the Muses in 3.4.27, and to Liber (= Bacchus) in 3.8.6–8. In those later references, the emphasis is on Horace's good fortune and the divine protection that it betokens. This poem dramatizes the event itself, the moment following the tree's collapse.

A central issue in interpreting this poem is its tone. Critics agree that much of the ode is humorous, but opinions differ about whether any parts of it are to be taken more seriously, and if so, which parts. My own view is that the ode intimates seriously held ideas about poetry, but overlays them with irony directed at the speaker for his indulgence in poetic convention. One could speculate that irony is employed precisely because Horace is expressing views that meant a great deal to him.

This ode is one of only a few that are addressed not to persons (or person-like entities, such as gods) but inanimate objects. When Pablo Neruda, in his *Odes to Common Things*, addresses an ode to a tomato or a fallen chestnut or a pair of socks, he is working against the traditional modern expectation that an ode should celebrate some lofty person or subject and adopting a Marxist perspective to celebrate the dignity of ordinary objects. Horace here does the opposite: by employing the elevated verbal register of lyric to excoriate a lump of wood, he opens up an ironic distance between manner and subject. Although Horace's bile is directed more at the planter of the tree than the tree itself, making the tree the formal object of address creates a humorous effect that would not have been achieved if the evil planter had been the person invoked.

James Michie's rendering brings out the slight illogicality in Horace's opening words: "Whoever was the first to plant you." Horace is not implying that the tree had more than one planter; he is instead drawing on a common trope of ancient invective, aimed at the person who was the first to practice some activity that is deemed undesirable (for example, the first to sail the seas or to slaughter animals for sacrifice). The reader gets an initial hint that Horace is filtering his experience through the lens of received ideas.

Evil that defies description is often called "unimaginable." The target of Horace's invective, however, is fully imaginable; Horace knows everything of which the miscreant is capable, because he has created him out of his own well-stocked mind. (Horace alludes to that process of invention with "I can imagine him" in 5 and "every abomination that one could conceive of" in 9.) His crimes, while outrageous, are also highly conventional: parricide and the murder of a guest were the ancient *ne plus ultra* of wickedness, and Horace piles on bloodcurdling details to ratchet up their horror. The following phrase reveals the stereotypical nature of this portrait by specifying "Colchic poisons," that is, poisons associated with Medea. The epithet may be intended only to suggest "as lethal as those used by Medea," but it raises for a moment the absurd thought that Horace's nemesis has inherited some of the potions of antiquity's most famous sorceress.

At line 13 Horace's tone suddenly changes to one of rueful generalization. Some critics read these lines in full earnest: West, for example, thinks that they "chill the blood" in the midst of an otherwise light-hearted poem.[5] The moralizing sentiments of this section are indeed delivered with poker-faced seriousness, but they are tinged with irony by the exaggerations that have preceded them.

---

[5] West 1998: 95.

Furthermore, in their language and imagery the lines are not particularly impressive. "The Carthaginian pilot" is not one of Horace's most vivid particularizing epithets. The Parthian is an even more hackneyed figure. The Parthian cavalry had developed the tactic of shooting while riding away in apparent retreat. The maneuver struck the Romans as unsportsmanlike, and it provided their poets with fodder for endless variations on the idea, among which Horace's must be one of the feeblest. (Michie somewhat enlivens Horace's words, which are literally rendered "The soldier [fears] the arrows and swift flight of the Parthian.")

Finally, the thought of the section does not fully cohere. The idea that "no one takes sufficient caution about the dangers to be avoided from one hour to the next" could well describe Horace, walking on his property without a thought of the tree about to come down on him. But the examples that follow move in different directions. The first introduces a distinction: the sailor fears what is near at hand but does not anticipate death from another quarter. In the second it is not clear what unexpected threat the Roman and Parthian troops are neglecting; it cannot be death itself, since that is exactly what each of them is afraid of, the Roman dreading the prospect of being picked off by an arrow and the Parthian of dying in a Roman prison. The concluding *gnome* is suitably grim, but in its vast scale (one thinks of a plague like the Black Death) it is grossly out of proportion to the situation that prompts it.

In these middle stanzas Horace has produced a parody of his moralizing manner, marked by a reliance on conventional figures and ideas.

Horace goes on to reflect on how close he came to seeing the underworld, showing by his phrasing that he did not see anything of what follows. The ode's final section, like much of the first, is spun out of a well-read poet's imagination.

To an educated Roman, the underworld would have been as familiar as his or her own home. Even though the most famous ancient description, in Book 6 of the *Aeneid*, was still a few years in the future when Horace was writing, previous accounts had standardized many of its features and inhabitants. So a reader encountering the dark realm of Proserpina, Aeacus (Michie's "dire judge") on his judge's bench, and the separate dwellings of the blest (lines 21–23) would have felt on well-trodden ground. That conventional lead-in, though, is a false start, as the focus shifts unexpectedly to Sappho and Alcaeus.

In ancient depictions of the underworld, its denizens are often shown carrying on the pursuits for which they were known in life. So Sappho and Alcaeus are shown doing what they had done so often when alive, declaiming their poems to an audience.

The following lines contain Horace's most detailed reference to his principal models in lyric poetry. Critics have naturally searched here for a poetic credo, and have seized on the greater prominence accorded Alcaeus as an expression of Horace's own allegiance. Horace's admiration for Alcaeus does indeed come across: he is in effect the poem's other addressee, and the warm "you" with which Horace salutes him in line 26 is a world apart from the bitter vocatives directed at the fallen tree (lines 1 and 11). But the passage also continues to look with irony at the conventional images that fill the speaker's mind.

Ancient literary criticism was fond of pairing exponents of a poetic genre for purposes of comparison and contrast. Thus Homer was matched against Hesiod, and Aristophanes in *The Frogs* pitted Aeschylus and Euripides against each other. Horace's dual portrait of Sappho and Alcaeus is in that tradition and partakes of its reductive tendency. His Sappho is reduced to lovesick mooning, while Alcaeus takes on a hypermasculine hardness ("hardship on land, hardship at sea"). Horace knew that there was more to their work than these caricatures, and his relationship to them is more nuanced than this passage, if read as a manifesto about his own poetry, would imply.

The final stanzas dwell on the effect Sappho and Alcaeus have on their listeners. Horace makes it clear that they enjoy the equal respect of their audiences ("the reverent hush due to them both"). But the shades are particularly riveted by songs of war and banished tyrants, and so they cluster more thickly around Alcaeus. It was an article of Callimachean poetic belief that the subjects that attracted the greatest popularity were the ones most assiduously to be avoided. So here the crowd of shades (which is called a *uulgus*) is displaying the literary tastes typical of all crowds.

In the last two stanzas, allusions to Virgil and Homer reinforce the literariness of Horace's underworld. In describing the reaction of Cerberus and the Eumenides (33–36) Horace recalls a scene in Virgil's *Georgics*, in which Orpheus's song pleading for the release of Eurydice has a similar effect: "Even the halls themselves were struck dumb and inmost Tartarus, seat of Death, and the Eumenides with blue snakes entwined in their hair; Cerberus gaping restrained his three mouths, and Ixion's wheel stood still in the air" (G. 4.481– 84). For the Greco-Roman world Orpheus was the supreme poet, and so the allusion further enhances Alcaeus's standing. But irony resurfaces in Horace's treatment of Cerberus. The description of the hound as hundred-headed, and by implication two-hundred-eared, is "deliberately grotesque" (Nisbet and Hubbard 1977); Horace's imagination is again in overdrive, this time through inflation of a poetic topos.

Virgil's reference to Ixion, one of the traditional sinners punished forever in the underworld, lies behind Horace's reworking of yet another conventional idea. He substitutes Prometheus and Tantalus ("the sire of Pelops") and introduces a new figure, Orion, the ancient hunter par excellence. Once again Horace's poetry-soaked imagination is at work. Homer's Odysseus, in his underworld journey, had seen Orion: "that huge hunter, / rounding up on the fields of asphodel those wild beasts / the man in life cut down on the lonely mountain-slopes" (*Odyssey* 11.572–74, trans. Robert Fagles). Thanks to the charm of Alcaeus's poetry, Orion ceases his Homeric activity; Alcaeus has the power to override Homer.

Prometheus and Tantalus are not the only ones "beguiled of their torments" by poetry: by the end of the ode Horace appears to have quite forgotten his near-death experience and the dastard who caused it, and so have we. The enchantment that Horace ascribes to Alcaeus is effected in a more modest way by his own poem, even as it pokes good-natured fun at the character who stands at its center.

The poem represents a variation on Horace's favorite structural arrangement. It is tripartite, with the central element the generalizing lines 13–20. That section is followed, surprisingly, not by a return to the situation of the opening but by an entirely new scene in the underworld. The structure might be described as ABC. There is a reason why this poem does not revert to the occasion that put it in motion: with few exceptions—Hercules, Theseus, and of course Orpheus—once one enters the underworld, one does not leave. The ode thus wittily demonstrates a truth that Horace elsewhere treats with more gravity.

Although the opening and closing sections are unrelated in content, a verbal link connects them. The verbs *concipitur* ("conceive of") in line 9 and *decipitur* ("beguile") in 38 appear at the same place in their respective lines, have the same form (third person singular present indicative passive), and are compounds of the same verb, *capere*; their kinship can be seen in their English derivatives "conceive" and "deceive." What is conceived by the imagination in the form of poetry can be the source of welcome deception.

I find this one of Horace's most enjoyable poems. The gentle mockery of his tendency to moralize is delightful, as is the exuberant hyperbole of the opening stanzas, while the scene in the underworld expresses Horace's admiration for his Greek models in a highly original way. In showing how poetry can take us to unexpected places and cast a spell over its audience, the poem pays implicit tribute to Horace's own poetic power, but it does so without the insistence of more overtly programmatic odes

· 6 ·

Friendship and Advice

> Of all the things wisdom provides for the blessedness of a complete life, far and away the greatest is the possession of friendship.
>
> Epicurus, *Principal Doctrines*

Poems offering some kind of advice, instruction, or exhortation to recipients who are addressed as friends form a significant subset of *Odes* 1–3, and a number of those poems are among Horace's most widely admired creations. Most of the poems treated in this chapter contain both elements, but I also include 1.9, which offers advice to an inferior (probably a slave), as well as 1.20, which celebrates Horace's friendship with Maecenas but does not contain any advice.

1.24

I begin with *Odes* 1.24, addressed to a close friend, the poet Virgil. The occasion is the recent death of a certain Quintilius. It is very likely that this is the same Quintilius whom Horace would later commemorate in the *Ars Poetica* (438–44) as an acute and candid critic of poetry—a trait that would have endeared him to both Horace and Virgil.

> How shall we keep in or limit our grief, so dear
> was this man? Teach me a funeral dirge,
> Melpomene, gifted by the Father with a clear
>   voice and the lyre's music.

> So the sleep that lasts forever now covers   5
> Quintilius. Honor, and the sister of Justice,
> unbroken Trust, and Truth who walks naked,
>   when shall they find his equal?
>
> He dies mourned by many good men,
> but by no man more deeply, Virgil, than you.   10
> Useless devotion to beg the gods for Quintilius,
>   he was not lent on those terms.
>
> What good would it do to play the lute more sweetly
> than Orpheus of Thrace, to whom the trees responded?
> Would the blood come back to his thin ghost,   15
>   whom Mercury once and for all
>
> (he does not take kindly to prayers to open the gates)
> with his grim staff has gathered to the flock of shades?
> It's hard: but patience makes those things lighter
>   that we have no power to change.   20
>   (Trans. Joseph Clancy)

    The poem is remarkable for its compression, combining elements of a eulogy for Quintilius and a *consolatio* for Virgil in a mere twenty lines. That economy comes as something of a surprise. The opening stanza is rather spacious, especially the invocation to Melpomene; we seem to be embarking on a poem of some extent. The next stanza does not alter that expectation, but the third stanza soon does: from a multitude of mourners Horace singles out one, Virgil, and begins the shift to consolation. The quickening of tempo reflects the movement from static grief to active coping with loss. Ancient consolations typically offered a form of emotional therapy along with sympathy, and Horace's poem exemplifies that aspect, attempting to move Virgil from grief to acceptance.

    Horace does so in part by seeming to make that transition himself. The implied answer to the opening rhetorical question is "none," and the implied answer to the similar question in the next stanza is "never." In lines 1–8 Horace appears to indulge in the unrestrained mourning that the poem goes on to deprecate; he could almost be imagined declaiming those lines at Quintilius's funeral. On a subsequent reading, it becomes clear that the opening lament is the first stage in Horace's strategy of consolation. By manifesting his own grief at the loss of Quintilius, Horace strengthens his standing to offer advice: he is only urging Virgil to do what he has already done.

Lines 11 and 12 are pivotal, setting the course for the remainder of the poem. A literal translation would read "Pious in vain (alas), you ask the gods for Quintilius, not entrusted on those terms." The juxtaposition of "pious in vain" and "alas" beautifully unites Horace's ability to empathize with Virgil and his awareness that the desire to call back the deceased is futile. Horace calls Virgil *pius*, the epithet that characterizes the protagonist of the *Aeneid*; since Horace undoubtedly had advance knowledge of the epic, the adjective may be a coded communication from one poet to another. The words I have rendered "not entrusted on those term," *non ita creditum*, can be interpreted in two ways: "The gods did not entrust him to you on such terms" (as in Clancy's translation) or "You did not entrust him to the gods on such terms," referring to a situation (illness, a dangerous voyage) in which Virgil had placed Quintilius in the care of the gods. Virgil would have known which sense was intended, but most of Horace's ancient readers would not. Ambiguity of that kind is not typical of Horace, and its presence creates an impression of intimacy in his address to Virgil.

The fourth stanza returns to the interrogative mode of the opening two. Just as the implied answers to the earlier questions were "none" and "never," the answers to these are "none" and "no," but the effect of the negative answers is now the opposite, to discourage grief rather than to yield to it. When Horace asks "Would the blood come back to his thin ghost?," he introduces the question with *num*, which presupposes a negative answer. By questioning Virgil in this way, Horace enlists his assent in support of his argument. That argument also has a philosophical dimension, since as Epicureans both Virgil and Horace would have denied the existence of an afterlife.

It is generally believed that Horace's reference to Orpheus alludes to Virgil's telling of the Orpheus and Eurydice story in *Georgics*

4. The allusion, though plausible, raises a problem, since in Virgil Orpheus *does* succeed in getting Eurydice released; he loses her again, but not because the underworld refused to grant his request. It seems likely that Horace is offering an implicit critique: "Your story of Orpheus and Eurydice is a fable; I am dealing with reality."

In the final line almost all translators speak of what it is impossible to "change," for which the closest Latin equivalent would be *mutare*. The verb Horace uses, however, is *corrigere*, which means "correct." Michael Putnam has noted that the Quintilius who is quoted in the *Ars Poetica* would not hesitate to say to a poet "Please correct this or that"; *corrige* is the first word Horace puts into his mouth. Putnam interprets Horace's use of "correct" as an evocation of their friend and as a way of bringing him back to life.[1] The term could also be understood in a less positive sense, one perhaps more in keeping with the stern tone of the conclusion: mortality, unlike faults of style, cannot be put right.

2.10

Neither should one, Licinius, beat forever
for the open sea, nor from a fear of gales
become too cautious, and too closely hug
    the jagged shore.

A man who cherishes the golden mean   5
has too much sense to live in a squalid house,
yet sensibly eschews the sort of mansion
    that begs for envy.

It is the tall pine that the wind more cruelly
buffets, the high tower that falls with the heavier   10
crash; and it is the crest of the mountain
    where lightning strikes.

---

[1] Putnam 2009: 200–201.

> A heart that's well prepared for shifts of fortune
> hopes in adversity, and in happy times
> is wary. Jupiter brings afflicting winter,   15
>   and the same god
>
> takes it away. Today's ill luck will someday
> change for the better: sometimes Apollo wakens
> the slumbering lyre to song, nor is he always
>   bending the bow.   20
>
> In every hardship show yourself to be
> both brave and bold; yet when you run before
> too strong a favoring breeze, wisely take in
>   your swelling sails.
>
>   (Trans. Richard Wilbur)

    The poem is atypical in being entirely generic; no situation is even hinted at. In the absence of specific details, structural elements assume greater importance. Formally it consists of three parts, an opening and closing stanza addressed to Licinius and advising him on how to act, and a middle section consisting of general statements. A division of that kind can be articulated in two ways: either the closing unit returns to the thought of the opening (producing an ABA′ structure), or the final section introduces a new thought (creating an ABC structure). I suggest that in this poem Horace evokes both types of arrangement, as well as playing those tripartite structures off against a bipartite division of theme. That skillful manipulation of structure is the spice that rescues the poem from blandness.

    The opening and closing stanzas are linked by the address to Licinius and by their shared sea imagery; each also prescribes behavior for a contrasting set of situations. The poem thus gives a first impression of an ABA′ structure. But in fact the opening and closing prescriptions are quite distinct: one advises avoiding extremes, the other adapting to changing conditions; in addition, the prescriptions themselves vary accordingly (don't *always* press out to sea or hug the shore; act *in opposition* to prevailing conditions so as to anticipate change). That shift is accomplished in the poem's central section, which begins (lines 5–8) by recasting the opposition of the first stanza in more general terms and with a change of image (the hovel versus the mansion), then focuses on one of the extremes to be avoided (9–12; the prominent are at greater risk, a development of the mention of envy in line 8). The fourth stanza then introduces what will become the poem's second theme, the need to anticipate and adapt to change.

By restating this new theme in the last stanza in language that recalls the opening, Horace calls attention to the shift of focus within the ode and invites the reader to recognize the connection between the original and the redefined idea: "a heart that's well prepared for shifts of fortune" will both avoid extremes and adapt itself to changing conditions. Indeed, on a subsequent reading it becomes clear that the second theme is potentially present in the opening stanza: "forever" and "from a fear of gales" contain in embryo the motifs of consistency and response to circumstances that will form the material of the poem's second half. A reader can now experience the end of the poem as simultaneously a departure from and a return to the opening. That reader can also observe how the formal tripartite structure acts in counterpoint to a bipartite division in which lines 1–12 deal with avoiding extremes while lines 13–24 concentrate on responding to change. Neither pattern entirely displaces the other in the reader's mind, and the interplay between the two corresponds to the relationship in thought between the two main themes.

1.9

The interplay of structural patterns is put to even more effective use in *Odes* 1.9, to my mind one of Horace's greatest achievements.

> You see Soracte standing white and deep
>   in snow; the toiling woods no longer bear
>   their burden, and the rivers
>   stand still, fixed by the piercing cold.

> Thaw out the chill, put a fresh pile of logs   5
> on the hearth, and be generous in pouring
>   a wine aged for four years
>   in its Sabine jar, Thaliarchus.
>
> Leave all else to the gods; when they have stilled
> the winds now battling on the churned-up sea,   10
>   the cypresses are at rest
>   and the old ash trees cease to stir.
>
> Do not ask what will come to pass tomorrow,
> and count as gain whatever span of days
>   fortune will give, nor as a boy   15
>   reject the pleasures of love and the dance,
>
> while gray hair and grumbling are still far off
> from your verdant youth. Now is the time to return
>   to the Campus and piazza, for soft whispers
>   as night and the agreed-upon hour come near,   20
>
> now is the time for the telltale lovely laughter
> of the girl hiding in some secluded corner,
>   for the token pulled from her arm
>   or snatched from a faintly resisting finger.

    The opening and closing scenes could not be more different in their physical details: the cold, bright light of a winter day seen from indoors and the warmth of evening outside in the Campus Martius in spring or early summer. This would seem to be a clear case of an ABC arrangement, with the generalizing middle stanzas acting as the hinge between the contrasting outer sections. When the poem is seen in those terms, its salient feature is the breathtaking poise with which it moves from start to finish, in defiance of chronology. In reality the entire poem must take place in the winter setting established at the outset, and the repeated "now" in lines 18 and 21 must mean "now that you are still young"; and yet the scene described in the closing lines is so vivid that it seems to be happening at the present moment.

But at the same time there is a strong thematic parallel between the opening and closing sections: each presents an image of enjoying the moment in the appropriate way. A. Y. Campbell accordingly concluded that the poem was a circle, not a parabola.[2] It would be more accurate to say that it is both at once, and that its success in combining those movements is one mark of its quality. As is regularly the case in Horace's finest poems, structure is a reflection of theme: cyclical and linear movement are simultaneously present, just as in our experience of time the circular progression of the seasons carries us forward on the path from youth to old age.

The ode contains the germ of a seasonal poem, although in this case the shift from winter to spring/summer takes place only metaphorically. That transition is reinforced by the imagery that associates winter with whiteness and old age (Soracte "white and deep," "gray hair and grumbling") and spring with the green of youth ("your verdant youth"). Here we see another aspect of the poem's complex treatment of time: in nature winter yields to spring, but in terms of the human equivalences that Horace establishes old age is succeeded by youth.

Thaliarchus appears only here in the *Odes*, and the only explicit information about him given by the poem is that he is young, still a *puer*, so perhaps in his mid-teens. But his Greek name (which ironically means "lord of the feast") provides a strong hint that he is not an equal but a servant; among his duties are tending the hearth fire and keeping Horace's wineglass full. If that is the case, it is remarkable that Horace should be so solicitous of him, and should even advise him to take advantage of his youth. Perhaps there is more to the relationship. Kipling thought so, as shown by the final lines of his "A Translation": "My steward (friend but slave) brings round / logs for my fire." Several critics have gone further, suggesting that Thaliarchus is also Horace's lover.[3] I would regard that

---

[2] Cited by Nisbet 1962: 191.
[3] West 1995: 43–44 states the case well.

interpretation as possible but not required, but there is no doubt that the poem gains enormously in poignancy if the final stanzas are Horace's way of gently easing Thaliarchus into the next phase of his life. In particular his admonition "nor . . . reject the pleasures of love and the dance" would take on added meaning, implying that Thaliarchus needs to be persuaded that it is time to leave the nest.

The closing scene's sharpness of detail might suggest that it is a recollection from the speaker's own youth. If so, it carries with it no bitterness at time's passage. The implied message is "this was once mine to enjoy; now it is your time," a thought rendered even more moving if we believe that the speaker is marking the end of his relationship with Thaliarchus.

Another aspect of the poem's artistry has only recently come into focus. On its surface the poem seems firmly rooted in Rome and environs, framed by Mount Soracte and the Campus Martius. But it has long been recognized that the opening contrast between freezing cold outside and warmth and wine indoors resembles a fragment of Alcaeus, and since 2014 we have been able to see that lines 9–12 are modeled on a poem of Sappho containing the lines "And as for / the rest of it, to higher spirits leave it / now, for calm seas often follow after the / squalling of a storm."[4] The context in Sappho is different, but her lines, like Horace's, act as a gnomic center between more specific opening and closing sections. To Sappho's image of a storm at sea Horace adds a land-based scene that looks back to the poem's opening: the cypresses at rest are the counterpart to the "toiling woods" on Mount Soracte. Such seamless integration of Greek and Roman elements is a hallmark of Horace at his most adroit.

Two odes of Book 2 share much thematic material, and so offer an opportunity to observe Horace's art of variation.

---

[4] Obbink 2014.

2.3

Remember to keep a level head in times
of trouble, and likewise in prosperity keep joy
    in bounds and free of excess,
        Dellius, you who are doomed to die,

whether you passed all your days in sorrow   5
or treated yourself on holidays, stretched out
    in an unfrequented meadow,
        with a choice vintage of Falernian wine.

Why do the towering pine and silvery poplar
love to join their branches into a welcoming shade?   10
    Why does the rushing stream work so
        as it bustles along in its winding course?

Here bid them bring the wine, the fragrant oil,
the lovely blossoms of the short-lived rose,
    while your age and your means allow it,   15
        and the black threads woven by the three grim
        sisters.

You will leave the pastures you bought up, your home
and the country estate washed by the yellow Tiber;
    you will leave them, and your heir
        will possess the wealth you heaped so high   20

Whether you are rich, a scion of ancient Inachus,
or a lowly pauper dwelling beneath the sky,
    it makes no difference; you are
        an offering to Orcus who shows no pity.

We all are herded there, the lots of all   25
toss in the urn; later or sooner they will
    leap out and place us on the boat
        bound for never-ending exile.

Odes 2.3, addressed to a Dellius, is a poem of undeniable power whose coherence—in my experience, at least—is not immediately obvious. Stanzas 3–7 go closely together: a shady spot near a stream suggests itself as the ideal place for an outdoor symposium, which Dellius is urged to enjoy while he can, for death will deprive him of that pleasure and of all his possessions, the death that awaits every one of us. We are in familiar *carpe diem* territory, even if the details and the setting are new. But what connection is there between that line of thought and the opening two stanzas, which enjoin Dellius to maintain his equanimity in the face of adverse or favorable circumstances? The answer, I think, is provided by the surprising way in which Horace first addresses Dellius: "Dellius, you who are doomed to die" (*moriture*). That is no mere vocative, but an explanation of the first stanza and a link to the second: if one's thoughts are trained on the inevitability of death, neither good nor ill fortune will seem important enough to disturb one's composure.[5] The second stanza carries on from this point: Dellius will die whether he has passed his life in misery or has enjoyed himself on occasion. The stanza also moves the argument a step forward. In the opening lines adverse and prosperous fortune receive roughly equal treatment, but in lines 5–8 the first alternative occupies one line, while the second is elaborated over the rest of the stanza. The unequal proportions suggest a conclusion: if one is to die no matter how one has lived, surely it is preferable to opt for pleasure from time to time. (Note the contrast between "all your days" and "on holidays": the hedonist does not neglect his duties but relaxes when it is appropriate to do so.) The attraction of the second course is enhanced by details such as the secluded meadow and the exceptional wine.

Up to this point the poem has given no hint of its setting; now in lines 9–12 Horace takes note of his and Dellius's surroundings. Ascribing to nature both human traits and human motivation, Horace asks why the trees and the stream behave as they do, with the implied

---

[5] Günther 2013: 328–29 helped me see the connections.

answer "if not to encourage us to enjoy this lovely spot." The trees who weave their branches together are like considerate hosts; the shade they create welcomes guests. The stream is like a hard-working servant who bustles about getting everything ready for the party.

The last stanza transposes the thought of the previous ones to the universal level. The lines are among the darkest in all the *Odes*; one verbal source of their power lies in enjambement: the thought runs over the boundaries of each line, suggesting the inexorable character of death. If one strand of the poem's argument is that contemplating death leads to imperturbability in the face of changing fortunes, these final lines present a particularly challenging form of that process.

Even when I had difficulty understanding how the poem hangs together, I was impressed by Horace's artistry in creating connections between its parts with binary oppositions and lists of three. Oppositions characterize the opening and closing sections: 1–4 good and ill fortune, 5–8 misery and enjoyment; 21–24 rich or poor, 26 later or sooner. (The last of these is a miniature opposition, in keeping with the accelerated pace of the closing lines.) Lists of three dominate the central stanzas and connect the present of the symposium (wine, oil, roses; age, means, threads woven by the Fates) with the goods Dellius will yield up when he dies (pastures, home, country estate).

What about Dellius himself? We can infer that he was rich, with a house in Rome, a villa on the banks of the Tiber, and holdings farther afield. About the latter Horace adds a detail: Dellius had "bought up" farmlands, combining separate properties into a single latifundium. If the picture of refined pleasure in lines 6–8 implies anything about him, he knew how to treat himself well and appreciated fine wine. The reference to the "unfrequented meadow" also fits: Dellius owned enough land to enjoy privacy when it suited him. Dellius is usually identified with Quintus Dellius, remarkable for having switched sides several times during the civil war: from Julius Caesar to Cassius to Antony to Octavian. His agility earned him the nickname "Circus-Rider of the Civil Wars" (i.e., a rider who could leap from one horse to another while both were racing at full speed) from Messalla Corvinus, a man who knew whereof he spoke, having executed a couple of timely shifts of allegiance himself. For Horace to urge consistency on such a character might seem to verge on sarcasm, but that would hardly have been tactful. The absence of any such allusion may be more to the point. The addressees of the first three odes of Book 2—Asinius Pollio, Sallustius Crispus, and Dellius—appear in the same passage of Seneca's *On Mercy* (1.10.1) as examples of former enemies who came to enjoy Augustus's favor. Their prominent place in Horace's collection may show Augustan *clementia* in action.

2.14

Alas, how quickly, Postumus, Postumus,
the years glide by, and all your piety
    will not put off the wrinkles
        and advancing old age and unconquerable death,

not if, my friend, for every day that passes   5
you sacrificed three hundred bulls to Pluto
    who cannot weep, who imprisons
        three-bodied Geryon and Tityos the giant

in those gloomy waters, the ones that all of us
who feed upon the bounty of the earth   10
    must sometime cross over,
        whether we be kings or hungry sharecroppers.

No use our avoiding the bloody god of war
and the stormy Adriatic's crashing waves,
    no use when autumn comes again   15
        fearing the unhealthy wind from the south.

We must set eyes on the slowly winding stream
of black Cocytus, on Danaus's ill-famed brood,
    on Sisyphus son of Aeolus,
        condemned to everlasting labor.   20

> Land, home, and loving wife must all be left
> behind, and of these trees you tend so well
>   none but the hated cypress,
>   tree of death, will follow its short-lived master.
>
> A worthier heir will drain the Caecuban   25
> you kept locked up with a hundred keys, and splash
>   the stone floor with better wine
>   than is served at the banquets of the high priests.

The poem opens with an exclamation of sorrow, followed by a plangent repetition of the addressee's name. While several odes begin with the O that accompanies formal address, no other poem starts with an exclamation of that kind. Repetition of the "Postumus, Postumus" form is also exceedingly rare in Horace; in all of the other instances it conveys powerful emotion. (2.17.10 *ibimus, ibimus* [see 112], 3.3.18 *Ilion, Ilion*, 4.4.70 *occidit, occidit*, 4.13.18 *illius, illius* [see 162]). The mention of wrinkles might make us think for a moment that we are listening to a mock-serious complaint about the woes of growing old, but the wrinkles prove to be only the first member of a tricolon that progresses to "advancing old age" and ends with "unconquerable death." ("Advancing"—more literally "pressing"—and "unconquerable" introduce a military metaphor, of a battle against old age and death that can never be won.) Having brought us face to face with death by the end of the first stanza, the poem has nowhere to go except to the underworld, which it does, remarkably, twice over, in stanzas 2 and 3 and 4 and 5; each time the thought moves from "there is no escape" to the places or sights of the lower world. In the first of these two sections Horace shifts the focus from Postumus and his hypothetical attempt to placate Pluto to human beings in general, introduced with the grand Homeric formula "all of us who feed on the bounty of the earth." That wider perspective is maintained through stanzas 4 and 5, and it appears to continue into stanza 6: I translated "Land, home, and loving wife must all be left behind" because the Latin does not specify whose land, home, and wife are meant, and the opening word of line 21,

Friendship and Advice | 79

linquenda ("must be left behind") seems to parallel the similar form *uisendus* ("must be seen / looked on") in line 17. But with the words that follow Horace brings us back to Postumus: "of these trees you tend so well." "These trees" must be in sight of where the poet's words are being spoken. We are somewhere on Postumus's property, perhaps walking in his garden. The final stanza looks beyond Postumus, now dead, to the heir who will drink up the fine wine that Postumus had kept so carefully secure. The closing image is one of Horace's most memorable, as the focus zooms in on the red wine staining the marble floor of Postumus's dining room.

To all appearances the ode is an unrelievedly grim set of reflections on mortality. The absence of any explicit injunction to enjoy life (such as lightens the middle of *Odes* 2.3) is striking: as David West nicely puts it, "This is an 'Eat, drink, and be merry, for tomorrow you may die' without the eating, drinking or merriment."[6] But perhaps the poem is not so one-dimensional. It contains two hyperbolical expressions involving large numbers: the "three hundred bulls" per day that will not earn Pluto's favor and the "hundred keys" Postumus uses to keep his precious wine safe. Their presence is not likely to be a coincidence. I think they are linked and that they encapsulate the message Postumus is meant to receive: there is no length to which you can go that will extend your span of life, and there is no amount of protection that will safeguard your most precious possessions if you fail to enjoy them while you can. If that interpretation is accepted, and the poem is read as containing an implied *carpe diem* message, we need to reconsider our understanding of the final stanza. Rather than a straightforward prediction of the future, it is predicated on an unstated condition: this is what will happen (if you do not make wiser use of your blessings). Classicists are happiest when they can point to a parallel for a proposed reading, and Horace does provide another example of this future with implied condition in the closing stanza of 3.6: (unless we Romans mend our ways) the

---

[6] West 1998: 96.

next generation will be even more degenerate than the present one. (See 134.)

We might wonder what to make of the stark difference between the underworld's appearance in the previous ode, 2.13, where the shades are entertained by joint recitals from Alcaeus and Sappho, and here, where the only characters referred to are monsters or criminals. As we have seen (62–64), the underworld of 2.13 is presented as the product of Horace's imagination; the return of the "real" underworld in 2.14 may underscore the fanciful character of the earlier description.

Of the eight odes addressed to Maecenas I have chosen one from each book. *Odes* 1.20 and 3.29 are both invitation poems, while 2.12 offers a sharp contrast of subject.

1.20

In 1.20 Horace invites Maecenas to dinner at his country estate.

> My dear Maecenas, noble knight,
> you'll drink cheap Sabine here tonight
> from common cups. Yet I myself
> sealed it and stored it on the shelf
> in a Greek jar, that day the applause
> broke out in your recovery's cause,
> so that the compliments resounded
> through the full theater and rebounded
> from your own Tiber's banks until
> the echo laughed on Vatican hill.
> At your house you enjoy the best—
> Caecuban or the grape that's pressed
> at Cales. But whoever hopes
> my cups will taste of Formian slopes
> or of the true Falernian
> must leave a disappointed man.
>
> (Trans. James Michie)

Michie's translation is freer than the versions I usually provide, and he does not reflect the division of the Latin into stanzas, but his rhymes are so clever that I couldn't resist using it, and the overall feel seems right.

The poem offers an introduction to the semiotics of wine—a topic close to Horace's heart, even if he would not have used that term to describe it. Five varieties are mentioned. Four appear in the final lines and are high-class types that Maecenas can enjoy at home but that Horace cannot provide. The fifth, "cheap Sabine," is all that Horace can promise. The numerical imbalance adds to the contrast between Maecenas's wine cellar and Horace's. One might expect Horace to be apologetic about his humble hospitality, but that is not the impression the poem creates. Instead he expects Maecenas to appreciate this *vin ordinaire* because of its personal associations: Horace has produced it himself, probably from grapes grown on the property—a property that was a gift from Maecenas. In addition, Horace put the wine away to commemorate an occasion on which Maecenas was cheered in the theater. The wine thus expresses Horace's gratitude for Maecenas's generosity and serves as a symbol of their friendship. In its lack of pretension, the wine characterizes the lifestyle that Horace purports to follow, and the combination of Italian grapes and a Greek vessel symbolizes Horace's Romanization of Greek lyric. If we recall that the wine Thaliarchus was to bring out in 1.9 had been aged for four years (see oo), it becomes clear that Horace stresses the unassuming character of this wine both to differentiate his manner of life from that of Maecenas and to demonstrate his confidence that he does not need to put on a show to impress his patron and friend.

2.12

You would not wish the long Numantine war
or iron-hard Hannibal or the Sicilian sea
purple with Carthaginian blood to be set
    to the gentle strains of the lyre,

or the savage Lapiths or Hylaeus maddened 5
with wine or the giant sons of Earth made tame
by the hand of Hercules, when their threats
    shook the gleaming house

of ancient Saturn. No, Maecenas, better
for you to tell of Caesar's wars in prose 10
histories, of the necks of menacing kings
    paraded through the streets of Rome.

As for me, my Muse has wished that I should speak
of the sweet songs of the lady Licymnia, of her eyes
brightly flashing, of her heart so true 15
    to a love that is shared.

She has held her own in the chorus of dancers
or the contest of wits, or offering her arms
in play to the girls adorned in finery
    on Diana's thronged holy day. 20

Surely you would not wish to exchange the realm
of rich Achaemenes, or Mygdon's Phrygian wealth
or the treasure-filled palaces of Araby
    for a lock of Licymnia's hair,

when she bends her neck to receive a passionate kiss 25
or with easy cruelty refuses them, though she
loves stolen kisses more than the one who asks
    and sometimes steals them first herself.

    The implied situation is that Maecenas has urged Horace to compose a poem to celebrate recent victories by Augustus (probably in the campaign against the Cantabri, concluded in 26); Horace declines to do so and instead praises the charms of a woman named Licymnia. The poem belongs to a type called a *recusatio* ("refusal"), in which a poet politely turns aside a request for a certain kind of poem, usually one of a panegyrical nature.

Friendship and Advice | 83

An earlier ode, 1.6, provides an example of a typical *recusatio*. It is addressed to Marcus Vipsanius Agrippa, the man responsible for Octavian's victory at Actium and Augustus's de facto second-in-command. Horace disclaims the ability to celebrate Agrippa's triumphs in the Homeric manner they deserve, ending with the disingenuous assertion that the only battles his poetry sings of take place at dinner parties, "battles of virgins / valiantly fighting off boys with manicured nails" (Joseph Clancy's translation).

Eduard Fraenkel thought that 2.12 lacked unity: "The tribute to Licymnia is here appended to . . . a wholly heterogeneous theme, a typical *recusatio*."[7] But in 1.6 and in all other surviving *recusationes* the poet both declines to write a poem of a certain sort and also specifies what kind of poetry he can or will write. So after the catalog of rejected subjects we expect a reference to a contrasting topic; what gives the poem most of its interest is the subject that Horace proposes, to which I will turn shortly.

The parts of the poem are also held together by verbal connections, of which the most important are forms of *uelle* ("to want," "to wish") and its negative counterpart *nolle*.[8] The first and last appearances are in the negative ("you would not wish," "surely you would not wish") and apply to Maecenas. The former brilliantly makes Maecenas himself responsible for Horace's refusal: *you* wouldn't want to see the Numantine War and the like narrated in lyric verse, and in the same way *you* wouldn't want to see Augustus's victories given the lyric treatment. The latter also ascribes a preference to Maecenas: you would rather have a lock of Licymnia's hair than all the wealth of Arabia. Maecenas is thus made to endorse both Horace's refusal and his substitute subject—a novel twist on the relationship in a *recusatio* between poet and addressee. The positive middle instance belongs to the Muse; it was she who willed that Horace praise Licymnia. The three taken together absolve Horace of all responsibility.

Much discussion of the poem has understandably focused on the intriguing figure of Licymnia and Horace's relationship to her. The

---

[7] Fraenkel 1957: 219.
[8] Syndikus 1972: 413.

natural assumption is that she is Horace's mistress, but that assumption entails problems. "I cannot celebrate Caesar's triumphs; I can only sing of my mistress" is just what an elegist would say, and just what Propertius had said in a poem (2.1) known to Horace and likewise addressed to Maecenas. But Horace was not an elegist—for more on that subject see 94–111—and several of Licymnia's features, most conspicuously "her heart so true / to a love that is shared," are antithetical to those of the elegiac mistress. Furthermore, when an elegist declines to write panegyric because of his commitment to a mistress, he is careful to describe his erotic relationship as producing only misery; he thereby avoids giving the impression that he is refusing because he has a more pleasant alternative. But if Licymnia is Horace's mistress, that is just what he would be saying.

A very different identification is offered by the late antique commentator known as pseudo-Acro. On this view "Licymnia" is a cover name for Terentia, the wife of Maecenas. The ultimate source of the identification is probably one of the treatises *On Characters in Horace* that began to circulate in the century after Horace's death.

Is it believable that Horace would describe the wife of his patron in blatantly erotic terms? In addition to the fact that the erotic elements are balanced by more decorous ones (faithful heart, mutual love, participation in sacred dances), we should recall that Maecenas was not a typical Roman and that Terentia may not have been a typical Roman matron. Seneca's portrait of Maecenas as an unbridled voluptuary cannot be taken at face value, but it does suggest that Maecenas's way of life, including his marriage, was the subject of much comment: "Was his style any more extraordinary than his manner of dress, his companions, his household, his wife?"[9] It seems possible that Horace here gives us a hint of the real Maecenas, rather than the sober character he created for him in other poems.

But while I think it is likely that Licymnia is Maecenas's wife rather than Horace's mistress, the language of the poem remains ambiguous on that point. It would have been easy for Horace to

---

[9] *Epist.* 114.4.

introduce a reference to "your Licymnia" or the like, and so the absence of an explicit marker is probably deliberate. The ambiguity may have been intended to soften any potential offense. In any event, Maecenas knew who Licymnia was, and that may have been enough.

3.29

Odes 3.29 is a great poem, but its greatness only gradually becomes evident. It begins as an invitation poem, like *Odes* 1.20, albeit one on a grander scale. Horace's hospitality now includes wine, rose petals, and a perfumed ointment (2–5), and the wine is smooth and of such high quality as to be drunk unmixed—a long step up from the cheap Sabine of 1.20. I suggested earlier that that wine symbolizes Horace's poetry; if that is also the case here, the improvement may reflect Horace's increased confidence in his poetic achievement at the end of the collection.

Horace urges Maecenas not to delay in leaving Rome for the country, describing his situation in almost ominous terms: "Abandon wearisome wealth and the mansion neighboring the clouds above" (9–10)—a dangerous sort of place, as we know from *Odes* 2.10. The following stanza (13–16), as so often in Horace, transposes the thought to a more general plane: a change of scene and a simple meal in a humble setting have often relieved the anxieties of the wealthy. Two further stanzas (17–24) tell us that the time is high summer, when shepherds seek a shady riverbank with their flocks, and no breeze blows.

As we approach the heart of the poem Horace turns back to Maecenas (25–28):

> Yet still you labour to perfect the pattern
> of government, Rome's anxious sentry keeping
>   watch on the farthest East,
>   Cyrus' old kingdom and the uneasy Don
>
> for plots of war.
>
> (Trans. James Michie)

That depiction both flatters Maecenas's sense of importance—he sounds almost like Augustus—and suggests that his preoccupation with affairs of state may be overdone. The foreign peoples named—the Chinese, Bactrians, and Scythians—were far distant and posed no credible threat. But rather than rebuke Maecenas himself, Horace invokes a greater authority, shifting the poem into a higher register (29–41):

> God wisely hides the future outcome
> in a veil of darkness, and laughs
> > if humans fret more than is right.
> > > Remember to set in order
>
> what is close at hand. All else is borne
> as by a river, now gliding peacefully
> > within its banks to the Tuscan sea,
> > > now rolling with it huge boulders
>
> and torn-up tree-trunks, herds and homes,
> as the mountains and nearby woods cry out,
> > when a savage flood stirs up
> > > once tranquil streams.

Leaving the sympotic setting behind, Horace offers a grander version of *carpe diem*—*carpe diem* without the hedonism, instead a sober setting of things in order. "What is close at hand" pointedly contrasts with Maecenas's far-off foreign worries. Although a second-person form persists, we sense that the words are no longer addressed only to Maecenas; in fact, as Oliver Lyne noted, Horace's advice does not really fit Maecenas's role as a statesman, who may have legitimate reasons to be concerned with long-term outcomes.[10]

The poem might have ended with the magnificent river simile, but it now goes even higher, rising to what is arguably Horace's most impressive single utterance (41–48).

---

[10] Lyne 1995: 113–14.

> Happy and in possession of his life
> the man who can say at each day's end
> > "I have lived. Tomorrow the Father
> > > may fill the sky with black clouds
>
> or clearest sunlight; yet he will not
> render void whatever is past, nor will he
> > remake or invalidate
> > > what fleeing time has once carried off."

As with many of Horace's most powerful statements, the language is studiously plain. The profusion of verbs ("render void," "remake," "invalidate") hammers home the limits of Jupiter's power, while the legal coloring of "render void and "invalidate" suggests that his inability to alter the past is a matter of universal law.

After a fortissimo passage like this we expect a descent of some kind. Horace meets that expectation in an unexpected way, introducing the figure of Fortune (49–52):

> Fortune enjoys her cruel business and
> persists in playing her proud game,
> > transferring her fickle honours,
> > > favoring now me, now another.
> > > > (Trans. David West)

At first this may feel like a change of subject, but on reflection we can see that the alternations of Fortune restate earlier forms of mutability: the differing moods of the river and the opposition of cloudy and clear skies. What is new is Horace's personal involvement—"favoring now me"—an idea that is developed in a stanza dominated by first-person forms, as Horace takes center stage (53–56):

> I praise her while she stays. If she shakes out
> her swift wings, I return what she gave, wrap myself
> > in my virtue, and look for honest Poverty,
> > > the bride who brings no dowry.
> > > > (Trans. David West)

The notion of Horace wrapped up in his virtue paying court to Poverty raises a smile, but the mild self-mockery does not conceal a powerful statement of independence, all the more remarkable if we recall that the primary embodiment of Fortune in Horace's life was Maecenas himself. When Horace says "I return what she gave," he uses the same verb (*resigno*) that he will soon use when declaring his readiness to return all of Maecenas's benefactions (*Epist.* 1.7.34; see 145).

The focus remains on Horace for the concluding stanzas (57–64):

> It is not for me, as the masts are moaning
> in blasts from the south, to go running to my
>   wretched prayers, bargaining with vows
>   so my goods from Cyprus and Tyre may not
>
> be added to the wealth of the hungry sea.
> At such a time, kept safe in my two-oared boat,
>   I am carried through Aegean storms
>   by the winds, Pollux, and his twin brother.
>
>   (Trans. Joseph Clancy)

The image of shipwreck flows naturally from the preceding stanzas, since the dangers of sea travel were a classic ancient example of the vicissitudes of Fortune. (See 69–71, on *Odes* 2.10.) There is again something amusing in the picture of Horace floating to safety in his dinghy, but underlying it is a serious paradox, that simple self-sufficiency is a surer bulwark against Fortune than vulnerable possessions. It has often been noted that Horace's little boat now provides the protection (*praesidium*) that in the opening ode of Book 1 came from Maecenas (1.1.2); the repetition is almost certainly deliberate and marks the completion of Horace's journey to independence. Another echo of an early ode points in the same direction. In 1.5 we learn that Horace had suffered shipwreck in love and had made a vow to Neptune if he was saved from drowning. (See 97.) Now he is beyond such bargaining.

After this poem, a veritable *summa Horatiana*, the proud words that open 3.30, "I have completed a monument more lasting than bronze," sound like a mere statement of fact.

·7·

Amatory Poems

Horace's love poetry has provoked a variety of responses. Even some devoted Horatian critics have been less than enthusiastic about this part of his work. Robin Nisbet flatly declared that "none of Horace's love-poems . . . reaches the first rank,"[1] and David West referred to their "generally tepid quality."[2] David Armstrong allowed that there was some merit in the criticism that "Horace is in the end no such profound or serious love poet as his contemporaries Catullus, Propertius, and Tibullus,"[3] and Eduard Fraenkel exercised an implicit judgment on the love poetry by electing not to discuss it: none of those poems receive an extended treatment, and several of the best-known odes (1.5, 1.11, 3.9) are ignored. One eminent Latinist has even denied the existence of love poetry in Horace: "Horace was undoubtedly a poet and erotic themes are to be found in his poems, but that he ever wrote anything that in the ordinary acceptance of the term could be called a love poem, I do most earnestly deny."[4]

The problem is in large part terminological, since "love poetry" carries with it associations that may lead to unfair assessments. For that reason I will speak instead of "amatory" poems, and I will usually call the women who appear in these poems Horace's "partners" rather than his "lovers."

---

[1] Nisbet 1962: 184.
[2] West 2014: 85.
[3] Armstrong 1989: 85.
[4] E. J. Kenney, quoted by West 1995: 85.

Horace's Odes. Richard Tarrant, Oxford University Press (2020). © Oxford University Press.
DOI: 10.1093/oso/9780195156751.001.0001

The citation from Armstrong is particularly useful in accounting for this mixed reception. Horace's reputation in this area has often suffered by comparison with other Latin poets, Catullus in particular. The youthful, passionate Catullus is regularly contrasted with the older and more detached Horace, often to the detriment of Horace. But such comparisons are only helpful if Horace set out to write love poetry in the manner of Catullus or Propertius. One of my aims is to argue that he did not, and that his purpose was in fact close to being the opposite. Another is to show that if we approach these poems without preconceived notions of what they should be, they are both successful and highly enjoyable.

Poems with significant amatory content account for about a quarter of *Odes* 1–3. Most of those poems deal with putative relationships of Horace himself, portraying him as having been involved with a number of women:

A. Current:
Lalage (1.22)
Glycera (3.19)
Lyde (3.28)

B. Former:
Pyrrha (1.5)
Anonyma (1.16)
Lydia (1.25); not certain, but likely
Myrtale + an unnamed "better love" (1.33)
Lydia (3.9)
Chloe (3.26)
Galatea (3.27)

C. Potential/desired/reconciled:
Leuconoe (1.11); possibly A
Anonyma (1.16)
Tyndaris (1.17); not certain, but likely
Glycera (1.19; cf. also 1.30, 3.19)
Chloe (1.23)
Barine (2.8); rejected

Lydia (3.9)
Lyce (3.10)
Lyde (3.11)

Ambiguous or dubious cases:
Thaliarchus (1.9): A?
Lydia (1.13): B?
Lalage (2.5): C, if poem is a soliloquy
Lyde (2.11): A?
Licymnia (2.12); A (according to some readings)

In some poems the situation is not entirely clear, and it is a further complication that we cannot know whether all the odes addressed, for example, to a Lydia refer to the same person. I have indicated the places where I think one person may figure in more than one poem, but even if one conflates women with the same name wherever possible, the overall picture remains unchanged.

Horace depicts himself as enjoying relationships with a multiplicity of partners. In some cases he is involved with different women in adjacent poems (1.22 Lalage and 1.23 Chloe; 3.9 Lydia, 3.10 Lyce, 3.11 Lyde; 3.26 Chloe, 3.27 Galatea [probably], 3.28 Lyde), and in one (1.33) he is simultaneously the partner of the freedwomen Myrtale and the desired partner of a "better love" (presumably a woman of higher social standing).

The erotic is an area where the temptation to connect the persona projected by the poems with the "real" Horace is particularly strong, so it is important to note that we have no reliable information about this aspect of Horace's life. We are on stronger ground in assuming that his sexual profile is strongly influenced by considerations of genre. A brief look at his other collections is revealing.

In the *Satires* sex is spoken of in pointedly unromantic terms. Just as the form distances itself from elevated poetry, Horace disparages affairs with high-born wives and sets his sights lower, preferring partners who are easy and available (1.2.119–27). In Book 2 Damasippus accuses him of being sexually omnivorous: "a thousand passions for women, a thousand for boys" (2.3.325);

and if Horace is the "you" of Davus's lecture in 2.7.46 ff., he is said to be enslaved by another man's wife (46). The only specific sexual encounter described, however, is a fiasco: on the trip to Brundisium Horace lies in bed waiting for a nameless "lying girl" who never appears, leaving him to pour out his pent-up desire in a wet dream.

The *Epodes* maintain a deliberately low register but take a large step in the direction of the *Odes* by depicting Horace as involved with a number of named partners: in 11 Inachia (previously) and Lyciscus (currently), in 14 the freedwoman Phryne, in 15 Neaera. In contrast to what we will see in the *Odes*, the Horace of the *Epodes* portrays himself in terms that resemble those of contemporary Latin elegy. For example, in 11 he professes himself unable to find pleasure in composing poetry because he is "struck by an oppressive love" (11.2). In *Odes* 1–3, love is never oppressive.

The Horace of the *Epistles* is an almost completely asexual—or more precisely postsexual—character. Two references to Cinyra (1.7.28–29 and 1.14.33) are explicitly set in the past. In 1.15.20–21 Horace seeks out a wine capable of lending him words with which he could commend himself to a Lucanian girlfriend as if he were still a young man. The scene sounds more hypothetical than real, and however read it underscores Horace's no longer youthful condition.

With the partial exception of the *Epodes*, the profusion of erotic relationships in the *Odes* has no parallel elsewhere in Horace's poetry; it must therefore be part of his identity as a lyric poet. Horace's decision to write lyric poetry in imitation of the classic Greek practitioners gave him access to a wide variety of subject matters and tones. That diversity is on full display in the erotic sphere, from Sappho's emotionally intense involvement to the more ironic attitudes taken by Ibycus and Anacreon. Drawing on the range of possibilities afforded by the Greek tradition, Horace crafted an erotic persona that is of a piece with his lyric self-presentation as a whole: as a rational and realistic person with an aversion to emotional extremes, who actively pursues life's pleasures knowing that they are fleeting and that death is final.

Horace differs from his Greek predecessors in giving names to all the women in his amatory poems; in Ibycus and Anacreon, boys addressed by the poet are usually named, but women are not. One result is an impression of greater specificity and aptness of what is said to the character being addressed or spoken of. However lightly sketched they may be, Horace's women are still characters with individual features. All of his female partners have Greek names. Their Greek identities do not, as one might think, transpose them to some Hellenic fantasyland, but rather situate them in a specific Roman context, as hetaerae (upscale prostitutes/courtesans). Some of Horace's female names, including Glycera and Myrtale, are attested as names of contemporary hetaerae. But one can also suggest a prudential reason for Horace to specify the Greekness of these women: it allows him to conduct a vigorous sex life without any suspicion of corrupting respectable Roman women or of engaging in adulterous relationships—neither of which activities would have endeared him to Augustus.

In another departure from Greek practice (and from Horace's own self-representation in the *Satires* and *Epodes*), Horace in *Odes* 1–3 represents himself as almost entirely heterosexual in his relationships. (1.9 is a possible exception; see 73–74.) One explanation is that he wanted to depict sexual relationships as affairs involving independent actors, and grown women were better suited to that end than passive boys.

Horace's relationship to Greek lyric helps to account for some of the features of his amatory poetry. A second genre-based consideration that helped to shape his erotic persona was a desire to set his poetry apart from that of his Roman predecessors and contemporaries.

In contrast to the rich corpus of Greek erotic verse, the only substantial collections of such poetry in Latin known to have been available to Horace when he embarked on the *Odes* were that of Catullus and the (now almost entirely lost) elegiac *Amores* of

Cornelius Gallus. In the years during which *Odes* 1–3 took shape (roughly 30–23), those texts were supplemented by the first two books of Propertius's elegies and the first elegiac collection of Tibullus. Catullus and the elegists share a conception of love poetry in which the lover-poet is deeply attached to a mistress in a relationship that yields moments of intense joy but more often leaves the poet disillusioned and frustrated.

A comparison with elegy makes several characteristics of Horace's erotic poetry more intelligible. For example, his involvement with multiple partners is the opposite of a grand passion for a single mistress, such as Catullus's for Lesbia or Propertius's for Cynthia. As Commager somewhat primly put it, "The very number of girls he addresses begs us to believe that no one of them affected him for very long."[5] From Horace's perspective, that is precisely the point.

In poetry books as in life, first impressions are especially powerful. That is one of many reasons to look closely at the first amatory poem in *Odes* 1–3, the ode to Pyrrha (1.5). It has generally been thought to be one of Horace's most attractive poems, and for a long time it was one of the most popular. (In 1962 Robin Nisbet could say "everybody knows Pyrrha."[6]) It also has the unique distinction of having been translated more than five hundred times and into all the major languages of the world.[7]

Before turning to the poem, we should take note of its place in the collection, following poems that deal with Horace's poetic ambitions, the current state of Rome, his friendship with Virgil, and reflections on the coming of spring and mortality. Eros occupies a prominent position in Horace's lyric corpus, but it is not the dominant theme. The contrast with Propertius and Tibullus is strongly marked: *Cynthia* is literally the first word of Propertius's first collection of elegies, and Tibullus's opening elegy ends with an address to Delia. We cannot speak with certainty about Catullus,

---

[5] Commager 1962: 156.
[6] Nisbet 1962: 181.
[7] See 198.

because we do not know the form in which Horace read his work, but poems involving Lesbia dominate the opening section of the Catullan corpus as it has been transmitted.

> What slender boy, hair dripping with scented oil,
> embraces you, Pyrrha, in a charming grotto
>   on a bed of rose-petals? For whose delight
>   are you tying back your honey-blonde hair
>
> in elegant simplicity? Alas! How often   5
> will he weep for broken faith and perjured gods,
>   will marvel at the unaccustomed sight
>   of seas made rough by storm-dark winds,
>
> who now enjoys you, thinking you are golden,
> who hopes you will ever be his, ever to be loved,   10
>   not suspecting the deceit that comes
>   from the shifting breeze? Poor fools, for whom
>
> you glisten yet untried! As for me,
> the votive tablet on the temple wall
>   bears witness that I have hung up my wet clothes   15
>   in thanks to the god who rules the sea.

In Latin the opening line, *Quis multa gracilis te puer in rosa*, is a masterpiece of mimetic word order that sets the scene even before the syntax is complete. The effect cannot be replicated in English, but the pattern can be illustrated:

Quis	multa		in rosa
	gracilis	puer	
		te	
What	amid many		a rose
	slender	youth	
		you	

Pyrrha is encircled by her youthful wooer, and both are surrounded by a bed of roses.

There is much that could be said about this poem, but I want to focus on the way Horace depicts Pyrrha's current lover, the unnamed young man, and uses him to poke gentle fun at some of the conventions of love elegy.

The first point is that Pyrrha's lover is young, scarcely out of boyhood. We might therefore expect him to be naive and credulous. The combination of the grotto and the abundant roses creates an impression of luxury, but his lavish application of perfume may suggest lack of experience. The only physical detail Horace provides is that the youth is *gracilis*, usually rendered "slender," but almost closer to "skinny." One reason may be to distinguish him from Horace, who was decidedly not slender and who at the dramatic date of the poem had long since ceased being a boy. There could also be a suggestion that the thinness has been brought about by love, a common motif of elegy.

Another elegiac detail is that the young man is unaccustomed to Pyrrha's ways, and perhaps to love affairs in general, as Propertius presents himself in his opening elegy as "previously untouched by desire" (1.1.2). The youth also resembles Catullus at an early stage of his affair with Lesbia, especially in his deluded hope that Pyrrha will "ever be his, ever to be loved." The idea of repeated lamenting ("how often will he weep") may point in the direction of elegy, which for Horace implies wallowing in erotic despair (as we will soon see in 1.33). Complaining of broken faith and changed gods also smacks of elegy.

The sea imagery connects the young man and Horace as victims of Pyrrha's fickleness, but it also differentiates them; they are not two representatives of the same type. The young man is like a sailor in calm water, unaware of the storms about to rise, while Horace has survived shipwreck long enough ago to have put up the votive tablet that commemorates his escape and thanks the god responsible for it. The contrast extends to the way they react to being disillusioned. The young man, Horace predicts, will be unable to comprehend the experience, and so will helplessly wring his hands, while Horace took action to extricate himself from danger.

The tone of the poem seems amused rather than indignant or bitter. The young man's infatuation is presented as extreme, and so is his reaction to Pyrrha's faithlessness. The "Alas!" in line 5, for example, represents the young man's emotional state, not Horace's empathy with it. If Horace had wanted to express sympathy for the young man, he would have addressed him rather than Pyrrha.

One function of the ode as the first love poem in the collection is therefore to establish Horace as an anti-elegist. By making Pyrrha's lover a character with elegiac traits, Horace may be implying that elegy as a genre suffers from a lack of maturity and knowledge of the world.

In addition to being the first amatory poem in *Odes* 1–3, 1.5 is also the first of a number of poems in which Horace is an observer of someone else's love affair, an advisor to a lover, or a real or potential rival in a love triangle.[8]

From this group I have selected 1.33 for discussion, in part because of its overtly anti-elegiac aspect. The poem is addressed to a man named Albius, who writes mournful elegies about his unhappy affair with Glycera. Albius is almost universally believed to be Albius Tibullus the elegist.

> Albius, give up this extravagant grieving
> For a sweetheart turned sour. "Why was she deceiving?"
> You ask, and then whimper long elegies on
> The theme of the older man being outshone.
>
> Lycoris, whose forehead is nearly all curls,   5
> Is burning for Cyrus. *His* favorite girl's
> Pholoe. *She* in turn throws him frown
> Meaning "Does and Apulian wolves will bed down
>
> Sooner than I with a peasant like him!"
> That's Venus's method. According to whim   10
> She puts bodies and minds to work her brass yoke
> In incongruous pairs—and enjoys the grim joke.

---

[8] Other examples: 1.8, 1.13, 1.17, 1.25, 2.4, 2.5 (if not addressed to Horace himself), 2.8, 2.12, 3.7, 3.9 (a quadrilateral situation), 3.12, 3.15, 3.20.

> I know. When a far better chance was presented
> I stayed with my freed-woman, chained and contented,
> Though she handed out stormier treatment to me   15
> Than dented Calabria gets from the sea.
>
> (Trans. James Michie)[9]

This must surely be the most crowded amatory poem on record: nine partners are referred to in sixteen lines. The actors are arranged in a symmetrical pattern of three triangles: the outer frame (the situation from which the poem takes its start) has Albius, his younger rival, and Glycera (Michie's "sweetheart turned sour"); the first inner triangle (which serves as an exemplum) is made up of Cyrus, Lycoris, and Pholoe, while the second (purporting to offer another illustration, this time from Horace's own experience) consists of Horace, the anonymous "better chance," and the freed-woman Myrtale.

Each triad occupies a different time frame. Albius is at risk of becoming Glycera's former lover, displaced by a younger man. The trio of Lycoris, Cyrus, and Pholoe is first shown in present terms, but Horace then opens the perspective to a future in which Pholoe will never join with Cyrus. His own relationship with Myrtale is set firmly in the past, and simultaneous with it was the attempt of another woman to win him.

This expansion of erotic situations beyond a basic duality might be another of Horace's ways of distancing himself from elegy, in which rivals often threaten but are hardly ever given a specific identity. Horace's recurring emphasis on mismatched lovers (described as Venus's "cruel joke") may be a way of undermining the elegiac conceit that the lover's mistress is uniquely destined for him.

There is a delightful irony in Horace's striking a pose as *praeceptor amoris* to an elegiac poet and instructing him as to the ways of Venus. But behind the humor is also a point about lyric versus elegy: the lyric poet who can see the larger picture versus the myopic elegist who (like the young man of 1.5) can only lament his wretched lot.

---

[9] In line 1 I have altered Michie's "Tibullus" to the "Albius" in Horace's text.

The suggestion that lyric provides a more mature response to *eros* takes on greater weight from knowing that Horace had portrayed himself as more susceptible to elegiac passions in his earlier poetry, the *Epodes* in particular. It is tempting to read the last stanza in a metapoetic fashion, and to think that Myrtale symbolizes part of Horace's poetic past.

In line 14, the words that Michie translates as "chained and contented," *grata compede* (literally "a welcome/pleasing shackle"), brilliantly encapsulate one of love elegy's psychological paradoxes: the male lover experiences his relationship with the mistress as an enslavement, yet he embraces his subjugation. Horace puts himself in that situation but refuses to glamorize it: Myrtale's low social status is underlined, and *compes* is more down to earth (a fetter such as a real slave would wear) than the *uincula* ("chains," "bonds") that the elegists themselves speak of (for example, Tibullus himself, 1.1.55: "As for me, I am held fast by the chains of a lovely girl"). Horace produces a similar deflation of elegiac imagery in 3.26, a poem in which he proclaims his retirement from love's warfare (an elegiac cliché) and prepares to dedicate his weapons to Venus: those implements include crowbars and axes,[10] with which this practical suitor had laid siege to his partner's door.

Disparagement of elegiac love, along with the hint of an alternative, forms a part of *Odes* 1.17. The poem consists of two main sections. In the first, Horace describes the preternatural serenity that his Sabine countryside enjoys when it is visited by Faunus (the Latin counterpart of Pan), a state of Eden-like peace in which she-goats (drolly called "wives of the smelly husband") can safely wander and predators pose no threat. In the second, Horace invites Tyndaris to join him there and enumerates the pleasures she will enjoy if she accepts.

> Fleet Faunus often exchanges Lycaeus
> for lovely Lucretilis, and while he's here
>   he keeps away the blazing heat
>   and the rainy winds from my flocks of goats.

---

[10] Reading in line 7 *securesque* (Bentley) for the nonsensical *et arcus* of the manuscripts.

> Safe in the protected grove, the wandering 5
> wives of the smelly husband seek out
> > the hidden arbutus and thyme,
> > > and the kidlings have no fear
>
> of green snakes or the wolves dear to Mars,
> whenever the valleys and the smooth stones 10
> > of sloping Ustica have resounded, Tyndaris,
> > > with the sweet sound of the pipes.
>
> The gods protect me; the gods cherish
> my devotion and my Muse. Here for you plenty
> > will pour forth to the full, rich with the fruits 15
> > > of the field, from the flowing horn.
>
> Here in the secluded valley you will escape
> the Dog Star's heat, and on Anacreon's lyre
> > you will sing of Penelope and sea-green Circe
> > > struggling for the love of one man. 20
>
> Here in the shade you will drink from cups
> of harmless Lesbian wine, nor will Semele's child
> > combine with Mars to mix up battles,
> > > nor will you fear the jealousy of hot-headed
>
> Cyrus, threatening to lay uncontrolled hands 25
> on you (a poor match), to tear the garland
> > that clings to your hair and the dress
> > > that has done nothing wrong.

The ode displays a strong formal symmetry: on either side of the central stanza (13–16) three stanzas focus, respectively, on the natural world and on human actors, with parallel elements in each section (avoidance of excessive heat, freedom from fear). The unifying factor in the middle of the poem is Horace himself: the divine favor he enjoys brings abundance and security to his fields and enables him to offer Tyndaris a similarly safe and pleasurable setting. That favor Horace attributes to his *pietas* (which I have translated as "devotion") and his poetry; one of the poem's attractions is the subtlety with which it reflects in miniature what the *Odes* do as a collection. We begin with Faunus, who often chooses to leave his cult site in Greece (Mount Lycaeus) for Horace's Sabine country and an Italian identity, just as Horace, in the conclusion to *Odes* 1–3, takes pride in "having transported [*deduxisse*] Greek lyric poetry to Italian measures" (3.30.13–14). The symposium Horace imagines for Tyndaris also blends Greek and Italian elements: Tyndaris will sing on Anacreon's lyre and will drink Lesbian wine, a clear allusion to Horace's domestication of the lyrics of Sappho and Alcaeus.

That poetic element has led some critics to treat the ode's world as a purely poetic one. Commager, for example: "The land that Horace conjures up for us has its truest existence in the private and inherently isolated world of the poet's imagination.... Its reality upon the page is, finally, its only reality."[11] Such a reading might be sustained if we look only at the opening stanzas, but even there Horace has combined elements of Golden Age descriptions (such as the harmless snakes and wolves) with strong assertions of specificity: Mount Lucretilis and Ustica, presumably local Sabine names, appear only here in Latin literature.

Taking the poem as a poetic idyll also fails to do justice to its final section. The most obvious threat to Horace's charmed world comes from the brutish Cyrus, whose potentially violent treatment of Tyndaris fills the last stanza. Cyrus's behavior is not atypical for an elegiac lover (see, for example, Propertius 2.15.17–18), but in the context of refined enjoyment Horace has created it seems shockingly discordant. To understand why Horace leaves us with these disturbing final images it is useful to recall the purpose of the poem, to persuade Tyndaris to join Horace at his Sabine estate. Dwelling on the abuse she might expect to suffer if she remains with her current lover is an effective way of enhancing the appeal of his invitation, but it also raises a question: Is Horace simply offering Tyndaris a safe haven, or does he have an erotic interest in her himself? The poem is not explicit on the matter, but we might see a strong hint in Horace's choice of subject for Tyndaris's musical

---

[11] Commager 1962: 350–51.

performance, a retelling of the *Odyssey* as a love triangle with two women vying for the love of one man, possibly suggesting her involvement in a triangle of the opposite configuration. Such a role would be appropriate for a Tyndaris, that is, a daughter of Tyndareus, like Homer's Helen, fought over by Menelaus and Paris. If Horace is presenting himself as an alternative to Cyrus, he does so with exquisite tact, perhaps recognizing that to Tyndaris in her current state of mind even an offer of respectful love would be unsettling. By highlighting Tyndaris's musical abilities, Horace may be hinting at another reason for her to escape Cyrus, who presumably lacks appreciation for her talent. Just as musical skill enhances physical attractiveness in women, the ability to value it properly forms a part of what Horace has to offer them.

A similarly understated expression of erotic interest forming a contrast with elegy is found in another invitation poem addressed to a singer, 3.28, in which Horace invites Lyde to join him in celebrating the Neptunalia.[12] This poem too falls into two halves, the first focusing on the excellent wine they will soon enjoy and the second on the singing they will then engage in until nightfall. Here are the last two stanzas (9–16):

> We will sing in turn, beginning
> > with Neptune and the green hair of his Nereids:
> you reply on the curving lyre
> > with Latona and swiftfoot Cynthia's arrows:
>
> the song's finale, she who rules
> > Cnidos and the gleaming Cyclades and comes to
> Paphos behind her team of swans.
> > Night also will be praised in appropriate song.
>
> > > > (Trans. Joseph Clancy)

The progression of subjects from Neptune and the Nereids to Latona and Diana to Venus and ending with Night is a clear sign that the singing is a prelude to lovemaking. The end of the ode may

---

[12] For the third of these poems, 4.11, see 163–64.

have inspired the conclusion of one of Propertius's loveliest elegies (3.10), in which he lays out an ideal order of celebration for his mistress's birthday. Venus and Night again combine, but the elegist spells out what Horace leaves unsaid:

> When the time has been completed with many cups of wine
>   and ministering Venus shall set up the rituals of night,
> let us carry out our annual custom in the bedroom
>   and so complete the journey of your birthday. (29–32)

Horace sometimes places himself in an elegiac situation in order to exploit the resulting incongruity. In *Odes* 3.10 he adopts the pose of a shut-out lover, camped outside Lyce's doorstep on an ice-cold night. Alongside conventional appeals and complaints he inserts barbs that puncture the elegiac mood, such as the notion that Lyce was not brought up to be a Penelope and the insinuation that her husband is enjoying an affair of his own. The coup de grâce comes in the final lines, where common sense triumphs over elegiac posturing: "This body of mine won't suffer the doorstep / and the water from heaven forever."

When Horace does purport to be experiencing feelings akin to those explored in elegy, one senses that he is not being fully serious.

One such passage is the opening of *Odes* 1.13:

> When you praise Telephus's
> rosy neck, Lydia, and Telephus's
>   waxen arms, Oh how my liver
> boils and swells in indigestible bile.
>
> At such a time neither mind nor colour   5
> stays in its fixed seat, and moisture trickles furtively
>   onto my cheeks, making clear how slow
> are the fires macerating me through and though.
>   (Trans. David West)

The enumeration of physical symptoms of jealousy recalls two famous earlier poems, one by Sappho and the other by Catullus (adapting Sappho).

Sappho 31.5–14:

> My heart 5
> flutters in my breast whenever
> I quickly glance at you—
>   I can say nothing,
>
> my tongue is broken. A delicate fire
> runs under my skin, my eyes 10
> see nothing, my ears roar,
>   cold sweat
>
> rushes down me, trembling seizes me,
> I am greener than grass.
>
>   (Trans. Diane Rayor)

Catullus 51.6–12:

> For as soon as I look
> at you, Lesbia, no voice remains
>   in my mouth.
>
> But the tongue is paralyzed, a thin fire
> spreads through my limbs, my ears ring with their 10
> very own sound, my eyes are covered
>   in a double darkness.

In Horace the motif is hard to take seriously, partly because the material is now being encountered at third hand and partly because Horace's language lowers the tone. The reference to bile in his liver sounds uncomfortably medical, and the verb West translates as "macerating," *macerer*, originally a culinary term (like "marinate"), is more at home in the language of comedy and iambic poetry.

Another is *Odes* 1.19:

> The cruel mother of the Loves,
>   Theban Semele's child and wild Abandon
> order me to give back my heart
>   to love that had been ended.

Amatory Poems | 105

I burn with Glycera's beauty,   5
    glowing brighter than Parian marble;
I burn with her delightful forwardness
    and her face, dangerous to behold.

Venus abandons Cyprus and rushes on me
    with all her might, forbidding me   10
to speak of Scythians, or Parthians bold
    in retreat, or anything irrelevant.

Come, boys, place here fresh altar turf,
    place wreaths for sacrifice,
incense and a bowl of two-year-old wine.   15
    She will come more kindly when a victim is
        offered.

Here, it would seem, we have the makings of a grand passion in the elegiac manner. Glycera is irresistibly alluring, and Horace duly burns with desire for her, even if his repeated "I burn" sounds almost stately. Glycera herself is overshadowed by a formidable array of divinities, who compel Horace to return to love: Venus with a posse of Loves, Bacchus, and personified Abandon. We may suspect that the piling up of divine forces dilutes rather than intensifies the emotional situation; those suspicions are heightened when we learn that Venus has left her favorite cult site of Cyprus just to devote all her attention to Horace. In the lines that follow, irony is unmistakable: Venus will not allow him to speak of Scythians or Parthians, subjects of the sort of patriotic poem that he never shows the slightest interest in writing. In the final stanza we discover why Horace was at pains to portray his infatuation with Glycera as godsent: Greco-Roman divinities were thought to be susceptible to bribes in the form of sacrifice, so if Venus is responsible for this new outbreak of passion, Horace has the means to secure gentle treatment from her. In the final line some translators introduce an element of hope or uncertainty (David Ferry: "Perhaps if I offer a sacrifice to Venus / Venus will be less cruel when she comes"; Robert Creeley: "May it lessen / the imperious impact of her arrival"), but the main verb is future indicative, "she will come." Horace knows the drill, and he can be confident of the result.

Horace was well aware that romantic love makes the lover behave in ways that to an uninvolved observer can only appear ridiculous. So even when he depicts himself as feeling the force of passion, he usually maintains some of that outsider's perspective on his own situation. Usually, but not always. In this respect 1.22 is an atypical poem. If I am interpreting it correctly, here Horace fully immerses himself in the guise of a besotted lover.

> The man who is pure of heart and free from crime
> needs no Moroccan spears nor bow nor quiver
> weighed down by its load of poisoned arrows,
> Fuscus my friend,
>
> whether he makes his way through the blazing Syrtes   5
> or ventures to the frozen Caucasus
> or the distant lands washed by the legendary
> river Hydaspes.
>
> For once in the Sabine woods as I wandered
> far from my land, my cares set aside, unarmed,   10
> singing of my sweet Lalage, a wolf
> ran away from me—
>
> no such monster did Daunia, land of soldiers,
> nurture in its broad forests of oak,
> nor does Juba's realm breed such a one,   15
> dry nurse of lions.
>
> Place me on a barren plain, where no tree
> is ever given new life by the summer breeze,
> a dismal region beset by looming fog
> and constant rain;   20
>
> place me right under the sun's chariot wheels,
> in a country uninhabitable for heat:
> I will go on loving Lalage, sweetly laughing
> and sweetly talking.

The humor of the poem lies mainly in the progression of its thought: (a) stanzas 1 and 2, proposition: the upright man can go anywhere without fear; (b) stanzas 3 and 4, proof: a wolf ran from me while I was singing about Lalage; (c) stanzas 5 and 6, conclusion to be drawn: place me anywhere and I will go on singing about Lalage. In order for the speaker's skewed logic to have its full effect, he must take it seriously, and must believe that he has constructed a perfectly valid syllogism. In this case the foolishness of the romantic outlook is exposed with no winking from the poet.

In the poem's final lines Horace converses again with Catullus and Sappho, and again introduces irony where there had been romantic absorption.

Catullus 51.3–5:
>who sitting opposite you over and over
>watches and hears
>>your sweet laughter

Sappho 31.2–5:
>whoever sits beside you
>and close, who listens to you
>>sweetly speaking
>and laughing temptingly.

(Trans. Diane Rayor)

Horace's "sweetly laughing" echoes the same phrase in Catullus, but the following "sweetly talking" looks further back to Sappho, who refers to both laughing and speaking. To this combination Horace adds the significant name Lalage, which derives from Greek λαλεῖν and which probably connotes constant chatter. "Sweetly talking" now sounds wryly amused ("I love her, but she does go on"), and the humor of the poem's mock-serious argument is enhanced: it is amusing that Horace should attribute his escape from the wolf to his devotion to a woman, but the likelihood that the woman in question is a chatterbox makes the assertion even funnier.

I come now to a final contrast between Horatian lyric and contemporary elegy. Catullus and the elegists aspire to a lasting love. In one of his more hopeful statements, Catullus prays that he and Lesbia "be allowed to continue our whole life long this eternal bond of sacred friendship" (109.5–6), and Propertius writes that "since one woman has robbed me of my senses, my funeral procession will set out from her house" (2.1.55–56; similarly 2.15.36, "I will be hers in life, I will be hers in death").

The notion of lifelong love appears only twice in the *Odes*, and in neither case is it presented as something Horace hopes to attain for himself.

The first occurrence is in the closing stanza of 1.13.[13]

> Three times blessed and more
> are those held in an unbroken bond, whose love
> torn asunder by no bitter complaints
> will not release them before their final day.
>
> (Trans. David West, adapted)

Here the ideal is placed at a distance by the hyperbolic "three times blessed and more are those," which implies that such fortunate couples are rare and suggests that Horace and Lydia are not among them. Furthermore, this positive vision is intriguingly dominated by negative words and expressions: "unbroken," "will not release them," "torn asunder," "bitter complaints." Is Horace adding to the implication that these couples are rare by enumerating the risks of such a relationship? One of those negated terms, "complaints," *querimoniae*, deserves a closer look. It is related to the verb *queror* ("to complain") and the noun *querela* ("complaint"), terms frequently used of lovers' complaints in elegy. The negation may hint that one requirement for a lasting love is the absence of elegiac emotions.

---

[13] On later uses of 1.13.13–16 see 216–17.

The other appearance of the idea is in the mouth of Lydia at the end of *Odes* 3.9.

"As long as I was dear to you,
 and there was no other, a sweeter boy, to put
his arms about your glowing neck,
 I lived more blissful than the king of Persia."

"As long as you burned for no one~ 5
 else, and Lydia was not second to Chloe,
Lydia was a noted name
 and I lived more famous than Rome's own Ilia."

"I'm now ruled by Thracian Chloe,
 who knows pretty songs and is clever with a lute, 10
for whom I would not fear to die
 if the Fates spared my soul and allowed her to live."

"I'm now on fire, and he burns too,
 for Calais, son of Ornytus of Thurii,
for whom I would gladly die twice 15
 if the Fates spared my boy and allowed him to live."

"What if the early love returned
 and joined those now apart with unbreakable yoke,
if blonde Chloe were brushed aside,
 and the door opened wide for cast-off Lydia?" 20

"Though he is far more lovely than
 he stars, and you lighter than cork and angrier
than the stormy Adriatic,
 with you I'd love to live, with you I'd gladly die."
                    (Trans. Joseph Clancy)

Among the amatory poems 3.9 is unique in giving a voice to a woman. The ode is a genuine duet with the partners on equal terms; in fact the woman has the more prominent role by virtue of speaking second and having the last word. Gordon Williams called the poem "a blithe Mozartian duet."[14] The analogy is most apt if one compares duets such as "La ci darem la mano" from *Don Giovanni* and "Bei Männern" from *The Magic Flute*, in which the two voices sing the same tune in succession, but with different words and, in the former instance, initially opposed feelings that in the end find common ground. But the musical comparisons also highlight a distinctive aspect of the ode: in both Mozart duets the male and female voices eventually join, while Horace and Lydia remain separate in their speeches and, it may be, in their attitudes as well.

In each pair of stanzas Lydia caps Horace, and in the last pair she takes his carefully hedged offer of reconciliation a large step further. It is tempting (especially for readers who would like Horace to show more feeling than he usually does) to think that he finds Lydia's proposal attractive or even that he accepts it, but the poem does not commit itself or him, and a cynical reader might conclude that Horace gets what he wants (another turn with Lydia) at a minimal cost (admitting that it was he who dumped her in the first place). I would be inclined to resist that reading, but it might get some support from the following ode, where Horace appears outside another woman's shut door, suggesting that any reconciliation with Lydia was short-lived. Lydia's final line evokes a union that is uncomfortably similar to marriage, so perhaps Horace felt it necessary to move smartly away from that prospect.

So far I have been highlighting ways in which Horace's amatory odes distance themselves from the treatment of love being developed by elegiac poets. Generic interaction of that kind plays a large part in Augustan poetry, but Horace's approach to the erotic was also shaped by other factors, of which I will briefly mention three.

One is his adherence to Epicureanism. Horace's philosophical outlook is sometimes characterized as superficial and eclectic, but his enjoyment of sexual encounters while avoiding emotional entanglements is perfectly in line with Epicurean doctrine. To make

---

[14] Williams 1969: 76.

one's own happiness depend on another person would entail a loss of the self-sufficiency that Epicureans considered indispensable for a good life.

Horace's generally detached attitude toward erotic relationships contrasts with the warmth that he displays in odes addressed to friends, in keeping with the high value that Epicureans placed on friendship. Horace's references to Virgil as "the other half of my soul" (1.3.8) and to Maecenas as "part of my soul" (2.17.5) are stronger than any endearment in the amatory poetry. It is in the context of friendship, specifically with Maecenas, that he introduces the motif of "united in death" that is more often found applied to lovers: the whole of *Odes* 2.17 develops that idea, in particular lines 5–12:

> Ah, if some force carries you off sooner, you who are part of my soul,
> why do I keep the other part alive,
>   no longer as dear and not surviving whole?
>   That day will bring ruin to us both.
>
> I have taken my oath of loyalty, and I will not be false to it:
>   we will go, we will go, whenever you lead,
>   comrades ready to take the final journey.

There is no more heartfelt passage in all of Horace; it is characteristic of his normal restraint that, having made such a forthright avowal, he should modulate immediately into a lighter key with mythological hyperbole ("not the fiery breath of the Chimaera, nor the hundred-handed Gyges, should he rise again, will ever tear me from your side").

A second factor is Horace's preoccupation with temporality. For Horace, erotic experience takes place within time and is bounded by time; it can never be constant because the people involved are forever changing. So for him the elegiac ideal of a perpetual (and therefore timeless) love is an impossibility. That is one reason why the panorama of Horace's relationships includes former, current, and potential future partners. Many of his partners and the recipients of his erotic advice are situated along a temporal spectrum that runs from "not ready" (2.5) through "on the cusp" (1.4) and "ready" (1.9, 1.23) to "too old" (1.25, 3.15). One of the principal breaches of what Horace regards as erotic decorum is to pursue a relationship at the wrong time. It is worth noting that for Horace there is apparently no reason why the passage of time should diminish the capacity for friendship or the enjoyment of it, as seems to be the case with time and erotic relationships.

My third contributing factor is admittedly speculative. I find it tempting to think that Horace keeps erotic feelings under careful control because he is aware of being highly susceptible to them. His habitual detachment would thus serve not as a sign of indifference but as a form of self-protection. That hypothesis could help to explain why on several occasions he attempts to shut down that side of his life. In his first erotic poem, 1.5, he is already an ex-lover, a survivor of love's shipwreck. In 1.19 (midway through Book 1) he speaks of loves as "over with." *Odes* 3.26—the counterpart to 1.5 in the architecture of *Odes* 1–3—has him declaring that his career as a lover is done. Within *Odes* 1–3, however, all such declarations are undercut; even the final-seeming 3.26 is followed by two poems in which Horace is erotically engaged.

In this context it is telling that the most powerful expression of love in Horace is placed in the mouth of a mythological character. *Odes* 3.11 is a fascinating—a polite equivalent of puzzling—poem. Horace begins by invoking the persuasive power of Mercury and the lyre to overcome the resistance of young Lyde to marriage (1–12). Further praise of the lyre recalls its use by Orpheus to captivate the inhabitants of the underworld, including the daughters of Danaus (13–24). Then, at the rough midpoint of the ode, Horace specifies that Lyde should hear of their horrendous crime—at their father's instigation all but one of the fifty killed their husbands on their wedding night—and its everlasting punishment (25–32). The final section of the poem singles out the virtuous exception, Hypermestra, and reports the speech with which she spared her husband and sent him to safety.

> One of the many was worthy
> of the marriage torch, and to her treacherous father

told a shining lie, a maid whose name 35
    will live to all time.

"Rise!" she said to her young husband,
"Rise! Or a long sleep will be given you
by a hand you do not fear. Deceive
    my father and cruel sisters. 40

They are like she-lions—O the horror of it—
each tearing the flesh of a young calf.
I am gentler. I shall not strike you
    or keep you behind bars.

Let my father heap cruel chains upon me 45
for taking pity on my defenceless husband.
Let him send me with his fleet
    to Numidia's distant fields.

While night and Venus grant their favour,
go where feet or wind may speed you. 50
Go with good omen and in my memory carve
    a lament on my tomb."

(Trans. David West)

    The distance between the opening of the poem and its conclusion has been seen as indicating a lack of unity, but the problem is not so much one of unity as one of scale. Lyde is resisting marriage, unreasonably; to move her Horace wants her to hear the story of those rabid anti-marriage girls, the Danaids, and what happened to them. As a positive example he introduces Hypermestra, who showed mercy to her husband and won eternal glory. But we are still faced with the disparity between silly little Lyde and the grandeur of the Danaid myth. I would say that the end of the ode grows out of the beginning, but that it also grows considerably beyond it. Many interpreters look for irony or humor: Giorgio Pasquali called the poem a "light-hearted jest,"[15] and Nisbet and Rudd (2004) call

---

[15] Pasquali 1920: 144.

Hypermestra's speech melodramatic. But Horace's introductory lines (33–36) do not suggest irony, and the speech itself reads to me as noble and moving. (Comparison with the speech of Europa in 3.27 shows what a melodramatic rant looks like.) In this case Fraenkel's habit of taking Horace seriously seems justified: "In the speech of the heroine a dignity of thought and expression, worthy of tragedy, is maintained throughout."[16]

Fraenkel's reference to tragedy raises the issue of genre. Michèle Lowrie treats Hypermestra as an elegiac figure,[17] but while she may be built in part out of elegiac material, the resulting character is unlike anything in elegy.[18] To take one example, Hypermestra's final word, "lament" (*querela*), does not denote "lover's complaints" (as in 1.13 and 2.9) but instead reaches back to the older connection between elegy and lamentation for the dead. Horace here transmutes the language of elegy into something more mature and impressive.

In a throwaway comment, Commager refers to 3.11 as an "Ovidian ramble,"[19] presumably meaning an excursion into the sort of amatory myth for which Ovid is known. The comparison with Ovid can perhaps be pressed a bit further. When purporting to recount his own erotic experiences in the elegiac *Amores*, Ovid adopts a light, sometimes cynical manner; but in the mythological narratives of the *Metamorphoses*, he presents several instances of a deeper and more lasting bond between lovers or spouses. Myth may have given Horace as well a freedom he did not enjoy (or did not choose to enjoy) when speaking in his own person.

The emotional poise that Horace strives to maintain in the erotic sphere comes at the cost of a limited range. To that extent the comparisons with Catullus that find him lacking in vitality have

---

[16] Fraenkel 1957: 197.
[17] Lowrie 1997: 275–97.
[18] A possible exception is Propertius's Cornelia in 4.11, a noble wife and mother. It seems to me conceivable that Horace's Hypermestra contributed something to Propertius's portrait.
[19] Commager 1962: 174.

some merit, however compelling Horace's reasons may have been for adopting that attitude. But fortunately for us, his career as a lyric poet did not end with *Odes* 1–3. The collection known as *Odes* Book 4 (on which see chapter 10) opens a new phase in Horace's amatory poetry.

· 8 ·

Political Poems

About a fifth of the poems of *Odes* 1–3 can be grouped under the heading "political," although only a few of them treat politics in the modern sense of the term; "public" or "civic" might be more appropriate descriptions. The poems form three overlapping subgroups: odes dealing with the civil wars and their aftermath (1.2, 1.14 [probably], 1.35, 1.37, 2.1, 2.7), poems that reflect on the current state of Roman society and morals (2.15, 2.16, 2.18, 3.1–6, 3.24), and poems that relate to Rome and Augustus (1.2, 1.35, 3.4, 3.5, 3.14, 3.25). This chapter will focus on examples of each subgroup.

That Horace chose to devote a substantial part of his collection to publicly oriented poems calls for some comment. The choice was not mandated by his ambition to become a Roman counterpart to the Greek lyric poets, since civic engagement was not universal among them; Horace could have opted to confine himself to personal subjects, as Sappho and Anacreon had done. The influence of Alcaeus may have been decisive: in *Odes* 1.32 Horace names Alcaeus as his lyric forebear, calling him "the citizen of Lesbos," who sang of wine, poetry, and love in the midst of fighting for his city. It is also possible, although I think less likely, that Horace chose Alcaeus as his main model because he represented the mix of private and public themes that Horace had already decided to treat.

Factors of genre aside, as a Roman writing under the patronage of Maecenas during the first years of the Augustan principate, Horace would have been expected to engage with public themes. The main challenge in doing so was how to avoid producing blatant panegyric of Augustus, which would have been uncongenial to the poet and distasteful to its recipient. The problem was compounded by the personal focus of Horace's chosen genres: unlike Virgil, who could comment on contemporary events through the filter of pastoral or didactic or epic, Horace had to speak in his own voice.

For some modern readers, political poetry is intrinsically suspect because there appears to be a conflict between what poetry is meant to do—in particular, to articulate complex feelings and attitudes—and the simplistic idiom that is associated with political discourse. In addition, we tend to prefer that our poets be either apolitical or voices of opposition. A poet whose talent is placed at the service of a regime arouses discomfort even if the regime in question is not in itself objectionable.

As a result, the presence of Augustus in Horace's poetry creates special problems. Most readers do not greatly differ in their opinions about the beauty of springtime and the brevity of life, but in the case of Augustus the range of views is extraordinarily wide. At one end is the benevolent *Pater patriae* ("Father of the Country"), who delivered Rome from civil war and gave her the stable government that the Republic had failed to maintain. At the other is the crafty tyrant of Tacitus's *Annals* and Gibbon's *Decline and Fall*, the man who destroyed the Republic and its freedom while pretending all the while to restore them. The view taken of Augustus will inevitably color the response to the poems that relate to him.

Assessing Horace's apparent support for Octavian/Augustus is further complicated by the fact of his having fought with Brutus against Octavian and Antony after the assassination of Julius Caesar, which suggests that in his youth he was opposed to Rome's becoming a de facto monarchy. A cynical view would hold that he was co-opted by Maecenas and abandoned his republican beliefs for personal gain; a more charitable interpretation would be that his views changed in response to political developments. In 42 the dream of preserving the Republic was still alive, even if in hindsight that outcome appears highly unlikely. Ten years later, the choice facing Romans may have seemed one between two autocrats, Antony and Octavian, with the prospect in one case of Rome being ruled in part by the queen of Egypt. Seen in that light, a decision to back Octavian appears defensible; the relative stability of the years that followed may have made it seem justified.

Although Horace was a member of Maecenas's circle from around 37 onward, that does not seem to have entailed automatic support for Octavian. Indeed it looks as though Horace held off making overt statements of support for several years. The first book of *Satires* contains only one glancing and ostensibly apolitical reference to Octavian (1.3.4). A change is evident around 30, in the Actium-centered epodes 1 and 9 and in the opening of *Satires* Book 2, where to a suggestion that he celebrate Caesar's accomplishments Horace responds with the polite excuse "I am eager to do so, but my powers fail me" (2.1.12–13). He may have declared his full support only after Octavian's preeminence was clear.

1. Civil War

The *Epodes* presented two strikingly different responses to Rome's civil wars. Poems 1 and 9, which are set before and after the battle of Actium, voice wholehearted support for Octavian, while poems 7 and 16 treat the wars more broadly as a national disaster, the result of Romulus's primal act of fratricide and a cause for despair of Rome's future. In the epode collection those views are kept separate and unresolved. (For fuller discussion see 22–23.)

Odes 1–3 wrestle with the same dual perspective. In *Odes* 1.2 the dark view of civil war as a crime is set against the hope that Octavian/Caesar may be able to rescue Rome from its guilt. In 1.35 hopes for Caesar's success in foreign wars are juxtaposed with agonized expressions of shame at what Romans had inflicted on each other. Then 1.37 and 2.1—which face each other across the slight 1.38—present the fullest development of the competing viewpoints, 1.37 celebrating Actium as the triumph of Rome over Egypt and 2.1 brooding on the tragedy of civil conflict. In the *Odes* the relationship between the poems is more subtle than in the

Epodes: rather than an opposition that the collection declines to resolve, the two odes offer complementary visions of the war and its conclusion, as both an escape from the threat of eastern despotism and an abomination that stained the seas with Roman blood.

1.37

Now is the time to drink, now the time
to beat the earth with unfettered foot,
    now, comrades, time to load the couches
        of the gods with Salian banquets.

Before this it was wrong to bring out Caecuban   5
from ancestral storerooms, while the mad queen
    was plotting ruin for the Capitol
        and death to our empire

with her squalid flock of diseased half-men,
helpless to restrain her hopes and drunk   10
    on sweet fortune. But the rescue of barely one
        ship from the flames diminished

her frenzy, and Caesar brought her mind, deranged
by Mareotic wine, back to face genuine fears,
    pressing close upon her with his oars   15
        as she flew away from Italy,

just as a hawk pursues the gentle doves
or a swift hunter tracks a hare
    in the snow-covered fields of Thessaly,
        preparing to throw in chains   20

this monster sent by fate. She, seeking a nobler death,
showed no woman's fear at the sight of a sword,
    nor with her swift fleet did she search
        for a place of refuge on secret shores,

>   daring to look upon the ruins of her palace   25
>   with face serene, brave to take the sharp-toothed
>   serpents in her hands, eager to drink
>   their black venom with her whole body,
>
>   fiercer than ever with her death determined,
>   no doubt she would not let the rude Liburni   30
>   convey her, no longer a queen, to a haughty
>   triumph—she, no submissive woman.

This is a classic example of a poem that ends in a very different place from its opening, through the mediation of a middle section. It is also a poem that establishes apparently clear-cut oppositions that by its end have come to seem more complicated.

Horace launches the poem with a phrase that translates the first words of an ode of Alcaeus: "Now is the time to drink" (*nunc est bibendum*). In Alcaeus the occasion is the overthrow of the tyrant Myrsilus, and Horace adopts a similar perspective. Antony and his Roman legions are nowhere to be seen, and the victory at Actium is cast as the triumph of Rome over Egyptian despotism.

The opening section establishes a strong contrast between Cleopatra and the Romans in their styles of drinking: the Italian Caecuban from ancestral cellars is set against the eastern Mareotic (a similar opposition of Italy and the East is established in *Odes* 2.7 [see 57]). The Romans drink as a group, Cleopatra alone (both at the beginning and when the motif returns in 27–28), reflecting the opposition between Romans as a people and a solitary despot. Other oppositions are suggested rather than made explicit. The Romans drink only when it is proper to do so, and their drinking has religious sanction if, as seems likely, the wine is to be brought out for the banquet of the Salii, the priests of Mars mentioned in the first stanza. On the other hand, it is implied that Cleopatra's drinking is both excessive and premature: she is drunk with hope as well as maddened by Mareotic wine.

Toward the end of the third stanza the poem begins to move in more interesting directions. Having portrayed Cleopatra and her entourage in viciously harsh terms, Horace now adopts an almost wry tone: the loss of her fleet has the sobering effect of a spell in rehab for an alcoholic, and Caesar acts like a therapist in bringing Cleopatra back from delusions to face reality. But then the chase is on, and pursuer and pursued are figured in highly unequal terms: the doves are no match for the hawk, nor is the hare for the hunter (it is he who is swift, not the animal). It might seem that Horace, in stressing Caesar's control, risks making Cleopatra an object of sympathy. Almost as though sensing that danger, he re-inflates Cleopatra's standing: seen through Caesar's eyes, she is something both more and less than human, a "monster sent by fate." Then the next word ("she") redirects us again, back to Cleopatra as a woman—but a woman whose first action is not to behave like one ("showed no woman's fear"). In a stunning demonstration of the difficulty of categorizing Cleopatra, she cycles through all three gender categories within two lines: from a neuter monster to a quasi-masculine woman.

 The rest of the poem belongs to Cleopatra; having been temporarily forced into the position of an object, she regains and tenaciously holds on to the agent position through the long sentence that runs from line 21 to the end. Her actions complicate the neat opposition of Rome versus Egypt established at the start; her self-possession and her defiance elicit admiration because they make her more like a Roman; her end is "worthy of a Roman noble."[1]

 The final stanza combines the perspectives of Cleopatra and Horace. Horace describes the motive that drove Cleopatra to suicide, determination to avoid being led in a triumphal procession. He probably knew that the historical Cleopatra had expressed a similar determination. But Horace also calls attention to himself as interpreting Cleopatra's state of mind: the word I have rendered as "no doubt" is *scilicet*, here a particle that affirms the truth of an inference and so marks the transition from omniscient narrator to self-conscious interpreter. Horace surmises that to this descendant of the Ptolemies, the Liburnian sailors who would transport her to Rome are *saeui*, not merely "cruel" but "rude," "uncivilized."

---

[1] Syme 1939: 299.

The presence of both perspectives creates an ambiguous space in which a reader might believe, if only for a moment, that Cleopatra has exploited Horace's word order to make the final line of the poem her own statement: *non humilis mulier triumpho,* "No humble woman, I triumph."[2]

Horace's glorification of Cleopatra in her final hours is sometimes interpreted as an indirect tribute to Caesar: "The adversary must have been redoubtable indeed!" as Syme sarcastically expressed it.[3] That may have been part of Horace's intention, but I do not believe that any reader of the poem's ending ever gave much thought to Caesar.

2.1

Civil unrest since Metellus was consul,
the causes, crimes, and phases of the war,
    the game played by Fortune, the fateful
      friendships of leaders, and arms

smeared with blood not yet expiated—   5
a work fraught with the hazard of the dice—
    these are your themes, and you walk on fire
      still smoldering beneath deceptive ash.

For just a while let your strict tragic Muse be gone
from our stage; soon, when you have set affairs of state   10
    in order, you will resume your high vocation
      as the bard of Attic theater,

Pollio, stout bulwark for anxious men on trial
and esteemed councilor in the Senate's debates,
    for whom the victor's laurel brought forth   15
      eternal glory in Dalmatian triumph.

---

[2] As noted by Feldherr 2010: 231.
[3] Syme 1939: 299.

Even now you batter our ears with the threatening roar
of the horns, now the trumpets blare, now the sheen
    of armor puts fear into runaway horses
        and into their riders' faces   20

Now I seem to hear of mighty generals
filthy with dust that carries no disgrace,
    and of a whole world subjected
        but for the unyielding soul of Cato.

Juno and any other gods partial to Africa,   25
who had left the land they were powerless to avenge,
    have brought back the grandsons of the victors
        as funeral offerings to the shade of Jugurtha.

What field made more fertile with Latin blood
does not bear witness with its graves to impious strife, 30
    does not proclaim the collapse of Italy—
        a sound heard in far-off Parthia?

What sea, what river is there that is unaware
of lamentable war? What ocean has not been turned
    red with the slaughter of Daunus's sons?   35
        What shore lacks its share of Roman gore?

But come, my impertinent Muse, do not forsake
your cheerful ways to rehash ancient dirges;
    together with me in Venus's grotto
        let's look for music in a lighter vein.   40

    Asinius Pollio, though scarcely a name to modern readers, was a figure of considerable importance. He first appears as a bright young thing in Catullus's poetry; he went on to a significant political/military career, reaching the consulship in 40 and celebrating a triumph in the next year. When the final confrontation between Antony and Octavian loomed, he declared himself neutral, adding loftily, "I will be the victor's prize." As a writer he was known first for tragedy, later for history; his history of the civil wars (unfortunately lost) was an important source for subsequent historians. He was also a patron of letters, creating Rome's first public library and initiating the practice of public reading (*recitatio*) of new work or work in progress. (A mixed blessing, by most accounts.) Finally, Pollio has the distinction of being the addressee of Virgil's fourth *Eclogue*, sometimes called the "Messianic Eclogue" because its prediction of a new Golden Age inaugurated by the birth of a child was read by Christians as foretelling the coming of Jesus.

Odes 1.37 avoided all suggestion of civil war; 2.1 adopts the opposite perspective: civil war, as narrated by Pollio, is present from the opening words. Lines 1–8 could almost be a poetic version of Pollio's preface, with a summary of the contents of the work to come and a reflection on the historian's boldness in taking on so sensitive a subject. The next two stanzas are an unsuccessful attempt to push the subject aside, but from 17 to 36 Horace finds himself drawn ever more deeply into it—itself a tribute to the power of Pollio's work.

We do not know how far Pollio's history went. If it included Actium, the contrast with 1.37 would be very strongly marked. Most scholars opt for an earlier terminus; the reference to bloodstained seas would make best sense if Pollio went at least to the death of Sextus Pompey after the naval battle of Naulochus in 36.

But for our understanding of Horace's poem it does not really matter where Pollio's history ended. Horace is responding to a historian's treatment of the civil war; his thoughts do not need to be limited by what that history actually contained, or by how much of it he had read or heard. In that light the three stanzas (25–36) that respond in the most emotional terms could be entirely Horatian. If so, the reference to seas red with Roman blood could include Actium without Horace needing to say so explicitly. In fact, it is difficult to imagine a Roman reading those lines and not thinking of Actium. (Propertius, in a poem written at nearly the same time, used Actium to epitomize the ruinous effects of the entire civil war [2.15.44].)

Although the focus of 2.1 is different from that of 1.37, it is hard to resist the impression that 2.1 corrects the Rome versus Egypt scenario of the earlier ode. That would be apt in a poem addressed to a historian, who would be interested in events as they actually occurred and not in some propagandistic version.

The swerve away from the war at the end of the poem, in addition to making a distinction of genre (this is not a suitable subject for my kind of lyric), is also perhaps a suggestion that any remembrance of the civil wars will inevitably lead to unbearable thoughts. Writing about the civil wars threatens to derail both Horace and Pollio from their proper pursuits (which in Pollio's case, according to Horace, is writing tragedies, not recollecting real-world disasters). By implication, the proper response to those wars is to forget them—which is what Horace explicitly advocates a few poems later, in 2.7, when he welcomes the diehard republican Pompeius back to Italy. (For fuller discussion of 2.7 see 53–58.)

2. Poems of Social Comment

Toward the end of Book 2 we find a group of poems (15, 16, and 18) featuring denunciations of luxury and excess, as manifested in lavish dwellings adorned with the choicest materials. Earlier poems (such as 2.14) had made the point that riches are no protection against mortality, but now extravagant living is itself the target of criticism. Poem 15, unusually, has no addressee, and 18 is directed at an unnamed "you"; the suggestion is that the lifestyle in question is not limited to particular individuals but is a more general phenomenon.

The reader of the *Odes* will soon realize that the strain of social criticism introduced by these poems will be taken up on a larger scale at the start of the next book, but it is worth asking why Horace chose to introduce it at this point rather than earlier in the collection. One explanation is that a focus on Rome's societal problems only seemed appropriate once the aftereffects of the civil wars had been laid to rest, a process that, as we have seen, reaches its conclusion in the first half of Book 2.

The opening of Book 3 presents readers with a unique sequence of six successive poems in the Alcaic meter, all with a focus on public themes. Several are longer than average, and two of them, 3.3 and 3.4, with 72 and 80 lines, are the longest poems in *Odes* 1–3. None is addressed to a named individual: 3.4 invokes the Muse Calliope, and 3.6 addresses a collective "Roman." That something unusual is happening is clear from the opening stanza of 3.1:

> I scorn the secular crowd and keep them out.
> Be silent. I am a priest of the Muses
>   and I chant for young men and maidens
>   poems that have never been heard before.
>   (Trans. Joseph Clancy)

Gone, at least for the moment, is the genial Horace with his praises of wine and friendship; in his place is an austere hierophant with lessons for the youth of Rome.

Since the late nineteenth century it has been customary to refer to these six poems as the "Roman Odes," a designation that usefully evokes their civic focus and their coherence as a group. Horace himself marked the boundaries of the sequence with a verbal correspondence that has not received the attention it deserves. The opening poem ends with a reference to "riches that are more burdensome," *divitias operosiores*, and the sixth poem ends with a reference to "descendants that are yet more degenerate," *progeniem vitiosiorem*. The two lines have the same shape, consisting of a noun of four syllables and a comparative adjective of six syllables; they are the only two instances of that form in the entire corpus of *Odes*. (On the connection between them see also 134.)

Horace's ancient commentator Porphyrio went so far as to regard *Odes* 3.1–6 as a single poem, a view that has been revived by Stephen Heyworth.[4] That is not likely to be true, but in practical terms the difference between considering 3.1–6 as six poems that

---

[4] Heyworth 1995: 142–44.

form a closely connected cycle or as one poem articulated in six distinct sections may not be all that great.[5]

I will try to give some sense of the contents of the cycle, singling out a few highlights, and then look more closely at the final installment.

Odes 3.1 ranges widely and unexpectedly; its abrupt transitions and elevated tone—features that characterize the series as a whole—are reminiscent of Pindar. The poem eventually settles on a familiar Horatian theme, the superiority of a simple but tranquil life to the anxieties of wealth and high status, and the closing stanza finds Horace literally back on home territory: "Why would I exchange my Sabine valley for riches that are more burdensome?" (47–48). The next poem is centered on the concept of *virtus*, or "manliness," especially as displayed by soldiers. It contains the famous line *dulce et decorum est pro patria mori*, "It is sweet and glorious to die for one's country" (called "the old lie" by Wilfred Owen in a poem detailing the horrors of actual warfare in World War I).

The two longest poems occupy the central position in the series. *Odes* 3.3 opens with two stanzas that have echoed across the centuries, from Seneca, Prudentius, and Boethius to George Eliot and Robert Browning:[6]

> The just man who holds fast to his resolve
> is not shaken in firmness of mind by the passion
>   of citizens demanding what is wrong,
>   or the menace of the tyrant's frown, or the wind
>
> of the south, rebellious king of the unquiet Adriatic,
> or by the mighty hand of Jupiter who wields the lightning.
>   If the round world were to break and fall about him,
>   its ruins would strike him unafraid.
>
>   (Trans. David West)

---

[5] Griffiths 2002 offers a reading of the cycle as a "monster mega-poem" (78) articulated in blocks that cross traditional poem boundaries.
[6] Tarrant 2007: 283–85; Harrison 2017b: 132; Maynard 1977: 301.

As examples Horace cites Pollux and Hercules, Bacchus and Romulus, all of whom have attained a place in heaven for their merits; a similar destiny is foretold for Augustus—the first reference to him in the cycle. The mention of Romulus leads to an extended account (based on a scene in Ennius's epic *Annales*) of the divine council at which Romulus's apotheosis was approved; it consists almost entirely of an impassioned speech by Juno (lines 17–68), in which she consents to Romulus's divine status and predicts worldwide rule for Rome on the condition that no attempt be made to rebuild the ruins of Troy. (Her insistence on that point closely corresponds to the position taken by Juno in the last book of the *Aeneid*, written at about the same time. The contemporary significance of these anti-Trojan sentiments remains unclear.)

Odes 3.4 is the most ambitious member of the cycle, and Horace's most Pindaric composition in *Odes* 1–3. After summoning the Muse Calliope, Horace devotes nearly half the poem to himself and the special protection he enjoys as a poet. He relates a story from his infancy, when he was lost and birds covered him with bay and myrtle. (Similar tales were told of Pindar and other poets.) Poetry provides the link between Horace and Augustus, who is said to have been refreshed by the Muses after he had settled the veterans from his campaigns; the Muses give him "gentle counsel," probably an allusion to the policy of clemency adopted by Augustus toward his former enemies. With no transition Horace recounts the defeat of the heaven-storming Titans by Jupiter and the other Olympians; that event had long been used to typify the victory of civilization over barbarous forces, and it may function likewise here to represent Octavian's triumph over Cleopatra. A gnomic stanza draws the lesson and looks forward to the final section of the ode (65–68):

> Force without wisdom falls by its own weight;
> force under control is increased and made greater
> by the gods; they detest force that plots
> all manner of evil in the heart.

Horace calls to witness malefactors punished for lack of self-control, several for crimes of a sexual nature (Orion, Tityos, Pirithous). An oblique allusion to Antony is likely.

A prediction of Augustus's future divinity opens *Odes* 3.5, but it is made conditionally: "Augustus will be deemed a god in our midst when the Britons and troublesome Parthians have been added to our empire." In 53 a Roman army led by Marcus Crassus had been defeated by the Parthians at Carrhae; the Roman legionary standards had been seized, and ten thousand Romans had been taken prisoner. Efforts to avenge this disgrace went on through the 30s and 20s; finally in 20 a negotiated settlement secured the return of the symbolically important standards (but not the soldiers). Horace adopts a peculiar attitude to the issue, condemning Crassus's soldiers for settling down among the Parthians and contrasting their behavior with an example from earlier times. In 255 Marcus Atilius Regulus and several hundred of his men had been captured by the Carthaginians; Regulus was allowed to go to Rome on the condition that he arrange for the ransom of the captives, but he instead urged the Senate to reject the arrangement and himself returned to Carthage, knowing that he would be tortured and killed. Regulus's story allows Horace to contrast the degenerate present with the illustrious past, a theme that will also figure prominently in the following ode. The best part of 3.5—and one of the best moments in all of the *Odes*—comes at the end, in two stanzas describing Regulus returning to Carthage as if heading off for a well-earned vacation (49–56):

> And though he knew what the foreign torturer
> was preparing for him, yet he pushed away
>   relatives who were blocking his way
>   and those who tried to delay his return,
>
> just as if, with a lengthy lawsuit settled,
> he were leaving his clients' cases behind,
>   taking a trip to Venafrum's fields
>   or Tarentum, once settled by Spartans.
>
>   (Trans. Joseph Clancy)

A reader who approaches the Roman Odes expecting to find
them full of patriotic sentiment and encomium of Augustus will be
surprised by much of what they actually contain. That reaction is
perhaps strongest in the case of *Odes* 3.6.

> You, though innocent, will pay for your fathers' crimes,
> Roman, until you repair the crumbling temples
>   and shrines of the gods, and their images
>   befouled and blackened by smoke.
>
> You rule because you act as lesser than the gods;   5
> make them the beginning and the end of all.
>   Neglected, the gods have bestowed
>   much woe on suffering Italy.
>
> Twice now Monaeses and Pacorus's forces
> have crushed our ill-omened assaults,   10
>   and, grinning, enrich their skimpy neckbands
>   with the loot of Roman legions.
>
> The city, gripped by internal strife,
> was nearly wiped out by Dacian and Ethiopian,
>   this one formidable with ships, the other   15
>   excelling with his flights of arrows.
>
> Fertile in vice, our age first polluted
> the marriage vow, the family, and the home;
>   flowing from this source, a river of ruin
>   has flooded our land and its people.   20
>
> A young girl thrills to learn Greek dance steps,
> even now adept in the arts of seduction;
>   thoughts of forbidden love fill her
>   right down to the tips of her toes.
>
> Soon, at her husband's parties, she seeks out   25
> younger lovers. Not for her the choice of one
>   to whom she gives illicit pleasure
>   hurriedly in the dark;

> instead she gets up in plain sight when bidden,
> with her husband's knowledge, whether a salesman   30
>   summons her or a Spanish sea captain,
>   ready to pay top dollar for her shame.
>
> Not sprung from parents like these were the young men
> that stained the sea with Carthaginian blood
>   and struck down Pyrrhus and mighty   35
>   Antiochus and dread Hannibal.
>
> No, they were the manly sons of farmer soldiers,
> trained to turn over the furrows with their Sabine hoes
>   and carry home the wood they chopped
>   following the instructions of their strict   40
>
> mother, as the sun shifted the shadows on the hills
> and lifted the yoke from the weary oxen,
>   bringing on the welcome hour of rest
>   as its chariot departed.
>
> What does time's decay leave undiminished?   45
> Our parents' age, worse than their parents, bore
>   us who are more wicked, who soon will breed
>   descendants yet more degenerate.

The reference in the opening stanza to rebuilding the crumbling temples must be connected to a program of that sort carried out by Augustus and recorded in his *Res Gestae*: "In my sixth consulship I restored eighty-two temples of the gods in the city on the authority of the senate, neglecting none that required restoration at that time."[7] That notice dates the project to 28; Horace's language might suggest that the poem was written before that year, but it should not be taken too literally: the compliment to Augustus would be all the greater if he had already carried out the restoration for which Horace calls.

The poem's twelve stanzas divide into three sections of equal size. Lines 1–16 describe the disastrous effects on Rome of its neglect of the

---

[7] *Res Gestae* 20.4.

gods: military defeats and near conquest by foreign enemies. Lines 17–32 focus on another source of ruin, the perversion of marriage. Lines 33–48 look back to a very different past and reflect on the phenomenon of decline over successive generations. This clearly demarcated structure corresponds to the poem's black-and-white moral outlook.

The public voice that characterizes the cycle as a whole is particularly evident here; it represents not just a voice different from Horace's usual manner but one that contradicts it. Take, for example, the pejorative picture of the girl who "thrills to learn Greek dance steps": condemnation of Greek dances as morally objectionable is in keeping with the traditional Roman suspicion of all things Greek and of dancing in particular, but it comes oddly from a poet who elsewhere—as at the end of *Odes* 1.1 (28)—employs images of Greek dances to embody the essence of his lyric form.

If we can put aside reservations about Horace in the role of strict moralist, there is much to admire. The images of present vice and former virtue are not subtle, but they are vividly imagined and effectively contrasted. Horace makes good use of the Roman habit of treating the behavior of women as a barometer of a society's health: the loose-living wife who surrenders all agency and becomes her husband's tool is set against the strict mother who exercises firm control over her adult sons. The poem also contains a marvelous instance of "false closure": the peaceful end of day described in the penultimate stanza makes the gloom of the final lines all the more shocking.

The last stanza seems to contradict the opening of the poem, where the innocent Romans of today must pay for the sins of their elders. Some interpreters think that the qualified optimism expressed at the opening is prompted by the success of Augustus's program of rebuilding temples, while the pessimistic conclusion alludes to the failure of an early attempt on his part to regulate marriage.[8] But it would be tactless of Horace even to hint at an unsuccessful effort by Augustus, and still more so to suggest that the failure overshadowed the positive results of the building program.

---

[8] So Nisbet and Rudd 2004: 100, following Williams 1962: 32–33.

A more promising approach is to take the final stanza as a warning of what the future holds if the present condition of Roman morals is not corrected; in Giorgio Pasquali's formulation, Horace's cry of anguish is an admonition, not a prophecy.[9] It demonstrates the need for the kind of moral reform by legislation that Augustus would in fact embark on a few years later.

I noted earlier the parallel wording of the last lines of 3.1 and 3.6, "riches that are more burdensome" and "descendants that are yet more degenerate." That link may point to another cause of Rome's current state. It is not difficult to see a causal relationship between the two phrases, and between the two comparative adjectives in particular: the future generation will be more degenerate because of the corrupting effect of riches that are more burdensome. Once the underlying economic argument is recognized, we can see that greed is responsible for the most damning instance of immorality in the poem, the husband who pimps out his wife to the highest bidder.

Looking back to the end of 3.1 has another effect on the way we read the end of 3.6. The picture of robust Roman youths hauling wood under the eye of a stern mother might seem to be merely a nostalgic flashback to a lost past. But then we recall that Horace had preferred the simplicity of the Sabine countryside to oppressive riches, and we notice the analogy between Horace's Sabine valley and the Sabellian hoes wielded by the youth of an earlier time. So perhaps an antidote to modern-day materialism and the pursuit of wealth does exist.

3. Augustus

It is a remarkable fact that Horace's reflections on the state of Rome under Augustus make no reference to the supposed "restoration of the Republic" that was the foundational fiction of Augustus's

---

[9] Pasquali 1920: 710; similarly Lyne 1995: 174–75 and West 2002: 71.

principate. (The last ode of Book 4 does employ the language of restoration, but applies it to a restoration of order or morality, not to political institutions or titles.) Indeed, a reader for whom the *Odes* were the only source of information for the period might conclude that Augustus had established a virtual monarchy in which he occupied a position second only to that of Jupiter. The end of *Odes* 1.12 could hardly be more explicit: "O Father and guardian of humankind, / son of Saturn, the Fates have placed in your hands / the care of great Caesar: you will rule with Caesar / second in command" (trans. Stanley Lombardo). By describing a political system centered on one man, Horace was able to square the expectation of support with a certain degree of honesty.

Horace's unwillingness to kowtow to his addressees, even when they outranked him in social position, made addressing Augustus a delicate challenge. In *Odes* 1–3 Augustus is directly addressed only once, in 1.2, the opening poem of the collection if 1.1 is seen as prefatory. That position is obviously a mark of honor, but Caesar figures in that poem not as a political leader but as a quasi-divine savior assimilated to Mercury. The distancing that this conceit of divinity creates is a sign of the care with which Horace constructs his relationship with Augustus: he cannot address him as an equal, but he avoids adopting a subservient attitude to a mere head of state.

Elsewhere in *Odes* 1–3 Horace maintains a certain distance between himself and Augustus by referring to him in the third person. Several of those poems have been touched on earlier. Another that merits notice is *Odes* 2.9, which contains the first appearance in the collection of the title "Augustus," conferred by the Senate in January of the year 27. Horace is encouraging Valgius, a writer of elegy, not to continue mourning the loss of his lover Mystes; as an alternative subject he proposes that they both sing of the "recent triumphs of Augustus Caesar," probably referring to the eastern conquests for which Octavian celebrated a triumph in 29. The placement of the poem is significant, coming almost immediately after a poem in which Horace declares an end to memories of the civil war. (For fuller discussion of *Odes* 2.7 see 53–58.) Caesar's victories over the Medes and Geloni are suitable material for panegyric, whereas his defeat of Brutus and Cassius, Mark Antony, and Sextus Pompey could not be openly praised.

I have chosen to focus on *Odes* 3.14, a poem that very clearly shows Horace grappling with the fact of Augustus's dominance and what it means for him. It is also the last poem in the collection in which Augustus has a prominent place. (The only later reference is in 3.25.3–6, where Horace imagines himself under Bacchic influence writing a panegyric of Caesar.)

> Citizens! Caesar, recently reported
> to have risked his life seeking a laurel crown,
> is coming home victorious from Spain in the
>   manner of Hercules.
>
> Let the lady who takes joy in this matchless spouse   5
> come forth having propitiated the just gods—
> our dear leader's sister too—and, adorned with
>   suppliant garlands,
>
> the mothers of the young women and men
> recently saved from death. You boys, and you girls   10
> without experience of men, avoid any
>   ill-omened language.
>
> This day, truly festal for me, will dispel
> my dark worries. I will not fear riots, nor
> a violent death as long as Caesar has   15
>   control of the world.
>
> Get going, boy, find some perfumed ointment, some
>   wreaths,
> and look for a jar of wine that remembers
> the Marsian War, if any somehow escaped
>   Spartacus' looting.   20
>
> And tell that soprano Neaera to hurry,
> with her myrrh-scented hair tied back in a knot.
> But if her odious doorman holds things up,
>   just leave and come back.

> My greying hair is smoothing out my temper,   25
> which used to itch for a fight. I would never
> have put up with this in my hot youth, back when
>   Plancus was consul.
>
>   (Trans. Stanley Lombardo)

The occasion for the poem is Augustus's return to Rome in 24, after three years away campaigning in Gaul and Spain. During his absence his health, never robust, was so poor that there were fears for his life; Horace's opening lines allude to the threat but treat Augustus's illness as if it resulted from a heroic resolve to pursue glory at all costs. The comparison to Hercules turns on the fact that one of Hercules's labors, the conquest of the three-headed monster Geryon, took place in Spain, after which he passed through the future site of Rome on his way back to Greece.

Horace's treatment falls into two distinct halves, with a central stanza (13–16) providing the transition. In the first he describes (or imagines) the public welcome prepared for Augustus, led by his wife Livia and his sister Octavia, and also including "the mothers of the young women and men recently saved from death." The reference is to the young men who had fought in Spain and are now safely home, and to the young women who had been awaiting their return, probably with the prospect of marriage. This part of the poem concludes with a word to the children present, warning them not to mar the solemn ceremony with ill-omened words.

In the prominent roles assigned to Livia and Octavia the poem offers early evidence of the showcasing of Augustus's closest relatives as a sort of "first family of Rome," with clear dynastic implications. Neither is named, which heightens the symbolic character of their depiction as ideal wife and sister.

The middle stanza introduces a personal perspective ("truly festal for me," "I will not fear") and spells out the meaning of the event for Horace: Augustus's safe return, and the continuing control it promises, offer security from fear of upheavals and violent death, probably a way of describing a return to civil war.

Acting on that sense of security, in the second section of the poem Horace sets about celebrating Augustus's return in his own way, with a drinking party. It seems to be an intimate affair; the only guest mentioned is Neaera, described as "clear-voiced" (*argutae*, translated by Lombardo as "that soprano"), who will presumably provide both musical and sexual entertainment. (That combination is more explicit in *Odes* 2.11.21–24, where Lyde, invited to bring her lyre to a similar party, is called a prostitute [*scortum*].) But Horace is even prepared to forgo Neaera's company if her doorkeeper creates problems, so much has he mellowed from the days of his hot-tempered youth.

A good deal of the poem's artistry lies in the ways the two main sections are both linked and differentiated. The main connection lies in the voice of Horace himself: in stanzas 2 and 3 and also 5 and 6 he is issuing instructions. To secure that link Horace rather unrealistically assumes the role of a master of ceremonies organizing the welcome for Augustus. (There are precedents in Callimachus's *Hymns* for the poet in that role, but it seems a stretch for Horace.)

The participants in the respective celebrations are neatly contrasted. The collective freeborn "boys" are balanced by Horace's singular slave "boy." Similarly the several groups of anonymous women in the first half ("mothers," "young women," and "girls") are set against a single named woman, Neaera.

So the poem seems at first to offer a clear opposition of public and private celebration. But since it is always a good idea to scrutinize apparently neat distinctions in Horace, it is worth asking whether the respective scenes contain elements of their opposites.

Such contamination is evident in the latter section, which incorporates allusions to several historical events. The wine Horace's slave boy is to seek out retains memories of the past, of the Social War of the 90s; it also prompts recollection of a later upheaval, the slave revolt of Spartacus, and of the depredations it entailed. A wine sixty-five years old could not have been easy to find; Horace seems to go out of his way for the historical connection. The references probably represent the kind of tumult and violent death that Romans no longer need to fear under Augustus.

The concluding reference to Plancus's consulship, that is, to 42, the year of Philippi, has a more personal significance, recalling that in those days Horace was not acquiescent in matters of more weight than the availability of an entertainer. On a straightforward reading, the lines gracefully renounce Horace's earlier republicanism; but, as Putnam observes, "Even if we view the ode's final words as an apologia for his being on the Republican side at Philippi, Horace has succeeded in restoring the event to our minds."[10]

The first part of the poem might seem impervious to a similar approach, but a line that has attracted much attention may offer a way in. Horace describes Livia as "the lady who takes joy in this matchless spouse" (5). The word rendered by Lombardo as "matchless" is *unicus*, and while it can convey the idea of "beyond comparison," its more normal meaning is "one and only." Applied to a wife it would characterize Livia as what the Romans called an *univira*, a woman who had had only one husband, a status as highly regarded as it was rare among the upper classes. The problem is that Octavian was not Livia's only husband; she had been married previously to Tiberius Claudius Nero, the father of her sons Drusus and Tiberius, from whom Octavian stole her in a scandalous divorce in 39. (Livia for her part was Octavian's third wife.)

Various explanations have been offered for Horace's choice of adjective: (1) Since the most common sense would not be accurate, we should ignore it and fix our attention on the meaning that does fit the facts. But a reader's reactions may not be so easily directed; as Kenneth Quinn comments, "*Unico* comes dangerously close to reminding us that Livia was in fact a divorcée."[11] (2) Horace was paying Livia a compliment by describing her as an honorary *univira*;[12] but that concept is as hard to imagine as an honorary virgin. (3) Horace is using the word in its natural sense and falsely describing Livia as *univira*; that interpretation assumes that Augustus believed that his and Livia's past marriages could be forgotten or

---

[10] Putnam 1996: 458–59.
[11] Quinn 1980: 270.
[12] Williams 1969: 92–93.

overlooked if they conducted themselves long enough as a devoted couple. In the case of a ruler using every available means to craft a favorable image of himself and his regime, it is hard to be sure where the limits of falsification lie.

Another possibility would be to understand *unicus* in the sense "one and only" as referring to Livia's fidelity: she "rejoices in this one husband." The compliment would fit the image of model wife that Livia cultivated, but it could also trigger awkward associations, since the fidelity of Livia was not reciprocated by her husband. According to Suetonius, Augustus's adulteries were notorious; the examples cited come mainly from his youth, but the biographer adds that even in his later years he enjoyed deflowering virgins, some of whom were procured by Livia herself.[13] That scandalous detail might be the product of a historiographical tradition hostile to Livia, but the core of Suetonius's account is credited by sober historians.[14]

Where does this leave us? One reading of the poem would see it as enacting an unsavory bargain, in which Horace endorses the charade of marital bliss performed by Augustus and Livia in return for permission to live in his own very different way. Another would find Horace subversively hinting that Augustus's life actually resembled Horace's unfettered bachelor existence more than that of the dutiful husband. The fact that such extreme interpretations can be formulated highlights the difficulty Horace faced in dealing directly with Augustus and his family.

On any reading of the poem, Augustus is made responsible for Horace's ability to pursue a lifestyle at odds with the ideals promulgated by Augustus himself. That paradox suggests that the balance between public and private that Horace is striving to uphold is precarious; the Augustan odes of Book 4 will show that it is one that could not in the end be sustained.

---

[13] Suetonius, *Life of Augustus* 69, 71.
[14] So, for example, Wardle 2014: 449.

· 9 ·

After the *Odes* 1
The Book of Epistles

Some works of literature seem predictable, at least with the benefit of hindsight. Readers of Horace's *Satires* and *Epodes*, taking note of his eagerness to master new genres and his metrical versatility, might have foreseen that he would produce a Roman counterpart to the lyric poetry of Greece. But no reader of *Odes* 1–3 could have expected the *Epistles*, a collection of twenty poems ranging in length from 13 to 112 lines, written in dactylic hexameter, the meter of the *Satires*, and taking the form of letters to a variety of addressees. Some relate to specific occasions, such as an invitation to dinner (5), a letter of recommendation (9), instructions for delivering a package (13), or a request for information to help plan a trip (15). Others are inquiries after a friend's health or current activities (3, 4, 11), while still others seem to offer unsolicited advice (16, 17, 18).

It is conceivable that Horace thought of ending his poetic career with *Odes* 1–3, as Rossini retired from opera at a comparable age after producing his magnum opus, *Guillaume Tell*. But if Horace did consider retiring, the thought did not last long. The *Epistles* are dated to late 20 or 19, about three years after the appearance of *Odes* 1–3. Three years is not a long time for a poet as painstaking as Horace, so the composition of the *Epistles* must have begun soon after the publication of *Odes* 1–3.

Horace introduces the collection with a poem addressed to Maecenas, who, it seems, has been urging him to write more lyric poetry. Horace declines, comparing himself to a gladiator who has retired from the arena or a racehorse that has run its last race. Furthermore, he has a new interest:

> so now I am putting aside verses and other trivial pursuits;
> I seek to know what is true and fitting, and am wholly engaged in this.
>
> (1.10–11)

It is often said that Horace turned away from lyric because *Odes* 1–3 had been coolly received in some circles. I will return to that issue later, but other reasons for the shift in genre can be suggested.

A further generic ascent would have required Horace to compose either an epic, as Virgil was doing with the *Aeneid*, or a tragedy, as Varius and Asinius Pollio had done; but Horace seems not to have been attracted by either of those genres. (If that is a pose, it is one that he carried off quite convincingly.) But by presenting his letters as essays in moral philosophy, he was able to compose in a formally less demanding medium while claiming the high status that philosophy enjoyed among educated Romans. (We may compare Virgil in the *Georgics* expressing admiration for those who, like Lucretius, could investigate the causes of things, and Propertius implausibly professing that he would turn to higher subjects such as natural philosophy when his career as an elegist was over.) It is from that philosophical perspective that Horace can say that he is putting aside all trivial pursuits, including poetry—as if the *Epistles*' poetic form were a mere accident.

Horace could also boast that with the *Epistles* he had created a new poetic genre. The philosophical letter in prose had a distinguished Greek tradition—Plato, Aristotle, and Epicurus being conspicuous examples—and isolated instances of poems in the form of letters can be found in Lucilius, Catullus, and Propertius. But a corpus of verse letters was new. Horace found an early follower in Ovid, who used the epistolary form for a collection of letters from women of myth (the *Epistulae Heroidum*) and later for the nine books he composed in exile, the *Tristia* and *Epistulae ex Ponto*. The form then enjoyed something of a revival in late antiquity, in the work of poets such as Ausonius and Paulinus of Nola.

For our purposes it will be most useful to focus on the ways in which the *Epistles* represent a next step for Horace after *Odes* 1–3.

From the opening lines of the first poem Horace speaks in a different voice: as he says to Maecenas, "My age and state of mind are not as they were" (1.4). The air of greater authority that he projects is partly the result of additional years and a turn to ethics, but it is hard not to associate it as well with the achievement of *Odes* 1–3 and the enhanced status Horace believed it had earned for him.

The consequences are most obvious in Horace's choice of recipients and his way of addressing them. Gone are the grandees such as Asinius Pollio or the contemporaries such as Virgil. With the exception of Maecenas, the addressees of the *Epistles* are younger men (there are no women), toward whom Horace can adopt a superior tone and offer advice of a more specific and pointed character than that offered to friends in the *Odes*. So Celsus is warned against plagiarism in his poetry (3.15–20), and Horace ends a later poem to him with the caution "As you bear your good fortune, so we will bear you" (8.17). Julius Florus is strongly urged to repair the rift between himself and Munatius (3.30–34), and Quinctius is admonished to pay less attention to the public's estimation of his virtues (16.17–23).

The ethical precepts Horace imparts are a mix of mostly Epicurean and Stoic elements. His undoctrinaire approach allows him to treat both schools with cheerful irreverence, describing the Stoic wise man as "king of kings and preeminently sane—except when he has a cold" (1.107–8) and calling himself "a pig from Epicurus's herd" (4.16). The only philosopher Horace treats with respect is Aristippus (17.23–32), famous for his adaptability and his skill in cultivating people of all kinds: a fitting incarnation of Horace's blend of moral uplift and worldly wisdom, and a suitable model for the young strivers who make up most of his addressees.

Compared to *Odes* 1–3, the *Epistles* display a drastically narrowed range of subject matter. Some of the omissions are due to the nature of a letter collection, in which one would not expect to find, for example, hymns to the gods. Others are not so mandated and are therefore more interesting. Amatory themes are virtually absent;

Horace seems uninterested in the erotic side of his recipients' lives, and references to his own experiences are limited to two glances back to an earlier time, the "days of wine and roses" with a woman named Cinyra (7.28 and 14.33) and a hoped-for fling during an upcoming trip to the south (15.21). The sympotic element is also much reduced; the only invitation poem, to Torquatus (5), promises an evening of candid conversation among friends, not enlivened by an attractive lyre player, and while Horace is as eloquent as ever in praise of wine (5.16–20), it now shares the ability to banish cares with reason and forethought (11.25–26). References to Horace's poetry are with one fleeting exception restricted to the last two poems, which function almost as an epilogue to the book rather than as part of the book proper.

Themes that are carried over from *Odes* 1–3 undergo significant transformation. *Carpe diem* is restated in more discursive and elevated language: "Accept with a grateful hand whatever hour god has blessed you with, and do not put off enjoyment to next year" (11.22–23; sound advice to be sure, but hardly the stuff of bumper stickers). The countryside is still preferred to the city, but on subtly different grounds: the country is where Horace can be most truly himself, on the estate "that gives me back to myself" (14.1), and the country is where one can most readily live in accord with nature (10.12–14, a playful allusion to a leading Stoic precept). Denunciations of the pursuit of wealth are even more frequent in the *Epistles* than in *Odes* 1–3, but a new rationale for the simple life is offered, grounded in ancient ethical thought: the person who courts riches forfeits freedom and becomes a slave to possessions (10.39–41).

Maecenas is an important structuring element in the collection, addressed in 1, 7, and 19, and Horace's relationship with him is still central, but there are new aspects to it, most notably a more outspoken independence on Horace's part. So the first letter begins with a *recusatio* that reverses the position of the two men in *Odes* 1.1: in the ode Horace credited Maecenas with the ability to make him happy by judging his poems worthy of the Greek lyricists; in the letter Maecenas cannot prevail on Horace to carry on in that medium. Poem 7 is a *recusatio* of a more personal sort: Horace had promised to join Maecenas in the city but has stayed away all summer; what is more, he proposes to spend the coming winter at the seacoast and to see Maecenas again only when spring comes. Horace justifies his absence by appealing to his advanced years: if Maecenas wants him to be constantly available, he would need to give him back his youth (7.25–28). But Horace also uses the occasion to offer a portrait of the ideal patron-client relationship, in which the patron consults the best interests of the client and the client is not corrupted by accepting the patron's benefactions. The argument is carried on through a series of negative examples: a trio of thoughtless or manipulative patron figures are implicitly contrasted with Maecenas's enlightened behavior, while the fable of a vixen that crawled into a granary, gorged itself and became too fat to leave illustrates the dangers of exploitation on the part of the client. Horace draws the conclusion: "If I am convicted by this story, I give everything back" (*cuncta resigno*, 7.34); he had used the same verb in *Odes* 3.29.54 (also addressed to Maecenas), where the reference is to returning the gifts of Fortune (see 89).

An apparently casual phrase early in the poem reveals the tact with which Horace tempers his self-assertion. Speaking of his plans for the winter, he writes, "Then your bard will go down to the sea and look after himself, huddled up with his books" (7.11–12). The word for "bard" is *vates*, a high-flown term for a poet that Horace had applied to himself in *Odes* 1–3 (e.g., 1.31.2); in this context it is amusing (with something of the flavor of "Shakespeare on the beach"), but it also reminds Maecenas of who it is that he is dealing with.

The *Epistles* also depict Horace's connection to Augustus and his family in a new light. The *princeps* himself is never addressed; the closest Horace comes is in a poem (13) that instructs an intermediary on delivering a copy of *Odes* 1–3 to him. Despite the anxiety Horace expresses about having his directions followed, he seems confident that his poems are such as to "captivate the eyes and ears of Caesar" (13.17–18). Elsewhere Augustus hovers in the background, reflecting the way in which his centrality had now become a fact that could be taken for granted. A nice example is the dinner invitation to Torquatus (5): Horace points out that Torquatus can afford to stay out late that night, since the next day is Caesar's birthday and therefore a holiday (5.9–11).

Three of the letters have links to Augustus's stepson Tiberius: 9 is addressed to him; 3 is addressed to Julius Florus, who is traveling with him; and 8 is addressed to Albinovanus Celsus, recently appointed as his secretary. Horace was never slow to advertise his success in moving among the highest levels of Roman society; as he writes in the letter to Scaeva, "To have found favor with the leading men is not the lowest achievement" (17.35). His letter to Tiberius seems more concerned to show off the extent of his influence than to perform its ostensible function of recommending Septimius for Tiberius's service.

Perhaps the most remarkable aspect of the *Epistles* collection is the way it ends, with a pair of poems that address a subject on which the book as a whole has been almost completely silent, Horace's career and achievement as a poet. Poem 19, to Maecenas, begins as a lighthearted disquisition on the link between the consumption of wine and poetic inspiration, then unexpectedly launches into an attack on imitators ("You herd of slaves, how often has your uproar provoked my rage, how often my ridicule!"), followed by an apologia for the *Epodes* and *Odes* 1–3. This extraordinary passage (19.21–34) deserves to be quoted in full.

> I was the first to plant free footsteps on unclaimed soil,
> soil trodden by no one before me. The bee that trusts itself
> will be the leader of the swarm. I was the first to show Italy
> the iambics of Paros, imitating the meters and spirit
> of Archilochus, but not the themes or the words that
>   hounded Lycambes.
> And so that you do not adorn me with fewer garlands
> because I feared to alter his rhythms and the form of his
>   poetry,
> know that masterly Sappho shapes her poetry with the
>   meter of Archilochus,

and so does Alcaeus, though he differs in subject and
 arrangement,
not seeking a father-in-law to smear with bitter verses
or weaving a noose for a bride with a slanderous poem.
Alcaeus too, not sung by any other's lips, I made known,
I, Latin's lyric poet. What joy it is to bring things
 previously unrecorded
to the freeborn, to be scanned by their eyes and held in
 their hands!

The opening word of the passage is *libera*, describing Horace's "free footsteps" and brilliantly connecting the artistic freedom of the truly creative poet with the ethical freedom that has been a principal goal of Horace's philosophical reflections. As the passage proceeds, pride in accomplishments mingles with resentment at ignorant criticism, such as the charge that Horace lacked originality because he imitated the formal aspects of Archilochus's iambics in the *Epodes*. The same, of course, could have been said of the *Odes*; it is crafty of Horace to rebut the accusation with regard to the *Epodes*, where he could appeal to the precedent of Sappho and Alcaeus, rather than the *Odes*, where no such argument would have been possible.

More defensiveness is to come. Horace rhetorically asks, "Do you want to know why an ungrateful reader praises and enjoys my little works at home, but unfairly disparages them in public?" and answers his question by saying that he has never curried favor with the fickle masses or deigned to seek the approval of the *grammatici*, the professional teachers of literature. When his reluctance to recite his work in public is taken as a sign of contempt and he is accused of saving his poetry for the ears of Jupiter (that is, Augustus), he declines to respond to his critics.

The poem sets up a tension with attitudes Horace has expressed earlier in the book. At times Horace seems to have felt the attraction of an extreme form of Epicurean withdrawal: he says he could happily dwell in an obscure town, "forgetting my friends and forgotten by them" (11.9), and that all he requires for "living for myself" is an ample supply of books and provisions (18.107–10). But that splendid isolation cannot coexist with a poet's desire to be read by others, with the joy he feels when his work is "scanned by their eyes and held in their hands."

The concluding poem presents that tension in dramatic form.[1] Dropping the epistolary pretense, Horace addresses the letter collection itself, imagined as a young male slave eager to decamp to the city and put himself up for sale. (The verb he uses, *prostare*, has clear connotations of prostitution, and Horace develops the image of the book as rent boy in the lines that follow.) In an attempt to dissuade his book from abandoning the principles on which it was raised, Horace paints a grim picture of the life that awaits it: when its charms have faded and its admirers have cooled, it will slink away to North Africa or be shipped off to Spain. The final indignity will be to become a textbook for teaching children in a back-alley school.

If *Odes* 2.20 and 3.30 present a poet's dream vision of an afterlife, *Epistles* 20 offers the nightmare equivalent, insisting on what being "fondled by the hands of the crowd" (20.11) actually involves. This is the voice of Horace the moralist—who knows that fame and popularity do not confer happiness—rebuking his own appetite for recognition.

But the moralist does not prevail. The book is undeterred, and Horace acquiesces in its desire to leave. He even instructs it on what to say about its author, a personal *Res Gestae* to match the record of poetic achievement in the previous poem:

> You will say that I was born of a freedman
> in humble conditions and that I spread wings
> greater than my nest, so adding to my virtues
> what you take away from my birth; that I
> pleased the leading men of Rome in war and peace;
> that I was short in stature, prematurely gray,
> fond of the sun, quick to anger but easily mollified.
> Should anyone happen to ask about my age,

---

[1] My reading of poem 20 owes much to O'Neill (1994), especially 170–75.

let him know that I completed my forty-fourth December in the year when Lollius named Lepidus as his colleague.[2]

That unusually forthcoming finale might suggest that Horace regarded the *Epistles* as his last work. If that was his intention, retirement was again brief: it is generally thought that he soon began work on an offshoot of the *Epistles*, a long verse letter to Julius Florus containing the beginnings of a more general discussion of literature. (The date of that letter is disputed; I discuss it in connection with the other two literary epistles in chapter 11.) What is certain is that within a couple of years Horace was once again writing lyric, prompted by Augustus's invitation to compose the *Carmen saeculare*.

---

[2] That is, 21.

· 10 ·

Lyric Revisited

The Carmen saeculare *and the* Fourth Book of *Odes*

We are usually ill-informed about the circumstances in which works of Latin literature were presented to the public. By contrast, we know that the *Carmen saeculare* (often translated as "Centennial Hymn") was sung in the late afternoon or early evening of June 3, 17 BCE. We know that the performers were a double chorus of twenty-seven boys and twenty-seven girls, all with both parents still living. We also know that the hymn was sung twice, first in front of the Temple of Apollo on the Palatine and then in front of the Temple of Jupiter on the Capitoline. We know all of this because the *Carmen* represents a unique meeting of Horatian lyric and Roman state religion, the latter characterized by a concern for meticulously recording significant occasions.

The event in question was the celebration of the *Ludi saeculares* ("Secular Games"), which took place over three nights and days at the end of May and beginning of June in 17, under the auspices of Augustus, Agrippa, and the other members of the Commission of Fifteen for the Observance of Sacred Rituals (the *Quindecemviri sacris faciundis*). These *ludi*, which were intended to mark the end of a *saeculum* (a period between 100 and 110 years, understood as surpassing the upper limit of a human life), are first reliably recorded in 249; a second observance took place in 146, but a third was prevented by the turmoil of civil war. Augustus revived the festival and redefined its purpose to celebrate the new era that had begun under his principate.

Horace's hymn was accorded an extraordinary place in the schedule of events. The inscription that preserves the details of the *ludi* specifies that the *Carmen* was sung after the completion of the final day's sacrifices; it was therefore strictly speaking not part of the ritual itself, but acted as a capstone of the entire festival. The inscription explicitly records Horace's authorship: "The hymn was composed by Q. Horatius Flaccus" (CARMEN COMPOSVIT Q. HORATIVS FLACCVS). That statement is immediately followed by the list of *Quindecemviri* in attendance, the first being "Imperator Caesar," that is, Augustus. Poet and *princeps* are tellingly juxtaposed.

The hymn consists of nineteen Sapphic stanzas. The Sapphic is one of the most regular of Horace's lyric meters, and it may have been chosen to suit the abilities of an amateur chorus. Horace's writing, though, makes no concessions to the youth of his performers; on the whole it is as dense and compressed as in any other ode. The rehearsal process—which we know from a later poem was overseen by Horace himself—must have been intensive.

The principal addressees of the hymn are Apollo and Diana, invoked at beginning, middle, and end. Although they always appear as a pair, Apollo is given greater prominence, in keeping with the special relationship Augustus claimed with him. (Apollo was credited with the victory at Actium, and the temple complex of Apollo on the Palatine, where the *Carmen* was first performed, was the first of Augustus's major building projects in the city.)

As befits its ceremonial character, the tone of the poem is stately and dignified. One of the central stanzas (45–48) will serve as an example:

> Gods, teach the young upright behavior,
> grant peace and quiet rest to the old,
> give to Romulus's race wealth, descendants,
>   and every honor.

There is little of a panegyrical nature, apart from the wish directed to the Sun God, "May you see nothing greater than the city of Rome" (11–12)—a sentiment that acquired fresh resonance in the Mussolini era. (See 197–98.) Instead the chorus project a serene confidence in Rome's current state, secure from foreign threats and internally reinvigorated.

In only one stanza (17–20) does the poem depart from generalities:

> Goddess, bring forth offspring, and prosper
> the decrees of the Fathers concerning the wedding
> of women, and the law of marriage fertile
>   in new children.

The reference is to laws enacted by the Senate in the previous year and intended to encourage Romans of the upper classes to marry and produce children, aims dear to Augustus. Critical opinion on this stanza has long been divided; I find it hard to believe that Horace, with his fine sense of generic propriety, would on his own initiative have asked a goddess in a hymn to promote a piece of legislation.[1] The impetus for this unfortunate idea probably came from Augustus or his advisors. The poem quickly recovers, but for a moment we may be reminded of Stalin-era paeans to the Five-Year Plan.

Augustus occupies a single stanza of the *Carmen* (49–52), but as the only individual Roman named in it, his unique status remains clear. He is introduced as "the noble blood of Venus and Anchises" and described as "superior to his opponent in war, and mild to the fallen enemy." The two phrases constitute a clear allusion to Virgil's *Aeneid*, published soon after the poet's death in 19, and specifically to the charge given to Aeneas by his father Anchises "to defeat the arrogant in war, and spare the conquered" (*Aen.* 6.851–53). Virgil's Aeneas did not obey that injunction at the end of the *Aeneid*, so Horace presents Augustus as not only the descendant of Aeneas but as a perfected version of Aeneas.[2] That depiction also

---

[1] Fraenkel 1957: 373–75 offers an impassioned defense of the lines.
[2] Putnam 2000: 80.

accords with Augustus's own later account of his actions in the *Res Gestae*: "When victorious I spared all citizens who sought pardon."[3]

In the final stanza of the *Carmen* the chorus steps back and reflects on its own performance, shifting from the first-person plural of the hymn to the first-person singular of choral poetry (73–76):

> I bring back home a sure and certain hope
> that Jove and all the gods support these prayers,
> I, the chorus taught to sing the praises
>   of Apollo and Diana.

The notion of the chorus going home reminds us that the singers are children, who will return home to their families when the performance is over. Their self-description as "taught" points indirectly to Horace himself, their instructor as well as the composer of the hymn.

The public recognition that the *Carmen*'s performance conferred was undoubtedly one of the greatest triumphs of Horace's life. Yet the very success with which the hymn expresses sentiments suitable for the Roman people effaces the qualities for which Horace's lyric poetry is most highly prized, above all the personal voice of the poet.

Augustus also had a part in Horace's decision to publish a second collection of odes, which appeared about four years after the performance of the *Carmen saeculare*, but the precise extent of his responsibility is hard to define. The statement of Suetonius that Augustus commissioned Horace to celebrate the victories of his stepsons Tiberius and Drusus "and for that reason compelled him to add a fourth book of odes to the original three" must be treated with some skepticism. The language of compulsion might fit Suetonius's own time but does not plausibly describe Augustus's dealings with writers, and even if Augustus did pressure Horace to produce poems in praise of his stepsons, he could hardly have forced him to compose the personal lyrics that make up much of

---

[3] Thomas 2011: 78.

the fourth book. It has been suggested that Horace padded out the new collection with poems that he had composed earlier but had not thought worthy of publication;[4] in fact only two poems (4.7 and 4.10) could be inserted in *Odes* 1–3 with no feeling of incongruity, and one of those (4.7) is generally regarded as among Horace's most powerful statements. (On 4.7 see 166–71.) It seems more likely that the experience of writing the *Carmen saeculare* led Horace to believe that he had more to say in the medium of lyric.

Odes 4 has often been seen as a poor relation of *Odes* 1–3. Even some commentators—who might be expected to make the strongest possible case for "their" texts—have been less than enthusiastic. Quinn, for example, writes that "one feels Horace knew his limitations and that his decision to abandon lyric poetry after *Odes* 1–3 was the right one. The very competence of *Odes* 4 (with one or two exceptions) underlines the poverty of invention."[5] In recent decades, however, the standing of *Odes* 4 has risen considerably. There are sympathetic book-length treatments by Michael Putnam (1986) and Timothy Johnson (2004), and a high-level commentary by Richard Thomas (2011).

Since it cannot be plausibly argued that *Odes* 4 represents a falling-off in craftsmanship, any sense that the book does not meet the standard of *Odes* 1–3 is probably due above all to its contents, in particular the prominence of panegyric. Poems with a strong element of praise make up slightly more than half the book (1, 2, 4, 5, 8, 9, 14, and 15). In that respect the content of *Odes* 4 corresponds more closely to the common understanding of an "ode" (that is, a praise poem; see 25) than do *Odes* 1–3.

The prominence of praise poems is only one way in which *Odes* 4 differs from its predecessor. Differences can be observed at every level, from content and outlook to minute points of meter.

The Horace we meet in *Odes* 4 is not the same person as his former lyric self: the achievement of *Odes* 1–3 has brought him

---

[4] See, for example, Bowra 1928.
[5] Quinn 1980: xii.

public recognition, and he is now pointed out by passers-by as Rome's lyric poet (4.3.22–23). If Horace had ever thought of himself as an outsider in Roman society or literary circles, by now such anxieties had been laid to rest.

Rome as depicted in *Odes* 4 has also undergone a transformation. The book contains no poems like those in Book 2 with their denunciations of excessive wealth and indulgence, and the urgency of moral reform expressed in the Roman Odes is no longer felt. Instead Horace presents the image of a city cleansed of its vices and safe from all threats (cf. 4.5.17–28 and 4.15.4–24). In both private and public spheres one misses the slight edge—a sense of goals to be striven for, of obstacles to be surmounted—that characterized earlier odes; now both Horace and Rome have made it.

The purification of Rome produces a striking difference in Horace's own self-positioning. The Sabine estate, which in *Odes* 1–3 served both as a retreat from the city and as an embodiment of the simple life, is nowhere to be seen. Instead, in the two poems (4.11 and 12) that invite their addressees to drink wine with Horace, he is probably or definitely in the city. Whatever other reasons there may have been for that shift of perspective, one was almost certainly ideological: the Sabine villa is no longer needed, because Rome has been purged of its undesirable features.

The private poems of *Odes* 4 focus on a narrower selection of topics than their counterparts in *Odes* 1–3: invitation poems (11, 12), seasonal poems (7, 12), addresses to aging lovers (10, 13), and poems reflecting on the celebrity Horace attained by composing the *Carmen saeculare* (3, 6). Poems of friendship and advice, which formed so large a part of *Odes* 1–3, are absent. Maecenas, the addressee of several of those poems, is also missing in *Odes* 4, except for a reference in 4.11 to his birthday, celebrated by Horace with a woman named Phyllis rather than with Maecenas himself. (On possible reasons for Maecenas's absence see 4–5.)

The eclipse of friendship and its replacement by a sense of Horace as a public figure is encapsulated in a verbal cross-reference. In *Odes* 2.6, addressed to a friend named Septimius, he singles out Tibur or Tarentum as places where he would wish to end his days; the poem concludes with the image of Septimius shedding a tear for "your friend, the poet" (*uatis amici*). The word I have translated as "poet," *uates*, has grand overtones, somewhat like "bard" in English (see 145, on *Epist.* 1.7.11–12); by juxtaposing it with the word for "friend," Horace gives it a more human and personal aspect. *Odes* 4.6 ends with Horace imagining one of the performers of the *Carmen saeculare* recalling the event and how she performed "trained in the meters of / Horace the poet." The last two words are *uatis Horati*; in place of the intimate *amici* we now have the formal *Horati* (used only here in Horace's lyric poetry), perhaps a nod to the inscription that records his composition of the *Carmen* (see 151).

Horace's relationship to the Greek poetic tradition has also undergone a change. Pindar now becomes the dominant influence, a position signaled by *Pindarum* as the first word of 4.2, the first poem after the prefatory 4.1. Pindar was the most eminent praise poet of antiquity, so his prominence announces the increased role of praise poetry in the book. Pindar was not absent from *Odes* 1–3; in fact, he is in the background in the opening lines of 1.1, with their reference to Olympic victors, the addressees of one book of Pindar's victory songs. But in that poem his praise poetry is set aside in favor of the lyrics of Alcaeus and Sappho, and he makes a belated entry with 1.12.

I will focus on three components of *Odes* 4: the treatment of eros; the seasonal poem 4.7 and its earlier counterpart, 1.4; and the panegyrics to Drusus (4.4) and Augustus (4.15). I begin, though, with brief remarks on the framing of the book.

Odes 4, like its predecessor, is framed by references to music, but the musical motif functions in a way that underscores the difference between them. In *Odes* 1.1 and 3.30 music relates to Horace's aspiration to join the ranks of lyric poets and his pride at being the first Roman to do so:

> 1.1.32–34   while Euterpe allows me
> her flute, and Polyhymnia does not refuse
> to tune for me the lyre of Lesbos.

| 3.30.13–14 | the first to have adapted Aeolian song to Italian measures |

In *Odes* 4, music is deployed in praise of others, Venus in 4.1 and heroes of the Roman past in 4.15:

| 4.1.21–24 | Thick incense you will breathe in, sweet to your nostrils, and you will delight in the lyre mixed with the sound of the Berecynthian flute and the panpipe. |
| 4.15.30–32 | In song mingling with Lydian flutes we will sing of Troy and Anchises and the offspring of kindly Venus. |

In the frame of *Odes* 4 the musical connections are particularly close: the Lydian (or Berecynthian) flute appears in both passages, and in each there is a sonic mixture, made up of different instruments in 4.1 and of song and accompaniment in 4.15. Given that Horace at the end of 4.15 submerges his own voice into that of the Roman people, it is probably significant that the lyre, his distinctive instrument, does not reappear in those final lines.

Venus also has a role to play in framing *Odes* 4. In the course of the book the goddess undergoes a radical transformation. In the opening lines of 4.1 she is the irresistible instigator of love, "the cruel mother of the cupids" (a phrase repeated from *Odes* 1.19). She reappears in the closing line of 4.15 as a very different sort of mother, Venus Genetrix, mother of Aeneas and ancestress of the Julian clan. Her metamorphosis effects a similar change in Horace: in 4.1 he is a middle-aged lover, in hopeless pursuit of the young man Ligurinus; he ends 4.15 surrounded by wives and children (it is not clear whose) and joining in their praise of Aeneas and other Roman leaders.

Another aspect of the book's frame is the interplay between public and private. In 4.1 Horace's erotic experience is set against a more decorous counterpart, the worship promised Venus from the young aristocrat Paullus Fabius Maximus. The poem's bifurcated focus has been seen as previewing the division of the book into roughly equal portions of public and private poems.[6] Within 4.1 the public element is enclosed and overshadowed by the personal, but by the end of the book the personal voice has been subsumed into a collective utterance.

1. Eros

The opening stanzas of *Odes* 4 both mark the temporal distance separating the book from Horace's previous collection and introduce a Horace whose years have made him resistant to amatory pursuits.

> Those wars, Venus, are long over,
>   and now you provoke them again? Please, please
>   spare me.
> I am not what I was when dear
>   Cinyra ruled me. Put an end to your efforts,
>
> cruel mother of sweet Cupids,
>   to soften the stiffness of a man now fifty
> by your gentle orders: go where
>   the young men invite you with flattering prayers.
>   (Trans. Joseph Clancy)

In *Odes* 1–3 Horace wrote as one *nel mezzo del cammin*, no longer young but not yet old. He is now a man of about fifty, and he looks back on a past love in a way that has no parallel in *Odes* 1–3: "I am not what I was when dear Cinyra ruled me." Readers who came to *Odes* 4 knowing the *Epistles* would have recognized Cinyra as the former mistress twice recalled in those poems: in 1.7, Horace tells Maecenas that if he wants him to be at his beck and call, he needs to restore him to youth; one of the memories of that vanished past (along with a full head of hair) is "lamenting over my wine when

---

[6] See, for example, Fraenkel 1957: 413–14.

saucy Cinyra left me" (28). In 1.14, Horace reminds the bailiff of his Sabine property, "You know that I pleased grasping Cinyra without bestowing gifts on her" (33). In those passages Cinyra resembles the fickle and mercenary mistresses of elegy, but the reference at the start of *Odes* 4 sounds an altogether different note, nostalgic and tender, a note that will be repeated in an even more moving form near the end of the book (see 161–63, on 4.13).

Horace's protest to Venus may have sounded reasonable to his readers, since the "old man in love" (*senex amator*) is a figure of ridicule in Roman comedy, and the elegists take it for granted that their style of love is incompatible with old age: as Ovid put it in *Amores* 1.9.4, "An aged soldier is a shameful thing, and so is an aged lover." When Horace bids Venus, "Put an end to your efforts" (*desine*, literally "cease, leave off"), he reuses an imperative that in two earlier odes he directed at a woman behaving inappropriately for her age (1.23.11 Chloe too mature to cling to her mother, 3.15.4 the wife of Ibycus too old to frisk with the girls).[7] Horace may have felt that he was on firm ground, but Venus is not so easily ordered about.

In an attempt to deflect the goddess, Horace offers her a more appropriate object for her attention, Paullus Fabius Maximus, twenty years younger than Horace and possessing high birth, good looks, and ready eloquence. He will excel in love's soldiery and will reward Venus lavishly for his success, building her a marble temple where she will be worshipped with constant music and dance.

After five stanzas extolling the attractions of Maximus, Horace returns to himself in language that recalls the opening (29–32):

> As for me, not woman nor boy
> > nor the hope that believes its feelings are returned
> pleases me now, nor drinking bouts,
> > nor having fresh flowers wound about my forehead.
> > > > > (Trans. Joseph Clancy)

---

[7] Ancona 1994: 89.

In terms of its logic the poem might appear to be over. Instead, it ends almost shockingly with the collapse of Horace's defenses, as longing for the youth Ligurinus overwhelms all of his resistance (33–40).

> But why, ah Ligurinus, why
> > does a tear now and then run trickling down my cheek?
> Why does my tongue, once eloquent,
> > fall, as I'm talking, into ungracious silence?
> At night I see you in my dreams,
> > now caught, and I hold you, now I follow as you
> run away, over the grassy
> > Field of Mars, over flowing streams, with your hard heart.
> > > (Trans. Joseph Clancy)

The symptoms of eros that Horace paraded with a touch of irony in 1.13 (104–05) are now set forth in serious terms. As in the earlier poem, Horace looks back to Catullus's reworking of Sappho (poem 51), specifically to Catullus's "but my tongue grows sluggish," which Horace intensifies into an embarrassing silence. In *Odes* 1.19, another poem evoked in 4.1, Venus imposed a partial silence on Horace, forbidding him to speak of Scythians or Parthians "or anything that isn't to the point." Now his subjection is total.

Elegy here has its revenge on Horace for his former superior attitude. His use of elegiac motifs in the early parts of the poem—love as warfare, Cinyra exerting rule over him, Paullus Fabius Maximus as the soldier of Venus—can be seen (at least on a second or subsequent reading) to anticipate his capitulation. When he pleads for mercy ("Please, please spare me") he sounds uncannily like Tibullus, for whom the cry for mercy is a recurring motif (1.3.5 "Hold off, black death, I pray," 1.3.51 "Spare me, father," 1.8.51 "Spare the youth, I pray").

The opening poem of a Latin poetry book usually has a programmatic function, often reflecting on the poet's choice of genre or ambitions for the work. *Odes* 4.1 never refers openly to Horace's poetry, but it is not difficult to read its scenario of resistance overcome as relating to Horace's return to lyric after an interval of a decade.

That interpretation goes back at least to the ancient commentary known as pseudo-Acro, which glosses the opening line as allegorically saying "I am forced to write again after I had stopped"; a similar reading probably contributed to Suetonius's notion that Horace was forced to compose a new book of lyric by Augustus. But the fact that a metapoetic reading has engendered some dubious offspring is not reason enough to discard it, and I find that such a reading enriches the poem and enhances the pathos of its ending.

Ligurinus would then function as a poetic symbol as well as an elusive object of desire, representing all that poets strive to encompass while knowing that they can never entirely capture it. It is remarkable to see Horace admitting, even if indirectly, to such anxiety, and even more remarkable to see him doing so in an opening poem. Is it possible that, after the triumph he had celebrated in 3.30, he felt genuine apprehension about returning to lyric?

In *Odes* 4 as a whole, and in the amatory poems in particular, time's passing weighs more heavily than before, and time itself seems to pass more quickly. In 4.1 Ligurinus is an unattainable object of desire; only nine poems later, Horace imagines a day when Ligurinus will look in the mirror and lament the loss of his youthful beauty.

Another sign of the changed atmosphere of *Odes* 4 and of the heightened awareness of time pressing on is the fact that two of the last poems, 11 and 13, depict the end of eros. (One could even add poem 10, which predicts the end of Ligurinus's erotic attractiveness.) Poem 13 comes later in the book but relates to a point in time earlier than 11, so I begin with it.

Horace is addressing a former partner, Lyce, a successor to Cinyra, who had at some point spurned the poet. The poem begins with Horace gloating over Lyce's advancing years and ruined beauty, but in the poem's middle section (lines 17–28) the tone shifts to one of regret for a lost past: Lyce's, Horace's—and Cinyra's:

> Where is the fresh complexion now, the charms, the graces
>   Of body that stole my self-command? What traces
>   Are left of her who long ago
>   Breathed love from head to toe?   20

> Queen after Cinyra, and pleased to have gained succession,
>   A famous face that knew each sweet expression?
>   The Fates dealt *her* an early grave,
>   But you they plan to save
>
> To linger on and on, Lyce, for years and years   25
>   Like an old crow: a target for the jeers
>   Of hot young rakes who'll come to gaze
>   At the ash of beauty's blaze.
>
> (Trans. James Michie)

Descriptions of Horace as a love poet lacking in real passion have not taken this passage into account. The pathos of the lines is heightened by their position within the book, near the end of Horace's last amatory poem and last personal ode. The reference to Cinyra's shortened life, along with the mentions of her in the *Epistles*, has led many readers to ascribe to her a reality not suggested by Horace's other mistress figures. (It is impossible to imagine Pyrrha dying young, or indeed dying at all.) The name "Cinyra" is attested in a number of inscriptions, one of them of late Republican or Augustan date commemorating a slave girl from Horace's native town, Venusia. But she cannot be a lover from Horace's early years (how then would the bailiff of his Sabine estate remember her?), and it may be more profitable to pursue another explanation for her prominence in Horace's late poetry. Latin poets were in the habit of giving their mistresses names with poetic associations. Catullus may have initiated the practice with "Lesbia," and the elegists followed suit: Cornelius Gallus with "Lycoris," Propertius with "Cynthia," and Tibullus with "Delia," all three epithets of Apollo, patron god of poetry. "Cinyra" coincides with κινύρα, the Greek form of a Hebrew word for a stringed instrument; to a learned reader it could suggest a lyre and symbolize Horace's lyric gift or his lyric poetry.[8] Read in that way, Horace's backward glance at his years "under the

---

[8] For this interpretation see Thomas 2011: 88–89.

reign of good Cinyra" (4.1.3–4), to whom the gods granted only a short life, becomes almost unbearably poignant.

In 4.11, Horace invites Phyllis to help him mark the birthday of Maecenas. The situation of the poem—an invitation to a woman who is identified as a singer—resembles that of 1.17 and 3.28 (on which see 100–04). As in 1.17, the prospective guest is involved with another man (Telephus), but here the situation is more complex: Telephus has been snagged by a rich rival, and Horace advises Phyllis to give up hopes of obtaining him and content herself with an equal partner. The last six lines present us with a distinctly new formulation of the musical-erotic scenario.

> Come then, last of my loves
> —for after this I shall never warm to any other woman—
> master these melodies to sing back to me
> with your lovely voice. Black cares
>   will be lessened by song.
>
>   (Trans. David West)

In contrast to Tyndaris and Lyde, who perform songs of their own composition or of one of the Greek masters, the song Phyllis is to sing is Horace's own, and the purpose of the occasion is for him to teach it to her. Phyllis is thus the erotic counterpart to the chorus of boys and girls taught by Horace to sing the *Carmen saeculare*, as recalled in the final stanzas of 4.6.

Those final lines do not only bring closure to the poem. Phyllis is addressed as "last of my loves," and the implication is spelled out in a parenthesis: "for after this I shall not warm to any other woman." Phyllis is usually thought to be a current lover, but that is not necessarily so: "last of my loves" can just as easily be understood to mean "you who were my last lover," and the advice that Horace gives her would well suit a former lover who retains a warm regard for her. In that reading his final injunction, that Phyllis learn the verses that she will sing for him, would represent the softening of eros into aesthetic pleasure. (Horace calls her voice *amanda*, literally "loveable," perhaps suggesting that her musical ability now exerts the attraction that was once sexually based.) In 1.17 and 3.28 song was the prelude to lovemaking; here it becomes its replacement and sublimation.

Horace's address to Phyllis as "last of my loves" is also accurate with regard to his poetic career, since the long literary epistles that constitute his last works have no place for amatory material. Read in that literary context, the phrase plays on the frequent use of *amores* to mean both a love affair and erotic poetry: Phyllis is "the last of Horace's loves" in both senses.

But even after that apparently definitive ending, there is more to say, namely, 4.13. Strictly speaking, there is no contradiction, since Horace's affair with Lyce lies in the past and so precedes the dramatic date of 4.11; but we may perhaps see an indication of how reluctant he is to say goodbye to that part of his poetic career. Because what remains for him? The loyal Augustan citizen of 4.14 and 4.15, with no life apart from that of the *Volk*.

2. The Seasons

Two of the three odes (1.4, 4.7, 4.12) that take their start from seasonal change are in Book 4, which makes it appropriate to consider that theme here, and to treat 1.4 in conjunction with 4.7. In addition, reading 4.7 in light of 1.4 mirrors the experience of that book's original audience, who would have noticed the several elements common to both and seen the later poem as a counterpart of the earlier. The most prominent of those elements are the dancing Graces and Nymphs of 1.4.6–7 and 4.7.5–6 and the warning against long-range hope in 1.4.15 and 4.7.6, more unobtrusively the reference to "life's brief sum" in 1.4.15 and "the sum of today" in 4.7.18.[9] It has been suggested that 4.7 might be an early poem that Horace held back, but that seems unlikely in view of the prominent place of Aeneas in Horace's underworld, which would have been

---

[9] Thomas 2011: 174 gives a full list of verbal correspondences.

particularly appropriate following the appearance of Virgil's *Aeneid* in 19 or shortly afterward. Aeneas is referred to in line 15 as either "pious Aeneas" or "father Aeneas"; the manuscripts divide between *pius* and *pater*. Both epithets are Virgilian, the former being almost a trademark of Virgil's protagonist.

Both poems have attracted ardent admirers. Lecturing on Horace at Cambridge in 1914, A. E. Housman called 4.7 "the most beautiful poem in ancient literature."[10] As for 1.4, Ezra Pound declared that its first line alone "has a week's work in it for any self-respecting translator."[11]

Comparisons of the poems often result in a clear preference for one over the other. My aim is rather to show how Horace has simultaneously connected and differentiated them. The pair provides an excellent example of his gift for creating variations on a theme.

1.4

Harsh winter thaws at the welcome change of spring and
  warm breezes,
    dried-out keels are hauled down to the water,
the flocks no longer delight in their stables, the plowman
  by his fire,
    and meadows are no longer white with frost.
Venus of Cythera leads the dances under a looming
  moon, 5
    the lovely Graces, joining hands with the Nymphs,
stamp the ground with rhythmical feet, while
  red-faced Vulcan
    inspects the ponderous workshops of the Cyclopes.

---

[10] Gaskin 2013: 12, and see 209–10.
[11] Pound 1929–30: 220.

Now is the time to garland glistening hair with
    green myrtle
        or with flowers that the new-released earth
            brings forth;   10
now is the time to sacrifice to Faunus in shady
    groves,
        whether he asks for a lamb or prefers a kid.

Pale Death knocks with impartial foot at the hovels of
    the poor
        and the palaces of kings. O fortunate Sestius,
life's brief sum forbids us to embark on long-term
    hopes.   15
        Soon night and the storied shades will press
            upon you

and Pluto's meager house; once you have gone there,
    you'll no longer cast the dice to rule the drinking,
nor gaze raptly at delicate Lycidas, for whom all the
    young men
        now burn and for whom the girls will soon grow
            warm.   20

4.7

The snows have fled, grass now returns to the fields
        and leaves to the trees;
the earth runs through its changes, and subsiding rivers
        flow within their banks.
    A Grace with her twin sisters and the Nymphs
        makes bold   5
            naked to lead the dance.
    Do not hope for immortal things, warns the year and
        the hour
            carrying off the life-giving day.

Cold grows mild with warm breezes, Summer tramples
   on Spring
      itself doomed to die, once   10
fruit-bearing Autumn pours out her bounty, and soon
      numb Winter rushes back.

Moons make speed to repair their heavenly losses,
   but we, when we have gone down
to be with pious Aeneas, rich Tullus, and Ancus,   15
   are only dust and shadow.

Who knows if the gods above are adding tomorrow's time
   to the sum of today?
Whatever you give to your own dear self will escape
   the greedy hands of an heir.   20

Once you have died and Minos has issued on you
   his august verdict,
no ancestry, Torquatus, no eloquence, no piety
   will bring you back to life.

Not even Diana sets chaste Hippolytus free   25
   from the darkness below,
and Theseus lacks strength to loosen the chains of Lethe
   from his beloved Pirithous.

In general terms, 1.4 is a poem of sharp contrasts of light and shade, while 4.7 is more of a piece, with a darker overall mood. The clearest example of that contrast lies in the way seasonal change leads to thoughts of mortality. In 1.4 the shift comes with the unexpected appearance of Death in line 13, more than halfway through the poem. In 4.7 the idea enters earlier, in line 7, and is folded into the temporal process: in a brilliant move (the effect of which becomes spookier every time I read the lines), the advice "Do not hope for immortal things" is offered not by Horace (as in the corresponding place in 1.4.15) but by time itself. Furthermore, in 4.7.13–14 Horace provides a transition from the natural to the human sphere, thereby smoothing the change of focus.

The opening words of each poem show the process of differentiation already at work. The earlier poem begins with a present tense ("thaws") and dwells for several lines on the signs that denote the return of spring, while the later one highlights the swiftness of time's passing by opening with a verb in the past tense ("The snows have fled"). Another detail in the first lines points in the same direction. In 1.4.1 we hear of the "welcome change" of winter to spring. In 4.7.3 the same noun appears in the plural, anticipating the wider temporal aspect the poem will develop. I translated "The earth runs through its changes" because I could not think of a way of capturing Horace's words literally: *mutat terra uices*, "The earth alters its changes." The combination *mutare* + *uices* underscores the motif of ceaseless change.

Even when the poems are closest in content, there is differentiation consistent with the mood of each. In 4.7.5 the Grace "makes bold" (literally "dares") to lead the dance unclothed. Daring suggests diffidence, a reluctance that must be overcome. The dancing of 1.4.5–7 is robust and uninhibited.

The tempos of the respective poems develop in opposite directions. The opening three stanzas of 1.4 are rather leisurely, enjoying the arrival of spring with no thought of what is to come next. Once Death has knocked at the door, however, the poem accelerates rapidly, rushing to the underworld and back again in eight lines. The opening words of 4.7 suggest time passing quickly, and the pace increases in lines 9–12. Once we reach the underworld, though, rapid action is replaced by stillness and absence of change.

As just noted, lines 9–12 of 4.7 are conspicuous for the speed with which the seasons succeed each other. The language of this stanza also contains hints of violence. Summer does not merely follow on Spring; it "tramples" on it. The rare verb *proterere* in its only other appearance in Horace (*Odes* 3.5.34) and its single appearance in Virgil (*Aeneid* 12.330) describes the trampling down of enemy warriors.[12] Summer itself is "doomed to die" at the approach

---

[12] Putnam 1986: 136–37.

of Autumn. We could be on a battlefield where one fighter kills another and is himself killed by a third. The progress of the seasons itself suggests mortality.

Both poems contain an element that is not logically required by the poem's argument. In 1.4 the dominant effect of Death's entrance is its suddenness, but Horace places at least as much emphasis on Death's impartiality, a motif that plays no obvious role in the final section of the poem. He may have done so to make the poem more relevant to its addressee, Sestius, described as "fortunate" and known from other evidence to have been extremely wealthy. In any case, the extraneous detail has probably not troubled most readers.

The intrusive element in 4.7, located in lines 17–20, is more damaging. As Quinn observes, "The reference to the uncertainty of life's span adds nothing to the argument of the poem, which is that death is inevitable and permanent. It is a natural further reflection, but one that weakens the impact of the poem."[13] The reference to the greedy heir in lines 19–20 has also caused consternation: Quinn finds the "satirical note" "misplaced," and Fraenkel calls it "conventional; one does not believe that the poet's heart is in it."[14] What is beyond doubt is that, as we saw earlier (79), Horace treated the motif with far greater vividness in the closing stanza of 2.14:

> A worthier heir will drain the Caecuban
> you kept locked up with a hundred keys, and splash
>   the stone floor with better wine
>   than is served at the banquets of the high priests.

Some critics have found this stanza of 4.7 so unsatisfactory as to doubt its authenticity, but the language and arrangement of words sound Horatian. Although I think the poem would be better without the lines, this grim, even spiteful version of *carpe diem* is of a piece with the character of the poem as a whole.

---

[13] Quinn 1963: 25.
[14] Fraenkel 1957: 421.

Horace's treatment of the poems' addressees is also carefully differentiated. Sestius was a member of the Roman aristocracy—he held the consulship for part of 23—but Horace depicts him in the Hellenized setting of a symposium, throwing dice to see who will regulate the wine and marveling at the beauty of young Lycidas. Torquatus came from an even more distinguished family, and Horace endows him with the qualities of an ideal Roman: noble ancestry, eloquence, and *pietas*, the virtue of honoring one's commitments, especially to family and the gods. The contrast corresponds to the larger distinction between *Odes* 1–3, where the private world of the symposium predominates, and *Odes* 4, in which Roman and public themes play a much greater role.

The endings of the two poems present the sharpest contrast. In 1.4 we return to life after a glimpse of the underworld; the pleasures that Sestius will not enjoy there are presumably ones that he can enjoy (or is imagined as enjoying) in the present. One implication is that present joys should be seen as more precious because of their brevity. But the carefree mood of the opening stanzas cannot be wholly regained, and the negatives attached to Sestius's actions ("no longer," "nor") cast a further shadow over the sympotic scene.

In 4.7 there is no return from the underworld; the poem enacts its theme in its structure. This underworld is also more fully furnished and inhabited than "Pluto's meager house" in 1.4. Some of the difference is probably due to the impact made by Virgil's richly imagined underworld in *Aeneid* 6, but it also contributes to the poem's overall effect: by the end of 4.7 the underworld seems (paradoxically for a world of "dust and shadow") more tangible than the fleeting scenes of spring with which we began.

And yet even the poems' endings have a common element, a fresh suggestion of temporality. In 1.4 the passing of time is implied by Lycidas's impending transition from object of male to female desire, from "now" to "soon." In 4.7 the suggestion of temporal change is less obvious, but potentially more powerful. If the "chains of Lethe" that bind Pirithous imply forgetting, the poem ends with a cruel image of time's effects: even if Theseus returned to the underworld to free his friend, he could not do so, and the friend would have ceased to remember him.

Read together, the poems help to interpret each other. The darkness of 4.7 becomes even more palpable when set against the varied mood of 1.4. The gain is greater with 1.4, which in isolation could be mistaken for an essentially light poem into which thoughts of death briefly intrude. One advantage of seeing it alongside its companion is that its mixture of light and shade can be more fully appreciated.

Limits of space rule out a full treatment of Book 4's other seasonal poem, 4.12; I will comment on just one aspect. The poem opens with three stanzas on the return of spring, conspicuous for avoiding any overlap with the corresponding sections of 1.4 and 4.7. At that point the reader is primed for a reflection on mortality, but what follows instead is "The season has raised a thirst," and the poem is revealed as an invitation to a person named Vergilius to join Horace for a drinking party. After the gloom of 4.7 the lighthearted shift of thought is surely meant to amuse.[15]

3. Augustan Poems

Horace's panegyrics for Drusus and Tiberius (4.4 and 4.14), together with three poems containing praise of Augustus himself (4.2, 4.5, and 4.15), form the nucleus of the collection. Praising Augustus and his family posed acute difficulties, of which Horace shows himself fully aware. In *Odes* 4 Horace asserts the ability to confer on others the poetic immortality he had acquired for himself by the composition of *Odes* 1–3. He makes that claim overtly in poems 4.8 and 4.9, addressed, respectively, to Censorinus and Lollius; as a passage from the latter poem puts it, "There were brave men living before Agamemnon, many of them, but they are all hemmed

---

[15] The identity of Vergilius (whether the poet, now dead for some years, or another) has been much debated; see Tarrant 2015.

in by a long night, unknown and with none to mourn them, because they lack a sacred bard" (4.9.25–28). But once Augustus was seen as a god-in-waiting, it would have been at best impertinent and at worst offensive for Horace to suggest that his future glory was contingent on praise from him.[16] To use the terms that have become standard in the analysis of Greek praise poetry, Augustus is the ultimate object of praise (the *laudandus*), and in his case Horace as the source of praise (the *laudator*) is insufficient. For all of Horace's Pindarizing, he knows that he does not enjoy the quasi-equality with which Pindar could address his victorious honorands; when in 4.2.1–4 Horace writes that whoever strives to equal Pindar is doomed to suffer the fate of Icarus, he may have been thinking in more than aesthetic terms. This problem is the counterpart to the one Horace faced in the *Satires*: there, lacking the freedom with which (as he thought) Lucilius could attack the leading men in the state, he contented himself with jibes at nobodies or fictitious characters. In *Odes* 4, Horace can promise immortality to middling figures like Censorinus or Lollius, but not to the *princeps* or his family.

To find a mode adequate to its object, Horace devises ways of making his praise more authoritative. The principal one is delegating the work of praise to others; a version of that tactic appears in each of the Augustan poems. In 4.2 Horace entrusts the task to his fellow poet Iullus Antonius, and the three stanzas that exalt Augustus (33–44) are placed in his mouth ("you will sing," and so on). In 4.4 and 4.14 conquered peoples and generals are mobilized to attest to the military prowess of Augustus and his stepsons. In 4.5 it is the fatherland that longs for Augustus's return and an unspecified "each one" who venerates him at the end of the day. In 4.15, the most ingenious example of the strategy, the age that Augustus has inaugurated is made responsible for the restoration of peace and harmony. Horace orchestrates the praise but does not lead it.

---

[16] Hills 2004: 118, 122–23.

Praise in Horace's own voice is correspondingly played down. In 4.2 Horace's contribution is modest (45–48): "Then, if I have anything worth hearing to say, the better part of my voice will chime in, and I will sing 'O glorious day! o praiseworthy one!'" After that unimpressive utterance Horace joins with the rest of the citizens (as he will again at the end of 4.15) in the formulaic cry of triumph. Similarly at the end of 4.5 he associates himself with a communal wish: "Dear leader, may you bestow long holidays on the land of Italy."

In addition to the complications caused by Augustus's unique status, Horace also had to deal with the fact that depictions of vice and disorder tend to be more engaging in artistic terms than descriptions of the ideal. We may compare *Odes* 3.6 and 4.5. The images of sexual license in the earlier poem (see 131–32) are almost cartoonish in their exaggeration, but they produce a more powerful impact than the anodyne enumeration of the blessings of Augustan peace in the latter (17–24):

> The cow now wanders safely over the fields,
> Ceres and kind Good Auspices nourish the fields,
>   sailors speed over seas now calmed,
>   honor fears to incur blame,
>
> no lechery taints the chaste home,
> custom and law have tamed the stain of evil,
>   mothers are praised for children like their fathers,
>   punishment presses close upon crime.[17]

The Augustan poems of *Odes* 4 have divided critics even more sharply than Horace's earlier political poetry. For Eduard Fraenkel they ranked among Horace's greatest achievements, and 4.5 in particular was "one of his most perfect poems."[18] That is now a minority view, although David Armstrong included the Augustan

---

[17] The repetition of "fields" reflects the Latin of lines 17–18: *tutus bos etenim rura perambulat, / nutrit rura Ceres almaque Faustitas.*

[18] Fraenkel 1957: 440.

poems in his positive assessment of the book as a whole: "[Horace] reconciles the world in which death, the passage of time, the transience of love and youth have complete and ultimate control over the individual, with the world in which it is possible to join in and celebrate the community, its history, and its triumphs, its hopes for as long and peaceful a life as the world allows."[19]

At the other end of the spectrum is the late Oliver Lyne, who argued that Horace was uncomfortable in the role of a court poet and that he signaled his resentment by a strategy of subversion, undercutting ostensible praise with a technique Lyne called "sapping."[20] A similar response in a less extreme form is visible in Richard Thomas's commentary, which discusses these poems under the rubric "reluctant praise" and speaks of deliberately "incompetent" writing.[21]

My own view is that the Augustan poems are uneven in quality. At their finest (and read on their own terms) they succeed magnificently, but there are passages—such as the lines of 4.5 quoted earlier—in which I have the sense that Horace's imagination has not been sufficiently engaged to yield the best he was capable of.

I have chosen two of the Augustan panegyrics for closer reading. One of them, 4.4, honoring Drusus for his campaign against the Vindelici, a Germanic tribe, is accounted a success even by critics who are generally cool toward poetry of this kind: "If poets must write panegyrics this is how to write them."[22] The other, 4.15, has proven to be much more controversial.

> As the eagle, bearer of the thunderbolts,
> who was given by Jupiter, king of gods,
>   rule over roving birds, for he proved
>   true in the fair-haired Ganymede affair,

---

[19] Armstrong 1989: 153.
[20] Lyne 1995. I have expressed my view of Lyne's approach in *BMCR* 96.9.15.
[21] Thomas 2011: 13–20, 157.
[22] Nisbet 1962: 215.

is driven by youth and natural vigor 5
to leave the nest, knowing nothing of struggle,
    and soon, for storms are over, the winds
        of spring have frightened but taught him to use

his untried powers, next with sudden assault
he descends, an enemy, on the sheep pens, 10
    and now desire for food and fighting
        thrusts him against the serpents, who strike back,

or as a lion, just weaned from the rich milk
of his tawny mother, is suddenly seen
    by a young doe, who was eager for 15
        good grazing and will die by his young teeth;

so Drusus, warring beneath the Raetian
Alps, was seen by the Vindelici (the source
    of whose custom that has been carried
        through all ages, arming their right hands with 20

Amazonian axes, I have not tried
to learn, nor can one know all things), but the mobs,
    conquerors so long and so widely,
        were conquered by a young man's strategy,

feeling the strength of a mind and a spirit 25
properly nourished in a favored household,
    the strength of Augustus' fatherly
        affection for the children of Nero.

Brave sons are begotten by brave and good men;
there in young bulls, there in horses, is the worth 30
    of their fathers, and the ferocious
        eagles do not beget pacifist doves.

But teaching develops natural powers,
and a training in goodness strengthens the heart;
    when a code of ethics was missing, 35
        faults have disfigured born nobility.

What you owe, O Rome, to the house of Nero,
witness the Metaurus River, and conquered
    Hasdrubal, and that glorious day
        when darkness was driven from Latium,   40

the first smiling day of blessed victory
since the grim African rode through the cities
    of Italy, like flame through pine trees
        or East wind over Sicilian waves.

After that, their efforts always rewarded,   45
young Roman troops grew stronger and in temples,
    ruined by the ungodly riot
        of Carthaginians, gods stood once more.

And at last the treacherous Hannibal said:
"We are like deer, the prey of ravenous wolves,   50
    pursuing them willingly, when to
        trick and escape them is a great triumph.

This race, still strong after Ilium's burning,
bringing through the beating of Etruscan waves
    its holy images and children   55
        and elders to Ausonian cities,

like an oak on fertile dark-leaved Algidus
that was stripped by heavy double-edged axes,
    through losses, through slaughter, it derives
        its power and life from the steel itself.   60

Not hydra grew stronger, its body cut up,
against Hercules, who could not stand defeat,
    nor was a greater wonder brought forth.
        by Colchis or Echionian Thebes.

Drown it deep, it emerges more glorious;   65
wrestle with it, great is its fame when it throws
    the unmarked man who thought he had won,
        and it fights battles the wives will talk of.

> Now I shall dispatch no more proud messengers
> to the Carthaginians: destroyed, destroyed,   70
>   all the hope and the luck of our name
>   after the total defeat of Hasdrubal."
>
> Nothing Claudian power shall not achieve,
> protected by Jupiter's favorable
>   wishes, and with prudent strategy   75
>   steered safely through the crises of war.
>   (Trans. Joseph Clancy)

    The vast opening sentence matches the description Horace gives in 4.2.5–8 of the style of Pindar: "Like a rain-fed river running down / from the mountains and bursting its banks— / seething, immeasurable, deep-mouthed, / Pindar races along in spate" (trans. David West). That expansive beginning is suited to the scale of the poem; only *Odes* 3.4 is longer (by one stanza). Such a long poem needs to be firmly held together, and Horace accomplishes the task of unification in several ways. One device is the use of recurring elements and images, in which this poem is especially rich: animals, specifically predators and prey (9–12, 13–16, 30–2, 50–51, 61–62); other natural phenomena— winds (7), fire and wind (43–44), the oak tree (57–60); youth (5, 16, 24, 30, 46, 55); and, most significant of all, the motif of strength or power, often combined with the idea of growth (5, 9, 25, 27, 33, 34, 46, 53, 60, 61, 73). Animals in similes are not usually shown changing, so the emphasis in the opening stanzas on the stages of the eagle's development is related to the theme of growth. Even the reference to "Amazonian axes" in the digression of lines 18–22—a passage that has occasioned much head-scratching among critics—has its counterpart in the "double-edged axes" in the simile of the oak tree (58). Another unifying element is the poem's strong forward movement, which is combined with a steadily widening focus: from Drusus to the Claudii Nerones and finally to the Roman people as a whole.

    The poem is so confident and imposing that it is easy to overlook the difficulties Horace had to contend with in writing it. Drusus's actions in Germany were not particularly glorious, and Horace is consequently sparing with details. A more serious challenge was the delicacy required in dealing with Drusus's relationship to Augustus. When Drusus was born in 38, his mother, Livia, had recently married Octavian after each had divorced their respective spouses. Drusus's father, Tiberius Claudius Nero, died when Drusus was five years old, but his existence complicates Horace's task, particularly as it involved the Pindaric theme of inherited excellence (see lines 29–32). Horace's solution is twofold. First, he insists on the importance of nurture in molding natural gifts (lines 33–36); in the case of Drusus that benign influence was exerted by the "fatherly affection" of Augustus. (The opening simile is also helpful here: the eagle is Jupiter's trusted agent, a role played by Drusus vis-à-vis the earthly Jupiter, Augustus.) Second, he interprets the idea of inherited virtue more broadly, linking Drusus to a remote ancestor, Gaius Claudius Nero, whose defeat of Hannibal's brother Hasdrubal at the Metaurus River in 207 was a turning point of the Second Punic War. That backward movement then opens the way for Horace's masterstroke, the introduction of Hannibal himself to pay grudging tribute to Roman resilience.

The poem's most puzzling feature, the aside of lines 18–22, may make more sense in the context of Horace's overall approach to panegyric: its almost self-mocking tone distances him from the serious business of praise, which is carried out by others.

There is nothing in the poem comparable to the speech of Anchises in Virgil's *Aeneid* that lays out a civilizing mission for Roman imperial power, nothing about "imposing custom on peace." The Romans simply impose their will on other people as eagles and lions dominate weaker species. One does not warm to the poem, but one is not meant to.

4.15

Phoebus, when I wanted to celebrate
battles and conquered cities, banged on his lyre
    to stop me from setting my small sail
        on the Tuscan sea. Your age, Caesar,

has brought rich harvests back to the fields 5
and restored to our Jupiter the standards
    torn from the Parthians' haughty doors
        and closed Janus's temple as a sign

that peace had returned, placed a curb
on licentious behavior that wandered 10
    beyond proper bounds, banished wrongdoing
        and recalled our ancient ways,

by which the Latin name and the forces of Italy
grew strong, and the fame of our empire
    and its greatness stretched from the sun's 15
        bed in the west to its eastern rising.

While Caesar keeps the state in his charge,
no civil madness or force will drive out peace,
    nor will anger beat sharp its swords
        and set city against unhappy city. 20

Nor will those who drink deep of the Danube
transgress the Julian laws, nor the Getae
    nor the Seres and deceitful Parthians,
        nor those born near the river Tanais.

And we, on working days and holy days, 25
amid the gifts of mirthful Bacchus,
    together with our wives and children,
        first offering due prayers to the gods,

in song mingling with the Lydian flute,
of generals brave in the way of their ancestors, 30
    of Troy and Anchises and the whole line
        of kindly Venus we will sing.

    For the purposes of this discussion the most interesting parts of the poem are its beginning and end. It opens with a hint of irony: the motif of a god warning a poet away from an enterprise for which he is unsuited would usually introduce a collection, not conclude one. The play with literary conventions continues: poets who are steered away from elevated subjects are normally deflected into a very different genre (for example, from epic to love poetry, as in Ovid's *Amores*). Horace is admonished not to diminish Augustus's military accomplishments by his praise, and instead turns to praise of Augustus's peacetime benefactions. A reader might be disposed to see an additional irony in the opening, in that "wanting to speak of kings and cities conquered" does not sound like Horace as he is ordinarily thought of, and yet it is exactly what he has just done in 4.14. Could the implied idea be that Horace is being steered away from more poems like the previous one?

Horace as a poet is strongly present at the outset, but he is, as it were, erased by Phoebus's admonition; it is almost as if the words beginning "your age, Caesar" are in a different voice, which by the end of the poem has become identified as that of the Roman people. We should also take note of how Caesar is positioned in these lines. While Horace addresses him directly, it is not to sing his praises but to have him hear an account of what "his age" has achieved.

Caesar re-enters the poem at its midpoint, and again his placement is significant. The words I have translated "while Caesar keeps the state in his charge" in Latin form a construction known as the ablative absolute, *custode rerum Caesare*. The function of the ablative absolute is to define the circumstances in which the action of the main verb takes place; here it specifies a condition that is necessary for the truth of the principal statements. Two other passages in the *Odes* use the same construction with reference to Augustus:

> 3.14.14–16 I shall have no fear
> of war or violent death while Caesar
> is master of the world (*tenente / Caesare terras*)

> 4.5.25–28 Who could tremble at the Parthian? At the chilly Scythian?
> At the shaggy brood that Germany produces,
> while Caesar is safe? (*incolumi Caesare*)

In each case Caesar is placed in a grammatically subordinate position, but he provides an essential foundation for his subjects' sense of security or for the health of the state.

The final two stanzas of 4.15 have elicited widely divergent responses. Do they represent a powerful enactment of civic engagement and an affirmation of collective identity, or an extinguishing of Horace's lyric voice?

Jasper Griffin offers an eloquent statement of the first position: "To insist that 'the public sphere edges out the personal' [Lowrie] is . . . a highly Romantic notion, which denies what Horace asserts: the possibility that the two can be one, that public events can be the subject of genuine emotions, and that the artist does not inevitably lose his independence when he makes himself the spokesman of those emotions."[23]

A good deal of the discussion has centered on the poem's last word, *canemus* ("we will sing"). The way Horace has structured the final two stanzas to culminate in that verb seemed so essential to the poem that I thought I needed to preserve it even at the cost of straining English word order. The future tense has been interpreted as signifying "not now," deferring (and thereby withholding) praise. I would understand it instead as implying "now and in years to come." If the "we" of these lines is "we Romans, now and in the future," Horace's assimilation of himself to Roman families with wives and children becomes slightly less jarring.

But even if Horace's "we will sing" is read in that way, the implications of the ending are still unsettling. Griffin is right to insist that a poet can identify with the sentiments of a community without forfeiting the ability to speak in a personal voice. A. E. Housman introduced *A Shropshire Lad* with a poem ("1887") containing the line "'God save the Queen' we living sing," but the poems that follow are couched in his distinctive first-person idiom. What makes the end of *Odes* 4.15 different is the fact that it *is* the end, of a poem and of a collection, and also that the poem is built around

---

[23] Griffin 2002: 331

the replacement of the singular "I" by the plural "we." To speak of a "disappearing act"[24] or of the extinction of Horace's lyric voice cannot be dismissed as a reflex of a post-Romantic outlook.

We should note, though, that as Horace is subsumed into the communal voice, Augustus is also subsumed into the line of Venus's descendants. By the end both Horace and Augustus as individuals have disappeared.

In this final ode Horace proposes a new answer to the problem of temporal limitation. In *Odes* 1–3, poetry offers Horace as poet an afterlife that transcends the limits of mortal existence, and in 3.30 that afterlife is presented as coterminous in time with the survival of Rome. In 4.15 what will survive is the *populus Romanus*.

But we cannot help reading these poems with historical hindsight, and that perspective does not work to their advantage. The picture Horace creates of Roman society is obviously idealized, but it was not as obviously false as it would have seemed only a few years later, after the banishment of Augustus's daughter Julia in 2 and of her daughter in 8 CE, both for offenses including adultery; by then the lines about curbing license and removing moral flaws could only appear either laughable or painful. Similarly, Horace's rhetorical question in 4.5.26–27 "Who could tremble . . . at the shaggy brood that Germany produces?" must have rung hollow after the loss of three legions in the Teutoburg Forest in 9 CE.

Not even all of Horace's skill could insulate Augustus and his Rome from such harsh realities.

---

[24] Oliensis 1998: 153.

· 11 ·

After the *Odes* 2

The Literary Epistles

Several of Horace's collections of poems create the impression of being his final word: *Odes* 3.30, *Epistles* 1.20, and *Odes* 4.15 could all mark the end of his career as a poet. It is therefore slightly paradoxical that the actual products of his last years do not convey a similar sense of finality.

The works in question comprise three long hexameter poems in epistolary form that touch on or more fully treat questions of literary theory and criticism; they are accordingly referred to as the "literary epistles."

One is addressed to Julius Florus, recipient of a letter in the *Epistles* collection (1.3). It is essentially a lengthy apology for not having written sooner and for not having sent poems (*carmina*, 25) that had been promised—apparently a reference to lyrics. Horace offers a series of excuses—I am a poor correspondent, I don't need the money, I am too old, Rome is a terrible place for poets—before producing his strongest argument, that a concern for upright behavior is far more important than composing poetry. Amid the excuses is a short but revealing description of the effort involved in writing good poetry (lines 106–25), to which I shall return.

Another is addressed to Augustus, and is generally thought to be Horace's response to a semi-serious complaint by Augustus that he had not been addressed in previous poems (perhaps referring to the *Epistles* book). Much of the letter is a defense of contemporary poetry against an alleged popular tendency to esteem only what is old, but it also contains reflections on the value of poetry to Roman society and to the *princeps*.

The third and by far the longest of these compositions is addressed to a father and his two sons, members of the Piso family. It ranges from precepts regarding the composition of a poem to a surprisingly long section on drama to miscellaneous thoughts on the role and value of the poet to society. Quintilian referred to it as the *Ars Poetica* ("The art of poetry"), and the title has unfortunately stuck, creating the misleading impression that the poem constitutes a systematic treatise, rather than a fascinating but in some ways enigmatic mix of strongly held principles and musty hand-me-downs from Hellenistic literary theorists (such as the rule that all plays should have five acts, a restriction quite foreign to Greek drama of the fifth century). The work was highly influential in the Renaissance and early modern period, especially in the years before Aristotle's *Poetics* circulated widely, but is now primarily known for a number of familiar expressions, including the "purple patch," Homer nodding, and *in medias res*—(Homer propels us) "into the middle of things."[1]

The chronology of these works is not entirely settled. The *Letter to Augustus* and the *Letter to the Pisos* are generally regarded as Horace's latest works, dating to the years 12–10. The *Letter to Florus* has traditionally been dated earlier, to about 19, but arguments have recently been made for placing it closer in time to the other two letters.[2] It is also unclear whether Horace saw the three letters as comprising a collection or as independent compositions: in the manuscript tradition the letters to Florus and Augustus are joined as a second book of *Epistles*, while the *Letter to the Pisos* is not associated with them. These uncertainties are mercifully irrelevant to our purposes.

---

[1] Hills 2004: 140 cites these and other examples.
[2] See Harrison 2008.

As I did with the collection of *Epistles*, I will treat the literary epistles as a means of enhancing our understanding of the *Odes*. That goal might seem difficult to achieve, since the literary epistles make no explicit reference to Horace's earlier poetry (unlike the retrospective in *Epistles* 1.19, on which see 146–47), and their subject matter does not allow for the sort of thematic comparison that I made between the *Odes* and the *Epistles* book. In place of those direct connections I would suggest that several of the general statements about poetry in the literary epistles apply to Horace's own work and constitute an implicit commentary on it.

One set of such observations relates to the craft of poetry. As might be expected, Horace insists on the highest standard of workmanship as a criterion for successful writing. In the *Satires* he had faulted his predecessor Lucilius for insufficient care; in the *Letter to Augustus* he extends a similar criticism to the whole of early Latin poetry. Some of his more specific statements bring us closer to grasping the effort that went into producing the *Odes*. Starting at the level of the individual word, the true poet will be acutely attentive to diction; like a censor, the Roman magistrate responsible for maintaining the lists of senators and knights, the poet will remove from the rolls words that are unworthy, restore vocabulary once held in honor but fallen into neglect, and add new words, thus enriching the Latin language (*Flor.* 109–21). He will exercise equal care in putting words together, and will enliven familiar terms by placing them in novel combinations (*Pis.* 47–48 *callida iunctura*, literally "clever collocation"); examples from the *Odes* would include *simplex munditiis* ("simple in her elegance," 1.5.5, of Pyrrha) and even *carpe diem* ("pluck the day," 1.11.8).[3] His words will give fresh form to well-known sentiments; that is probably the sense of a much-discussed line in the *Letter to the Pisos*, *difficile est proprie communia dicere* (128 "It is hard to treat universal themes in an individual manner"). Once again the *Odes* offer numerous examples.

---

[3] Many other examples are collected by Wilkinson 1959: 188–89, reprinted in Harrison 1990: 423–25.

The poet will also be rigorous in revising his work; like a gardener he will cut back excess, cultivate the rough, and remove what lacks vigor (*Flor.* 122–23; a similar eye for pruning is one of the gifts ascribed to the ideal critic in *Pis.* 445–50). Once a poem has been produced, it should not be rushed into circulation; Horace recommends holding it back for nine years (*Pis.* 388), which happens to be about the length of time that intervened between the composition of the earliest odes and the appearance of *Odes* 1–3.

A second theme of the literary epistles with a bearing on the *Odes* concerns the place of the poet in Roman society. It is most prominent in the *Letter to Augustus* but also makes a brief appearance toward the end of the *Letter to the Pisos*. In a passage of the former letter Horace is clearly speaking as the author of the *Carmen saeculare*:

> How would unmarried maidens together with chaste boys
> learn their prayers, if the Muse had not given them a poet?
> Their chorus calls upon the gods for help and feels their
>   presence,
> persuasive with the prayer they have learned they beg
>   for rain,
> they turn away disease and drive off fearful dangers,
> they secure peace and a year rich with bountiful harvests.
> Poems win the favor of the gods above and the gods
>   below. (*Aug.* 132–38)

The lines immediately preceding these describe the role of the poet in the moral formation of the young, recalling Horace's self-presentation at the start of the Roman Odes as a priest of the Muses singing poems previously unheard to girls and boys (*Odes* 3.1.2–4).

Horace argues that poets also contribute to Rome's greatness by their praise of Augustus. He contrasts Alexander, who showed poor judgment in patronizing the mediocre poet Choerilus, with Augustus, whose discriminating support of Virgil and Varius has been rewarded by poetry worthy of its patron (*Aug.* 229–50). Although Horace makes no mention of the Augustan panegyrics of *Odes* 4, and even professes himself unable to praise Augustus as he deserves (250–59), it is hard not to see a tacit reference to Horace's own efforts, particularly since his statement that "the features of great men are not more clearly made visible by bronze statues than are their character and virtues made known through the work of poets" (248–50) reprises a claim for poetry made in *Odes* 4.8. The entire passage marks a telling shift from Cicero's *In Defense of Archias*, where the Roman people as a whole are said to gain from the praise bestowed by a poet on one of their leading men. (See 00.)

An often-quoted line from the *Letter to the Pisos* provides an opportunity to bring together the two themes I have been tracing: "The one who combines the useful and the pleasurable wins everyone's vote" (343 *omne tulit punctum qui miscuit utile dulci*). The pleasure of poetry for Horace is largely the product of the poet's meticulous craftsmanship; its utility looks to its effect on a wider public. After what has been said in previous chapters I do not need to argue that the *Odes* give pleasure, but can they also be considered useful?

We can give an affirmative answer if, following Niall Rudd, we understand the utility of poetry in a broad sense, as "embracing everything that helps us to understand and cope with our human condition."[4] As examples from the *Odes* Rudd cites the several tonalities of the erotic poetry; the good humor of the invitation poems and the good sense of the poems of advice; the sensitivity with which Horace offers comfort, encouragement, or consolation; and the melancholy fortified by resignation with which he confronts the prospect of death.

If one adds to that list the political poems, which show Horace in the role of an engaged citizen at a critical point in Rome's history, we come close to a set of reactions to all aspects of life. In the *Odes* Horace shows what it means to be a mature human being, keenly aware of life's sadness and brevity but determined to enjoy it to the full and ready to help others do the same. From that perspective the various roles that Horace plays—friend, lover, citizen, hedonist—do

---

[4] Rudd 1989: 206 (note on line 343: also 230–33).

not imply inconsistency or hypocrisy, but rather the many-sidedness of a fully lived life. That is the lyric equivalent of the modeling of appropriate behavior that Horace engages in throughout his poetry, and it constitutes the particular *utilitas* of the *Odes*. Horace might have waved away so serious-sounding a description with an ironic smile, but irony is often employed by those who would be embarrassed by too obvious a display of genuine feeling.

Irony of some kind is certainly at work in the closing lines of the *Letter to the Pisos*, a strange passage rendered even stranger by the fact that, whether by accident or design, it constitutes Horace's final leave-taking of his readers. Describing a mad poet whose incessant versifying makes him a figure of ridicule avoided by people of sense, Horace concludes as follows (470–76):

> It's not clear why he keeps manufacturing verses; did
>   he commit
> sacrilege by pissing on his father's ashes or disturbing
>   a piece
> of consecrated ground? In any case he raves and, like a bear
> with the strength to break the bars blocking its cage,
> he puts learned and unlearned to flight with his pitiless
>   recitation.
> But the one he catches he holds fast and kills with his
>   reading,
> a leech not letting go of the skin until gorged with blood.

The image of the poet who, Ancient Mariner–like, fastens on an unsuspecting listener and bleeds him dry with an endless recitation is not likely to be a literal self-portrait; at least early in his career Horace made a point of reciting only to friends and only then when urged to do so (*Sat.* 1.4.73–74). But many critics have suggested that the picture contains more than a little of Horace's own experience. As Charles Brink put it, "This cautionary story could never have been written without a generous measure of the quality so caricatured."[5] Ellen Oliensis goes further and identifies

---

[5] Brink 1971: 516.

the "murderously exuberant versifier" as Horace himself, "who clings and clings to his readers for all 476 lines."[6] The *Letter to the Pisos* is more than half again as long as Horace's next-longest poem, *Satires* 2.3; Horace was probably still enough of a Callimachean to at least pretend to be appalled by its length. Oliensis also calls the ending "an ironic closural apology." The irony here has a strategic function: by depicting himself in terms more pejorative than any reader would be likely to imagine, Horace inoculates himself against the very criticism he seems to anticipate. Horace remains elusive to the last.

We find it particularly satisfying when the last works of an artist are that artist's best. In the musical sphere, the final phase of Mozart's or Beethoven's career and the marvelous products of Verdi's old age are obvious examples. In a classical context one can point to Sophocles's *Oedipus at Colonus* and Euripides's *Bacchae*. Virgil is a perfect specimen, dying with his magnum opus just short of completion. I doubt that any Horatian would claim that the literary epistles are Horace's finest work, despite their skillful composition and many vivid and quotable passages. That accolade is much more likely to go to the *Odes*. Their long and varied reception allows us to trace the presence of Horace's masterwork beyond the poet's own lifetime; that reception will be the subject of my final chapter.

---

[6] Oliensis 1998: 219.

·12·

Reception of the *Odes*

From Propertius to Seamus Heaney

> About half the bad poetry in English might seem to have been written under [Horace's] influence.
>
> Ezra Pound, "Horace"

An author's reception might naively be thought of as something distinct from the work itself, in which case the study of reception would have an essentially historical value. In fact, matters are more complicated, and reception cannot be neatly separated from interpretation. As Charles Martindale puts it, "Whether we like it or not, indeed whether we know it or not, our current images of Horace, our current readings of his poems, are shaped by that history."[1] To give one example, it seems likely that Horace's image as a genial dispenser of mellow wisdom—the image that much recent criticism has been at pains to reject—is as much a product of Horatian reception (in particular of eighteenth- and nineteenth-century readings) as of Horatian scholarship.

A full account of the *Odes*' reception would fill a small library. For this brief sketch I have limited my scope to literary works, and for the period since the Renaissance the focus is on material in English.

---

[1] Martindale 1993: 1.

"With Horace the Latin lyric stops dead."[2] That is not literally true, since Quintilian's statement that Horace is nearly the only lyric poet in Latin worth reading (*Inst. or.* 10.1.96) shows that there were others, but those unnamed figures were apparently not of much account. The *Odes* seem to be among the works of literature that so successfully embody their form as to render imitation in the strict sense impossible.

Within two or three years of their appearance, *Odes* 1–3 had prompted a reaction from a poet of the next generation, the elegist Propertius. Introducing his third collection of elegies, he cheekily appropriates and conflates imagery from several Horatian odes: "Shade of Callimachus and rites of Coan Philetas, / grant me, I pray, admission to your grove. / I enter first as priest of a pure-flowing spring / to render Italian mysteries in Greek dances." The "grove" of poetry echoes Horace's words in *Odes* 1.1.30–32 "The cool grove ... screens me off from the crowd," but Propertius turns the grove from one of lyric into one of elegy (suggesting an emphasis on "*your* grove"); poet-as-priest recalls the first lines of *Odes* 3.1 (Horace as "priest of the Muses"); and the interplay of Greek and Italian corresponds to Horace's similar claim in *Odes* 3.30.13–14 (2). Another younger contemporary, Ovid, wrote in a poem recalling his youth that "Horace with his many meters [*numerosus*] captivated my ears" (*Tristia* 4.10.49). If meant literally, the statement would suggest that Ovid, although not a member of Maecenas's circle, had been present at one of the rare occasions on which Horace recited his lyrics. Whether the captivation was literal or figurative, Ovid's words point to the powerful impression made by Horace's adaptation of Greek lyric meters—the same achievement emphasized by Horace himself in *Epistles* 1.19.32–33 (147). Ovid does not often draw on the *Odes* in his poetry, with one conspicuous exception. The proud boast with which he ends the *Metamorphoses*—"Now I have completed a work that neither Jupiter's anger, nor fire, nor sword, nor

---

[2] Mackail 1899: 113.

corrosive time will be able to destroy"—is a clear counterpart to the opening lines of *Odes* 3.30. To Horace's trio of destructive forces Ovid adds the anger of Jupiter, ostensibly a reference to the thunderbolt but almost certainly hinting at the displeasure of the earthly Jupiter, Augustus.

The influence of Horatian lyric is strongly felt in the choral odes of Seneca's tragedies, composed between the 40s and the 60s CE. Two plays, *Oedipus* and *Agamemnon*, contain choruses in meters generated by recombining elements of Horace's favorite forms, the Sapphic and the Alcaic, with results verging on the bizarre. Elsewhere, as in a chorus of the *Thyestes* (336–403), Seneca more successfully combines a Horatian metrical pattern with reflections on wealth and power that parallel (though in a more extreme form) sentiments found in the *Odes*:

> All I seek is to lie still.
> Settled in some secret nest,
> in calm leisure let me rest,
> and far off from public stage
> pass away my silent age.
> Thus when without noise, unknown,
> I have lived out all my span,
> I shall die, without a groan,
> an old honest countryman.
>
> (Trans. Andrew Marvell)

Statius's collection of occasional poems, the *Siluae*, dating from the end of the first century CE, contains one example each of poems in the Alcaic and Sapphic stanzas. Those isolated instances constitute a tribute to Horace rather an attempt to rival him, and in fact Statius's Alcaics, though competent, are no match for Horace's. Statius's familiarity with the *Odes* and his metrical dexterity are better displayed in passages where he adapts Horatian phrases to his preferred meter, the hexameter. In *Siluae* 2.1, a poem of consolation on the death of a slave boy, Statius renders the commonplace "We shall all die" as follows: "We shall all go, we shall go; Aeacus shakes his urn for numberless shades"

(218–19), weaving together the repeated "we shall go" of *Odes* 2.17.10, Aeacus as judge of the dead from *Odes* 2.13.22, and the shaken urn from *Odes* 2.3.25–26.

As that example suggests, reception of the *Odes* in the century after Horace's death is often a matter of allusion, a phrase echoed with the assurance that one's audience will recognize the source. In one of his *Epistles* (58.22–23) Seneca is describing the passage of time:

> None of us is the same in old age as we were when young; none of us is the same tomorrow as we were yesterday. Our bodies are carried along as if by a river [cf. *Odes* 3.29.49–50 "All else is carried along as if by a river"]. . . . I myself, while I am saying that those things are changed, have been changed [cf. *Odes* 1.11.7–8 "While we speak, envious time will have fled"].

And here is Martial on his favorite kind of girlfriend (1.57), giving an erotic interpretation of *aurea mediocritas*. The epigram is addressed to a "Flaccus," alerting the reader to a connection with Horace.

> Do you ask, Flaccus, what kind of girl I like or don't?
>   Not one who is too easy or too hard.
> The happy medium is what we want to see;
>   spare me that which tortures, or which cloys.

Quintilian can usually be counted on to articulate the received view of an author, and his description of Horace as a lyric poet is doubtless one that many ancient readers would have shared: "He is lofty at times and also full of grace and charm, versatile in his figures of speech and successfully daring in his choice of words" (*Inst. or.* 10.1.96). A generation earlier Petronius had put into the mouth of the poetaster Eumolpus a pithier and more acute summary, referring to Horace's *curiosa felicitas*, an aptness of expression that is the result of taking pains (*Satyricon* 118.5).

Horace had professed a horror of becoming a school author (*Epistles* 1.20.17–18), a fate that soon befell him, as it did his friend Virgil. A passage of the satirist Juvenal (7.225–27), on Horace and

Virgil in the school of the *grammaticus*, describes how their texts—or possibly their busts—get sooty from the smoke of the boys' lamps. Another document that links Horace and Virgil in a scholastic context is a papyrus of the first century CE from Hawara in Egypt in which *Ars Poetica* 78 (along with *Aeneid* 2.601) is used as a writing exercise; the papyrus is also evidence of Horace's early circulation around the Empire.[3]

Horace's place in the school curriculum also accounts for the composition of commentaries on his work. Material from two ancient commentaries survives: large portions of the work of Pomponius Porphyrio (late third century CE?) and a miscellaneous set of notes perhaps put together in the fifth century, to which in late manuscripts is appended the name of Helenius Acro (ca. 200 CE). Both commentaries place the *Odes* first among Horace's works, in defiance of chronology but in keeping with the prestige of lyric; that order is the one found in all manuscripts of Horace, and it has been perpetuated in all modern editions to date. Ancient editions and commentaries are also responsible for assigning titles to individual odes, often simply identifying the addressee (so 1.1 "To Maecenas" or 1.5 "To Pyrrha"); those titles are found in the medieval manuscript tradition but are not printed in modern editions.

Shortly after 400 CE Aurelius Prudentius Clemens, often called the first great Christian poet, published a collected edition of his works. Most of the poems were written in hexameters, but Prudentius framed the edition with two sets of hymns in a variety of meters, including some used by Horace; he also added an introductory poem in the Asclepiad meter in which he implicitly cast himself as a Christian Horace, noting his advanced age (fifty-six) as Horace had done in the opening lines of *Odes* 4 and vowing to turn aside from frivolous pursuits to the proper use of his talent, as Horace had done at the start of the *Epistles*. In other poems Prudentius gives a Christian meaning to Horatian expressions, inaugurating a practice that would recur in subsequent centuries. For Prudentius

---

[3] Dow 1968.

it is the martyr's death that is *dulce et decorum* (*Peristephanon* 1.25 and 51), and the vocative *dux bone*, "blessed leader" (*Odes* 4.5.5, 37), is transferred from Augustus to Christ (*Peristephanon* 3.87).

Nearly all classical Latin authors went through a period of hibernation between the mid-sixth century CE and their rediscovery at some point in the Middle Ages. Horace's dormancy was relatively brief. He is still a presence in the poets of the early sixth century, such as Maximian in Italy, Dracontius in North Africa, and Avitus in southern France. Avitus's epic on the Creation and Fall applies Horace's lines on the return of spring, "Grass now returns to the fields / and leaves to the trees" (*Odes* 1.4.1–2), to the changeless state of Paradise, "Grass stands forever on the hilltops / and leaves on the trees" (1.228–29); and Horace's phrase "I am not the man I was" (*Odes* 4.1.3) is echoed almost word for word by Maximian.

Horace was one of the first Latin authors to come back into circulation with the Carolingian revival of interest in the classics. Literary figures of the 780s and 790s, such as Alcuin and Paul the Deacon, were familiar with him as an eminent poet of antiquity, like Virgil or Homer—Alcuin was even known by the nickname "Flaccus"—but evidence for knowledge of his work is inconclusive. We are on firmer ground with the earliest extant manuscripts, six of which can be dated to the ninth century. By the third quarter of the century, knowledge of Horace was no longer a rarity. Heiric of Auxerre (died ca. 876) transfers expressions from the *Odes* to Christian contexts, as Prudentius and Avitus had done earlier. In his Life of Saint Germain of Auxerre, he connects Horace's appeal to Venus, "Are you stirring up war again? . . . spare us, I beg" (*Odes* 4.1.1–2), to a resurgence of the Pelagian heresy (4.378–82), and makes the claim of Lydia in *Odes* 3.9.15 that she would die twice for her lover's sake into an attribute of the saint prepared to die twice in defense of the Lord's commandments (5.369).

Horace had again become a school author by the year 1000, when Gerbert of Aurillac, the future Pope Sylvester II, was lecturing on him in the schools of Rheims. But scholastic interest may have begun earlier: in Paris BnF Lat. 7900A, a manuscript written around 900 in northern Italy, Horace appears along with

Lucan, Juvenal, Terence, and Martianus Capella, all provided with copious annotation. It seems likely that the collection was intended for teaching purposes. That manuscript illustrates another medieval practice with a possible pedagogical intent, marking the text of the *Odes* with musical notation. Nearly fifty manuscripts of Horace containing such notation have been registered, dating from the ninth to the twelfth century; one likely purpose was to assist in memorizing and explicating Horace's lyric meters.[4]

A musical connection is appropriate for a poet who prided himself on his control of complex measures. One of the most impressive examples of Carolingian poetry is a hymn to John the Baptist beginning *Ut queant laxis*, written in Sapphic stanzas and generally ascribed to Paul the Deacon. (The poem has a circumstantial link to Horace, since in the earliest extant copy only a few folios separate it from a text of the *Odes*.) The hymn was soon set to a melody that would make its first stanza famous in the history of music, because the notes corresponding to the initial syllables of the six half lines describe a scale in ascending order:

> UT queant laxis REsonare fibris,
> MIra gestorum FAmuli tuorum,
> SOlue polluti LAbii reatum,
> Sancte Ioannes.

In the eleventh century Guido of Arezzo turned that series of syllables into a mnemonic device for teaching music and produced the solfege system that with minor adjustments is still in use today. This chain of connections ends with a direct link to Horace: in an eleventh-century manuscript in Montpellier, *Odes* 4.11 is notated to the melody of *Ut queant laxis*.

The most remarkable example of medieval *Odes* reception is the twelfth-century *Quirinalia* of Metellus, a monk of Tegernsee in Bavaria, a collection of poems in honor of Saint Quirinus, a third-century martyr whose remains were translated to Tegernsee

---

[4] See Wälli 2002; Ziolkowski 2007.

in the eighth century. The work begins with a sequence of poems that matches the "parade odes" of *Odes* 1 meter for meter, and continues with poems in every Horatian lyric meter not represented in that opening group, followed by a set of poems in all the meters of the *Epodes*. Adding verbal to metrical allusion, Metellus begins many poems with a quotation from the corresponding Horatian ode, altered to fit the collection's hagiographical program. Poem 4, for example, begins *Soluitur acris hiems* (= *Odes* 1.4.1) *tersa niue persecutionis,* "Bitter winter is loosened as the snows of persecution are wiped away." Metellus's clerical audience was presumably expected to recognize both his metrical virtuosity and his redeployment of Horatian phraseology.

Horace retained his place in the canon of classical authors through the rest of the Middle Ages. One measure of his medieval reception is the size of his manuscript tradition, second only to Virgil's: more than eight hundred manuscripts written between 800 and 1500 survive, out of a once far greater number. For most of this period the hexameter *Satires* and *Epistles* were more widely read than the *Odes* and *Epodes,* partly because of their simpler metrical form and partly because of their more overtly moral content. The Horace who figures among the great poets of antiquity in Dante's *Inferno,* for example, is Horace the satirist ("Orazio satiro," *Inferno* 4.86). By contrast, for a poet of the next generation Horace is primarily the author of the *Odes,* "the monarch of lyric song," as Petrarch saluted him in a poem written in the same meter as *Odes* 1.1 (*Epistulae familiares* 24.10).

Petrarch is indirectly responsible for one of the most curious products of Horace's reception. A manuscript now in Florence, Biblioteca Medicea-Laurenziana lat. 34.1, is an elegantly written tenth-century copy of Horace. It was purchased by Petrarch in Genoa in 1347 and contains nearly 250 annotations in his hand. In the 1930s, the conjunction of Horace and Petrarch made the Florence manuscript an icon of the glorious Italian past that the Fascist regime was vigorously promoting. An exact facsimile was published with an accompanying essay by the eminent Latinist Enrico Rostagno. In his peroration Rostagno quoted the *Carmen saeculare* (11–12), "May you see nothing greater than the city of Rome," and claimed that Horace's wish was even then being brought to fruition through the energies of Il Duce.

The *Odes* were represented at the start of the transition from manuscript to print: *Odes* 4.7 appeared at Mainz in 1465, in the first printed book containing any of the Greek or Latin classics, in the company of Cicero's *De officiis* and *Paradoxa Stoicorum*. The first printed edition of all of Horace followed in 1471/2 and was succeeded by ten more editions by 1500. Horace was now firmly established in print and ready to begin the next phase of his reception.

From the seventeenth century to the end of the nineteenth, Horace is so pervasively present that it seems best to focus on a few representative or distinctive figures and themes.

The *Odes* have attracted translators of all kinds, from major figures such as Herrick, Jonson, Milton, Dryden, Johnson, and Smart to aristocratic poetasters. Several of the odes have been especially popular with translators, but no other poem has enjoyed the celebrity of *Odes* 1.5. In a wonderfully dotty display of British amateur scholarship, Sir Ronald Storrs (1881–1955), an architect of British colonial policy in Palestine, devoted years to collecting translations of the Pyrrha ode, amassing several hundred renderings into numerous languages. Further work by Charles Tennyson brought the total to 451, from which a selection of sixty-three English versions and eighty-one in other languages was published in 1959. It seems unlikely that 451 translators would have independently decided to tackle this ode; I imagine that at a certain point doing so became a sort of *rite de passage* in a number of literary communities, and that new translations were undertaken as both a tribute and a challenge to existing versions. The existence of translations into less widely spoken languages such as Latvian and Maltese may owe something to feelings of national pride.

The translators assembled by Storrs and Tennyson are an overwhelmingly male group (as has been true of most translators of Horace until recent times), which makes the "imitation" by Lady Mary Wortley Montague (1750) stand out all the more. In a pointed reversal of gender, a young man is the attractive but deceitful seducer, and his victim a "poor unhappy maid." The first stanza gives the flavor:

> For whom are now your Airs put on?
> And what new Beauty doom'd to be undone?
>   That careless Elegance of Dress,
>   This Essence that perfumes the Wind,
> Your ev'ry motion does confess
> Some secret Conquest is design'd.[5]

Although less common than translation into English, Latin verse composition in Horatian meters also had a robust following. The most accomplished of these composers was Anthony Alsop (1669/70–1726), "the English Horace," of whom two books of odes were published in 1752 by his stepson, Francis Bernard. The first ode in Bernard's edition is a version of the ancient hymn "Te Deum laudamus" in Sapphics.[6] A later specimen of the genre is C. S. Calverley's 1862 translation of canto 106 of Tennyson's *In Memoriam* (itself inspired by *Odes* 1.9) into the Alcaic meter of Horace's ode.

Throughout this period Horace was seen as a source of moral instruction. Ben Jonson spoke of him as "an Author of much Civilitie; and (if any among the heathen can be) the best master, both of vertue, and wisdom" (*Discoveries* 2590–92). A similar description in more practical terms appears in the anonymous preface to a 1741 edition: "Of all the gifts of the Muses, Horace's poems are the most useful, and he is the only Poet who can form the Gentleman, as there is none but he who lays before us the Duties of a civil life, and teaches Men to live happily with themselves, with their Equals, and with their Superiors."[7] Coleridge similarly called him "the man whose works have been in all ages deemed the model of good sense, and are still the pocket companions of those who pride themselves on uniting the scholar with the gentleman."[8]

---

[5] Carne-Ross and Haynes 1996: 167. The same reversal of roles appears in the 1684 version by Aphra Behn (ibid., 120–21).
[6] Edition and study by Money 1998.
[7] Quoted by Edmunds 2010: 343.
[8] Quoted by Thayer 1916: 33.

Ben Jonson (1572–1637) was called "the Horace of our age" by a contemporary. Jonson emulated Horace's generic variety, composing odes, epodes, epistles, satires, and more. His comic play *Poetaster* (1601) features as its protagonist a Horace who is a thinly disguised self-portrait; it dramatizes several of the *Satires*, and substantial portions are translations of the original. Jonson was particularly attracted to Horatian odes that proclaim the poet's ability to secure immortality for himself and for his addressees; he returned often to *Odes* 1.1, 3.30, 4.8, and 4.9. A single poem of 1600, addressed to Elizabeth Countess of Rutland, draws on all four odes to produce what Victoria Moul calls a "hit parade" of Horatian echoes.[9] The fame that Jonson promises Elizabeth is figured in images drawn from *Odes* 1.1 and 3.30: "There like a rich, and golden *pyramede*, / borne up by statues, shall I reare your head." In 1.1 it is Horace's own head that is uplifted, but Jonson adopts the perspective of *Odes* 4, in which the poet confers lasting renown on others.

In his "Ode to Himself," published in 1631 and written after the hostile reception given to his play *The New Inn* in 1629, Jonson exhorts himself to abandon the stage and devote himself to lyric in praise of Charles I:

> Leave things so prostitute,
>   And take the Alcaick lute;
> Or thine own Horace or Anacreons lyre;
>   Warm thee by Pindares fire: . . .
> But when they heare thee sing
>   The glories of thy king,
> His zeale to God, and his just awe o'er men:
>   They may, blood-shaken, then,
> Feele such a flesh-quake to possesse their powers
>   As they shall cry, 'Like ours,
> In sound of peace or wars,
>   No Harp e'er hit the stars.'

---

[9] Moul 2010: 24, and see 20–24 for fuller discussion.

As Horace had aspired in *Odes* 1.1 to be included in the company of lyric poets, Jonson aims to be associated with Horace, Anacreon, and Pindar. The poem concludes with an echo of the end of *Odes* 1.1 (cf. 1.1.35–36 "My uplifted head will strike the stars").

Andrew Marvell (1621–1678) may not have identified with Horace as Jonson did, but he certainly had much in common with him in character and temperament: ironically detached, holding opposing ideas in balance, passionate yet remote, obsessed by the passing of time, and striving to maintain an independence of outlook in a career largely spent dependent on others.

Marvell's best known poem, "To His Coy Mistress," is a wittily expanded counterpart to Horace's ode to Leuconoe (1.11), but his most impressive use of Horace is in his arguably greatest poem, "An Horatian Ode upon Cromwell's Return from Ireland," composed in 1650. Marvell's description of Charles I at his execution, which occupies the middle of the poem, has often been compared to the tribute Horace offers to Cleopatra in the final stanzas of *Odes* 1.37:

> *He* nothing common did or mean
> upon that memorable scene:
>   but with his keener eye
>   the axe's edge did try:
> Nor called the gods with vulgar spite
> to vindicate his helpless right,
>   but bowed his comely head
>   down as upon a bed.

Marvell's poem is more complex than Horace's, partly because it has a richer literary background but primarily because it is more about Cromwell than about Charles I, whereas in Horace Octavian plays a subordinate role in a poem firmly focused on Cleopatra. Marvell's Cromwell, "the Wars' and Fortune's Son," is an ambivalent figure, with traces both of Lucan's Julius Caesar (his lightning-like restlessness) and his Pompey (acting as the faithful servant of the Republic). In an impressive display of negative capability, Marvell combines a wholehearted admiration for the dignity of Charles with a hardheaded recognition of Cromwell as the man of destiny and of the future. In a nice touch inspired by *Odes* 4.4, Marvell has the defeated Irish testify to Cromwell's goodness and justice.

As often happens, the study of reception causes the original to be seen in a new light. Marvell's reflections on contemporary events have a sober weightiness that is rarely to be found in Horace's political odes.

As a representative of Horace's eighteenth-century reception I have chosen Samuel Johnson (1709–1784). Johnson's fondness for the *Odes* was already evident in his teens, when he produced translations of 1.22 and 2.9, probably among others. Boswell records that during Johnson's undergraduate years at Pembroke College, Oxford, "Horace's Odes were the compositions in which he took most delight, and it was long before he liked his Epistles and Satires."[10] Among his college compositions is a brief essay in elegant Latin prose offering a reading of *Odes* 1.20 as a testimony of the friendship of Horace and Maecenas.[11] (For the poem see 81–82.) For the rest of his life the *Odes* were never far from his mind, whether providing apt moral reflections or supplying mottos for the essays in *The Rambler* and *The Adventurer*. In his final illness he again turned to Horace, translating one of the greatest and saddest of the *Odes*, 4.7 (for which see 166–71).

A curious incident reported by Boswell suggests another use Johnson made of the *Odes*. When at the Thrales' house Johnson would often retreat to a corner of the room and murmur inaudibly to himself. "It used to be imagined . . . that he was praying; but this was not *always* the case, for I was once, perhaps unperceived by him, writing at a table, so near the place of his retreat, that I heard him repeating some lines in an ode of Horace, over and over again, as if by iteration, to exercise the organs of speech, and fix the ode in his memory."[12] (The lines were *Odes* 1.2.21–24.) Boswell's interpretation is not the only possible one: Johnson suffered almost all his

---

[10] *Life of Johnson* ed. Hill and Powell 1934: 1:70.
[11] Ibid., 1:60n7.
[12] Ibid., 1:483n4.

life from a fear of losing his mind, and would recite Latin poetry from memory to assure himself that he was still in possession of his faculties.

Horace's reflections on the passage of time and the fading of beauty had a personal meaning for Johnson. In March 1776 he wrote to Boswell, "You will see, Sir, at Mr. Hector's, his sister, Mrs. Careless, a clergyman's widow. She was the first woman with whom I was in love. It dropt out of my head imperceptibly; but she and I shall always have a kindness for each other." In a note Boswell quotes from a letter of Johnson to Mrs. Thrale in July 1770: "I have passed a day in Birmingham with my old friend Hector . . . and his sister, an old love. My mistress is grown much older than my friend. *O quid habes illius, illius / quae spirabat amores, / quae me surpuerat mihi*" (*Odes* 4.13.18–20; see 161).[13]

Johnson was aware of the darker side of Horace's outlook, and did not accept the by-then established view of him as cheerful and contented (as in Dryden's reference to his "briskness, jollity, and good humour"). When confronted with that image, he replied, "We have no reason to believe that; . . . we see in his writings what he wished the state of his mind to appear." Caroline Goad comments, "There is in this answer perhaps a reflection of Johnson's own melancholy, which felt the corresponding innate sadness . . . in Horace."[14]

Horace's popularity as a school author stimulated efforts to remove from his text anything that might be thought morally offensive. Jesuit educators took the lead in producing expurgated editions, beginning with one published in Rome in 1569. One might imagine that the *Odes*, with their chaste diction and delicate depictions of erotic behavior, would not offer much scope for pruning, but the editors thought otherwise: any reference to pleasure was grounds for excision. Some cuts involved entire stanzas, such as the last stanza of 1.9 (see 72), but others were on a

---

[13] *Ibid.*, vol. 2, 449–50.
[14] Goad 1918: 235.

smaller scale and were achieved by rewriting rather than removal. So in 1.9.15 Horace's "sweet loves" was altered to "dear loves," lowering the emotional temperature, and in 1.22.10, instead of singing of his Lalage, Horace was made to sing of cheerful Graces. Even a mention of "dances" in 1.9.16 seemed too risqué and was replaced by the more hearty-sounding "games."

A remote descendant of the Jesuit editions is the "Harvard Horace" of 1806, "undertaken for the use of students at Harvard University." The preface is explicit about the motive for expurgation:

> The consideration of the pernicious tendency, in a moral view, which certain obscene expressions and allusions of this otherwise excellent author might have, induced the governors of the University to procure the publication of this expurgated edition, as a substitute for that, hitherto used, which is entire. . . . The punctuation also is on a plan, somewhat different from that, generally received; the colon being altogether neglected. The reasons for this departure from the common method of pointing were, that the use of the colon is very unsettled and irregular, and that the other three points are sufficient, it is apprehended, to answer every purpose of correct punctuation.

The editors seem to have been as fond of the comma as they were hostile to the colon, and to have been as worried about improper punctuation as they were about loose morals. The edition was denounced by a Harvard alumnus in the *Monthly Anthology and Boston Review* for 1807, which suggests that the time when Horace could be expurgated on a large scale had passed. Even the most prim Victorian editions and translations limit themselves to omitting the obscene epodes 8 and 12 and the bulk of *Satires* 1.2.

In the nineteenth century, and in the Victorian era in particular, Horace's position at the center of the classics remained secure. "On the whole Horace, suitably selected, served the nineteenth century well as a kind of honorary Victorian, providing forms of words which said what people wanted to hear or feel, sometimes giving them opportunities to demonstrate their own superiority.

He was never in any danger of being blackballed at the club."[15] As that statement suggests, familiarity with Horace was strongly correlated with social class and was an effective means of advertising membership in an educated elite. That aspect of Horace's Victorian reception has been studied by Stephen Harrison with reference to Pierre Bourdieu's concepts of cultural and social capital.[16]

Horace's quotability made tags from his poetry a convenient shorthand in which to communicate with fellow members of the group. As late as the 1930s the practice could be satirized by Ronald Knox in his *Let Dons Delight*: "It seems to me quite certain that the whole legend of the 'English Gentleman' has been built upon Latin and Greek. A meets B on the steps of his club and says 'Well, old man, *eheu fugaces*, what?' and B says '*Dulce et decorum est pro patria mori*', and the crossing-sweeper falls to his knees in adoration of the two men who can talk as learnedly as that."[17] It is noteworthy that while Knox refers to the role of Latin and Greek in general, his examples come from the *Odes*.

When joined to the Victorian image of Horace as a guide to life, such quotations could take on greater weight. In a passage from Trollope's *The Prime Minister*, an older brother expresses concern about his younger sibling's emotional volatility: "*Aequam memento*—you remember all that, don't you?" "I remember it, but it isn't so easy to do so, is it?" Knowledge of Horace creates moral expectations that must be acknowledged even if they are not always met.

A memorable instance of familiarity with Horace creating a bond between enemies is the often-told story of Patrick Leigh Fermor (1915–2011) and the German general. At the age of eighteen, Leigh Fermor set out to walk across Europe, from the Hook of Holland to Constantinople. In his baggage he carried two books, the *Oxford Book of English Verse* and the Loeb edition of Horace's *Odes*, a gift from his mother. During World War II Leigh Fermor fought in Crete, embedded with a group of Cretan resistance fighters. Their

---

[15] Vance 1993: 216.
[16] Harrison 2007, 2017.
[17] Quoted by Harrison 2017: 21.

most daring exploit was the capture of the German commander General Heinrich Kreipe in 1944. One morning, as Leigh Fermor was keeping watch over their prisoner, the general looked out at snow-capped Mount Ida and spoke in Latin the first words of *Odes* 1.9, *Vides ut alta stet nive candidum / Soracte* ("You see how Soracte stands white in deep snow"; see 71). Leigh Fermor knew the ode by heart and continued the quotation in Latin to the end, prompting the general to look at him and say "Ach so, Herr Major." In Leigh Fermor's telling, "For a long moment, the war had ceased to exist. We had both drunk at the same fountains long before; and things were different between us for the rest of our time together."[18]

While knowledge of Horace most often served as a badge of belonging to an educated elite, studying Horace could also be a means of self-improvement and social advancement. The most famous example is a fictional one, Thomas Hardy's Jude Fawley, who teaches himself Latin and Greek in the vain hope of being admitted to the University of Christminster (modelled on Oxford). Jude's most intense experience of the classics comes when he is working through the *Carmen saeculare* and sees one evening the setting sun and rising full moon; overcome with emotion, he kneels and intones the entire hymn. But the study of Horace was also beneficial to the upwardly mobile in real life, and its advantages extended throughout the British Empire. Applicants to enter the Indian Civil Service had to pass an examination in which they might encounter questions like "What criticism of contemporary poets is to be found in Horace's writings?" or be invited to "compare in detail . . . the Sapphic metre in the hands of Catullus and Horace."[19]

In addition to being regarded as an honorary Victorian, Horace in the nineteenth century also acquired the status of honorary Christian. Edward Bulwer-Lytton, author of the best-seller *The Last Days of Pompeii*, wrote that Horace "has always found indulgent favour with the clergy of every Church . . . and the greatest

---

[18] Leigh Fermor 1977: 74.
[19] Vasunia 2013: 231, 233.

dignitaries of our own Church are among his most sedulous critics and his warmest panegyrists."[20] One Anglican prelate who fits that description was Christopher Wordsworth (1807–1885), nephew of the poet and bishop of Lincoln, 1869–1885, of whom we are told, "There was scarcely an incident in life that did not get capped with a Horatian quotation. . . . He used often to talk of giving a lecture on Horace to the theological students at Lincoln—not without some feeling that the tact, humour, and knowledge of life and grace of style possessed by that poet were just the qualities in which the technical teaching of a seminary is likely to fall short."[21] At least one Anglican clergyman, the Reverend Francis Kilvert (1840–1879), incorporated the *Odes* into his daily spiritual exercises: in his diary for August 17, 1874, he wrote "Rose early. Read the second lessons [*sic*] for the day in the Greek Testament and an ode of Horace, the first of the fourth book."[22]

Two prominent figures with close ties to Horace whose careers straddle the nineteenth and twentieth centuries are Rudyard Kipling (1865–1936) and A. E. Housman (1859–1936). I quoted earlier Kipling's recollection of his classics master at school, William Crofts (xx). In the same passage of his autobiography Kipling recalls a memorable day when the class was working through *Odes* 1.37. "I had detonated [Crofts] by a very vile construe of the first few lines. Having slain me, he charged over my corpse and delivered an interpretation of the rest of the Ode unequalled for power and insight."[23] That experience provided the basis for one of Kipling's best-known short stories, "Regulus" (published in 1917), in which Mr. King, a classics teacher, is dragging a mostly reluctant group of students through *Odes* 3.5. After the smell of chlorine gas emanating from the science class next door provides a distraction, King returns to Horace in a mode similar to that of Crofts on *Odes* 1.37—"passing thence to the next Ode . . . where he fetched up, full-voiced, upon

---

[20] Quoted by Harrison 2007b: 209.
[21] Overton and Wordsworth 1888: 508–9.
[22] Cited by Kenney 2005: 185–86.
[23] Kipling 1937: 32–33.

'*Dis te minorem quod geris imperas*' (Thou rulest because thou bearest thyself as lower than the Gods)—making it a text for a discourse on manners, morals, and respect for authority as distinct from bottled gases, which lasted till the bell rang."[24] Later in the day King has an exchange with his science colleague, Mr. Hartopp, who holds that after seven years of studying classics "your victims go away with nothing, absolutely nothing, except, perhaps, . . . one score of totally unrelated Latin tags which any child of twelve could have absorbed in two terms." To this King replies, "If our system brings later . . . a mere glimpse of the significance (foul word!) of, we'll say, one Ode of Horace, one twenty lines of Virgil, we've got what we poor devils of ushers are striving after." "And what might that be?" "Balance, proportion, perspective—life."[25]

In its original publication "Regulus" was followed by a version of *Odes* 1.1 in which the pursuits rejected are those of science and technology. Its opening stanza reads "There are whose study is of smells, / And to attentive schools rehearse / How something mixed with something else / Makes something worse." The poem is headed "A Translation. Horace, Bk. V. *Ode* 3"; together with two other pseudo-Horatian odes it formed the nucleus of a complete Book 5 containing fifteen poems. C. L. Graves contributed the other twelve English texts; they were translated into Latin by A. D. Godley, with some assistance from Ronald Knox, and published in a facsimile of a scholarly edition complete with Latin preface and an apparatus of variant readings.

In an edition of Horace published by the Medici Press and edited by E. C. Wickham (1910), Kipling entered glosses to fifty-five of the *Odes*.[26] Some are straightforward paraphrases, while others take the form of a commentary. The tone varies widely and offers a microcosm of Kipling's responses to Horace. The ode to Leuconoe (1.11) is reduced to a jaunty two lines: "Lucy, do not look ahead: We shall be a long time dead. / Take whatever you can

---

[24] Kipling 1917: 252.
[25] Ibid., 264.
[26] Published by Carrington 1978.

see: And, incidentally, take me." (Compare my reading of the poem, 52.) The paraphrase of *Odes* 1.24 (consoling Virgil on the death of Quintilius Varus) strikes a very different note: "They pass, O God, and all / Our grief, our tears, / Achieve not their recall / Nor reach their ears. / Our lamentations leave / But one thing sure, / They perish and we grieve / But we endure." Kipling's tribute to *Odes* 4.7 suggests the depth of his admiration for the *Odes*: "If all that ever Man had sung / In the audacious Latin Tongue / Had been lost— and this remained / All, through This might be regained."

A. E. Housman engaged with the *Odes* from a dual perspective. In his capacity as a classical scholar, he published a number of conjectures in the text of Horace; indeed, his first published article was a set of conjectures on the *Odes* and *Epodes*. The intimate knowledge of Horace that Housman acquired in his scholarly work also found expression in his poetry, often in subtle details of language. "On Wenlock Edge" opens thus: "On Wenlock Edge the wood's in trouble." "In trouble" seems at first an oddly anthropomorphic way of describing a forest; it was suggested to Housman by the opening lines of *Odes* 1.9, where the trees on Mount Soracte are "toiling" (*laborantes*) and cannot bear the weight of snow on their branches. That connection is clinched by the poem's third line, which paints a similar picture of trees bending under nature's assault: "The gale, it plies the saplings double." The second and third stanzas look back to a time when the same landscape was seen by a Roman occupier: "Then, 'twas before my time, the Roman / At yonder heaving hill would stare." As we have seen (73), Horace's poem establishes a connection between the seasons and the stages of human life. Housman follows suit: "Through him [the Roman] the gale of life blew high; / The tree of man was never quiet: / Then 'twas the Roman, now 'tis I." Housman's poem engages in a dialogue with Horace's ode, and its emphasis on the continuity of human experience parallels Housman's poetic connection to his Roman predecessor.

The two sides of Housman's relationship to Horace meet in the often-told story of a lecture on the *Odes* given at Cambridge in May 1914. The poem for analysis that day was *Odes* 4.7. One of the students present, Mrs. T. W. Pym, recalled, "This ode he dissected with the usual display of brilliance, wit, and sarcasm. Then for the first time in two years he looked up at us, and in quite a different voice said 'I should like to spend the last few minutes considering this ode simply as poetry.' . . . He read the ode aloud with deep emotion, first in Latin and then in an English translation of his own. 'That,' he said hurriedly, almost like a man betraying a secret, 'I regard as the most beautiful poem in ancient literature,' and walked quickly out of the room."[27]

In his play *The Invention of Love* (1997), which features Housman as its protagonist, Tom Stoppard suggests that Housman was so deeply moved by *Odes* 4.7 because of its final image, of Theseus unable to free his comrade Pirithous from the underworld; in Housman's translation, "And Theseus leaves Pirithous in the chain / The love of comrades cannot take away." In "the love of comrades" (stronger than Horace, who only speaks of "dear Pirithous") Stoppard sees a reflection of Housman's unreciprocated love for his fellow student at Oxford Moses Jackson. Elsewhere in the play Stoppard creates an analogy between Horace's quest for the ever-receding Ligurinus at the end of *Odes* 4.1 and Housman's futile longing for Jackson.

In the poem Housman wrote after parting with Jackson, he portrays himself in terms that recall the two great friendships of Horace's life:

> He would not stay for me, and who can wonder?
>   He would not stay for me to stand and gaze.
> I shook his hand, and tore my heart in sunder,
>   And went with half my life about my ways.

"Tearing my heart in sunder" echoes Horace's reference to Virgil as "half of my soul" (*Odes* 1.3.8) and to Maecenas as "part of my soul" (*Odes* 2.17.5), while "went with half my life about my ways" corresponds to what Horace would not wish to do if Maecenas were to die: "What would the other half do, / going on

---

[27] Gaskin 2013: 12.

living, neither / as dear as it used to be, / nor able to be by itself?" (2.17.6–8, trans. David Ferry).

In a talk given in 1925, J. W. Mackail referred to the *Odes* as "having been and still being the school-book of the European world . . . easily accessible to all who have such educational advantages as are now widely open to all classes." Mackail was right to foresee a time of expanded educational opportunity, but mistaken in his belief that the study of classics would retain its central position in the new era. For most of the century since he wrote, knowledge of the *Odes* in the original has been limited to a small minority. In Britain at least, it also seems likely that Horace's close connection to the establishment and its institutions—the elite universities, the Church of England, Parliament, the empire—worked against him as popular attitudes to those institutions shifted.

But the *Odes* have lost none of their appeal to poets. The list of distinguished twentieth-century poets who have translated individual odes or sets of odes includes Ezra Pound, Louis MacNeice, C. H. Sisson, Robert Lowell, and Donald Davie. The roster of poets who contributed to J. D. McClatchy's 2002 collective translation (xvii–xviii) contains such eminent figures as Robert Bly, Robert Creeley, Rachel Hadas, Daryl Hine, John Hollander, W. S. Merwin, Paul Muldoon, Robert Pinsky, Rosanna Warren, and Richard Wilbur.

A few years before his death, W. H. Auden (1907–1973) wrote that "the only classical latin poet I *really* like is Horace."[28] Like many others, Auden grew closer to Horace as he aged, and the strongest Horatian influences are to be seen in the poetry of his final decade. To James Michie he described "Thanksgiving for a Habitat" (1962) as representing "what I think Horace might write, were he alive today and were English his mother-tongue."[29] In the poem Auden writes of the satisfaction he derives from the farmhouse he had acquired in Kirchstetten, Austria, from being "dominant / over three

---

[28] From "The Fall of Rome," an essay that was commissioned by *Life* magazine in 1966 but rejected by the editors; it was published with an introduction by G. W. Bowersock in *Auden Studies* 3 1995: 111–19; reprinted in Bowersock 2009.

[29] Mendelson 1999: 454

acres and a blooming / conurbation of country lives, few of whom / I shall ever meet, and with fewer / converse." In "A Thanksgiving," one of his last poems (1973), Auden reflects on his intellectual biography, tracing a progress from Hardy, Thomas, and Frost to Yeats and Graves, thence to Kierkegaard, Williams, and Lewis, and finally to the present, when "Nature allures me again," and his chosen tutors are Goethe and Horace, "adroitest of makers, beeking in Tivoli."[30]

Auden's most overtly Horatian poem, titled "The Horatians" (1968), has some of the expansiveness and breadth of vision of *Odes* 3.29 and is written in an approximation of that ode's Alcaic stanza. In Auden's definition, Horatians are those who live lives of moderation, shunning operatic extremes of feeling or lofty ambitions, attached to "some particular / place and stretch of country," desiring only "a genteel sufficiency of / land or lolly." Many such people have found their Maecenas in the Church of England as country vicars or "organists in trollopish / cathedral towns," as keepers in zoos or botanical gardens, as museum curators. "Some of you have written poems, usually / short ones, and some kept diaries, seldom published / till after your deaths, but most / made no memorable impact / except on your friends and dogs." One stanza captures the reaction of many young readers to Horace himself: "Enthusiastic / youth writes you off as cold, who cannot be found on / barricades, and never shoot / either yourselves or your lovers." The poem ends with a direct address to Horace:

> You thought well of your Odes, Flaccus, and believed they
> Would live, but knew, and have taught your descendants to
>   Say with you: "As makers go,
>   Compared with Pindar or any
>
> Of the great foudroyant masters who don't ever
> Amend, we are, for all our polish, of little
>   Stature, and, as human lives,
>   Compared with authentic martyrs,

---

[30] Auden 1991: 892. "Beeking" is a Scottish term for basking in the sun, and "makers" is a Scottish equivalent for "poets."

>   Like Regulus, of no account. We can only
>   Do what it seems to us we were made for, look at
>   This world with a happy eye,
>   But from a sober perspective."[31]

The tone is hard to gauge; although the reference to Pindar takes up Horace's ostensibly modest comparison in *Odes* 4.2, surely there is some degree of irony in this minimizing description.

One of Auden's greatest admirers was the Russian-born poet Joseph Brodsky (1940–1996), awarded the Nobel Prize in Literature in 1987. In his "Letter to Horace" of 1995, Brodsky addresses Horace in the underworld, proposing (perhaps not entirely in jest) that he had been most recently reincarnated as Auden.[32] The idea was almost certainly suggested by *Odes* 2.13, where Horace imagines encountering Sappho and Alcaeus in the underworld (see 63). For Brodsky, as it had been for Ovid, what is most appealing about Horace is his metrical mastery. In a touching passage of the "Letter," Brodsky supposes that if he and Horace cannot understand each other's language, they could communicate in meter, tapping out Asclepiads or Sapphics like prisoners in adjacent cells.

A likely consequence of Auden's use of a metrical form based on the Alcaic stanza is a resurgence of interest in similar forms by more recent poets writing in English, some of whom have no direct knowledge of Horace.[33] Horace himself fades away like the Cheshire Cat, leaving his meter behind—not what he meant by *non omnis moriar* ("I shall not entirely die"), but a form of survival nonetheless.

Some modern poets who do know their Horace have produced modernized versions of odes, sometimes with humorous effect. One of those is Anthony Hecht (1923–2004), whose versions of 1.1 and 1.5 "freely from Horace" wittily update the poet to the contemporary United States. Hecht's delightful retake of *Odes* 1.1 turns

---

[31] Auden 1991: 772.
[32] Brodsky 1996: 428–58.
[33] See Talbot 2009.

the poem into a grant application to the Guggenheim Foundation, spelling out an appeal for support that Horace had left unexpressed in addressing Maecenas. After reviewing the pursuits that engross others (such as bartending, cheating the IRS, shell collecting, and obsessive exercise), Hecht ends with his own aspiration: "As for me, the prize for poets, the simple gift / for amphybrachs strewn by a kind Euterpe, / with perhaps a laurel crown of the evergreen / imperishable of your fine endowment / would supply my modest wants, who dream of nothing / but a pad on Eighth Street and your approbation."[34]

A more ambitious such enterprise is the collection *Museum of Clear Ideas* (1993), by Donald Hall (1928–2018), a former poet laureate of the United States. It contains thirty-eight poems (matching the number of Horace's first book) attributed to "Horsecollar" (a minor character in Disney films). Each poem is a modernized version of its counterpart in *Odes* 1. In Hall's response to *Odes* 1.37, Cleopatra is replaced by an odious candidate for re-election to the US Senate. Some of Hall's lines seem eerily relevant in 2019:

> Until this afternoon, it seemed unlucky
> to break out the cider we pressed last autumn.
> We feared that Senator Hell might win,
> wagging his sullied tail to celebrate
> fund-raising, bigotry, merde, contempt for art,
> and detestation of the First Amendment.

Yet another version of an ode that gives it a contemporary resonance is Seamus Heaney's reworking of *Odes* 1.34. Here is my rendering of the original:

> Grudging and infrequent in my worship
> of the gods I wandered, an expert in crackpot
>   philosophy; but now I'm forced
>   to reverse my sails and follow again

---

[34] *The Venetian Vespers* (1980), also in *Collected Earlier Poems* (Hecht 1990).

the path I abandoned. For Father Jupiter,
who normally splits the clouds with flash of lightning,
    has driven his thundering horses
        and swift chariot through a clear blue sky;

at that the inert earth and wandering streams,
at that the Styx and dreaded halls of loathsome
    Taenarus, and Atlas who marks the end of land—
        all shook. Powerful is the god

to exchange highest for lowest, humbling the great
and promoting the unregarded. With hissing wings
    Fortune swoops and snatches the crown from
        one head,
            delighting to have placed it on another.

And here is Heaney:

ANYTHING CAN HAPPEN
after Horace, Odes 1,34

Anything can happen. You know how Jupiter
Will mostly wait for clouds to gather head
Before he hurls the lightning? Well, just now
He galloped his thunder-cart and his horses

Across a clear blue sky. It shook the earth
And the clogged underearth, the River Styx,
The winding streams, the Atlantic shore itself.
Anything can happen, the tallest things

Be overturned, those in high places daunted,
Those overlooked regarded. Stropped-beak Fortune
Swoops, making the air gasp, tearing the crest off one,
Setting it down bleeding on the next.

Ground gives. The heavens' weight
Lifts up off Atlas like a kettle lid.

> Capstones shift, nothing resettles right.
> Telluric ash and fire-spores boil away.[35]

Heaney's opening lines strike a less than serious tone: for Heaney, even more than for Horace, Jupiter's thunder cart is merely a poetic figment. But from the repetition of "anything can happen" onward, the poem moves (as does Horace's) from the fanciful particular to the more fully felt general. In later versions Heaney altered the original reference to "the tallest things" (matching Horace's *summis*) to "the tallest towers," making the allusion to September 11, 2001 unmistakable.

To conclude this sketch, I would like to take a different approach and consider the afterlife of a single stanza of Horace, the final lines of *Odes* 1.13:

> Three times blessed and more
> are those held in an unbroken bond, whose love
>   torn asunder by no bitter complaints
> will not release them before their final day.

Earlier (109) I considered the stanza in the context of the poem it concludes; here I want to focus on its remarkable afterlife. For nearly a thousand years it has been read as an independent text, and the bond it describes has been understood in a variety of ways.[36]

The oldest of those interpretations takes the lines to be a description of an ideal marriage. They appear in the popular twelfth-century anthology known as the *Florilegium Gallicum* under the heading *De concordia coniugali* ("On marital harmony"). They were set to music by the early Lutheran composer Johann Walter (1496–1570) with the title *Laus matrimonii* ("Praise of marriage"). The matrimonial reading is still current: in 2016 a setting for eight-part choir by the British composer Gabriel Jackson received its first

---

[35] First published in November 2001 as "Horace and the Thunder"; collected in Heaney 2006.

[36] The discussion of this passage originally appeared in an anthology of tributes to my Harvard colleague Albert Henrichs, presented to him shortly before his death on April 16, 2017.

performance as part of a couple's celebration of their twentieth anniversary.

A different way of reading those lines brings me much closer to home. Less than a hundred yards from where I am writing these words in Widener Library, the lines are inscribed on one of the gates leading into Harvard Yard. The gate in question was commissioned by members of the class of 1857 in the years before 1900. Four years after the class of 1857 graduated, many of its members joined either the Union Army or the Army of the Confederacy. Nearly forty years later, the surviving members of the class turned to Horace's words as a means of affirming the bond of friendship that not even civil war could break apart.

Among the many people who have pondered Horace's words on the Class of 1857 Gate was the composer Randall Thompson (1899–1984), who taught at Harvard for many years. In 1953, to commemorate the seventieth birthday of his colleague Archibald T. Davison, Thompson set Horace's text in the style of Renaissance polyphony associated with Palestrina.[37] For Thompson, Horace's words must have seemed an appropriate way to express his affection for the work's dedicatee; he had obviously forgiven Davison for denying him admission to the Harvard Glee Club during his undergraduate years.

The union of husband and wife, the loyalty of classmates, the devotion of colleagues—set loose from their original context, Horace's words have been used to express all of these. It is a marvelous example of the capacity of the classics, and of Horace's *Odes* in particular, to find new ways of speaking to us, and of speaking for us.

---

[37] A performance by the Harvard University Choir may be found at https://www.youtube.com/watch?v=PqXtxbVrVoE.

Further Reading

Text, Commentary, Translation

The most accessible Latin text of the *Odes* is in the Loeb Classical Library edition (Rudd 2004); that edition also contains a prose English translation on the facing pages. Commentaries at various levels are available for readers with some knowledge of Latin. A good basic commentary is Garrison (1990); Quinn (1980) is on similar lines, with a more literary focus. More advanced readers will benefit from the commentaries in the Cambridge Greek and Latin Classics series: Mayer (2012) on Book 1, Harrison (2017a) on Book 2, and Thomas (2011) on the *Carmen saeculare* and Book 4. (A commentary on Book 3 in this series is being prepared by A. J. Woodman.) Still more detailed, and primarily for scholars, are the commentaries on Books 1 and 2 by Nisbet and Hubbard (1970, 1978) and by Nisbet and Rudd on Book 3 (2004). For each of the poems in *Odes* 1–3 West (1995, 1998, 2002) includes a Latin text, an accurate translation, and a brief critical essay.

Among the many translations of the *Odes* I have a particular fondness for those of Clancy (1960), who combines closeness to Horace's meaning with a graceful sense of flow. I am still getting to know Lombardo (2018), but it seems very promising. The translations in McClatchy's anthology (2003) vary widely in their relationship to Horace. The much-admired translation by Ferry (1997) captures Horace's tone well, but is often far from the literal sense. The translations by Michie (2002) and Lee (1998) are noteworthy for their metrical virtuosity. Carne-Ross and Haynes (1996) is a collection of translations from different periods.

Collections of Essays

Recent years have seen a proliferation of "companion" volumes on individual authors: collections of commissioned essays that aim to present the results of current scholarship in a form accessible to nonspecialists. Horace now has three companions. The volumes published by Cambridge and Blackwell (Harrison 2007a and Davis 2010) are each the work of a diverse team of scholars; there is almost no overlap among the contributors, so the two collections complement each other well. Every essay in each volume contains suggestions for further reading. The Brill companion (Günther 2013) is largely the work of a single scholar and has less to offer the general reader.

Other noteworthy collections of essays include Rudd (1993), Harrison (1995), Woodman and Feeney (2002), and Houghton and Wyke (2009). Lowrie (2009a) is a judicious selection of previously published articles; it contains English translations of several articles that originally appeared in other languages.

General Works

Armstrong (1989) and Hills (2004) are useful short treatments of all of Horace's works. Fraenkel (1957) is also wide-ranging and much more detailed; some of the author's views (e.g., that Horace was an ardent supporter of Augustus) have not worn well. Commager (1962) is arguably still the best book-length treatment of the *Odes*, remarkable for its acute close readings. The brisk overview in Nisbet (1962) retains the power to provoke and delight.

Specific Topics Relating to the Odes

Davis (1991) explores Horace's uses of rhetorical forms of argument. Ancona (1994) examines the amatory poems from the perspective of temporality. Lowrie (1997) concentrates on the role of narrative within Horatian lyric, while Lowrie (2009b) looks at the place of performance. Santirocco (1986) focuses on the arrangement of poems. Oliensis (1998) traces Horace's strategies of self-representation. Putnam (1986, 2000) offers sympathetic appreciations of *Odes* 4 and the *Carmen saeculare*, respectively.

Putnam (2006) situates Horace in relation to Catullus. From a growing body of work on Horatian reception I mention the essays in Martindale (1993), Moul (2010) on Horace and Ben Jonson, and Harrison (2017b) on Horace's reception in the Victorian era.

Finally, for readers fortunate enough to know Italian, the *Enciclopedia oraziana* (Mariotti 1996–98) contains articles on just about every conceivable Horatian topic.

Works Cited

Ancona, R. 1994. *Time and the Erotic in Horace's Odes*. Durham.
Anderson, W. S. 1982. *Essays on Roman Satire*. Princeton.
Armstrong, D. 1989. *Horace*. New Haven.
Auden, W. H. 1945. *The Collected Poetry of W. H. Auden*. New York.
Auden, W. H. 1991. *Collected Poems*, ed. E. Mendelson. London.
Bowersock, G. W. 2009. *From Gibbon to Auden: Essays on the Classical Tradition*. New York.
Bowra, C. M. 1928. "Horace, Odes IV.12." *Classical Review* 42: 165–67.
Brink, C. O. 1971. *Horace on Poetry: The "Ars Poetica."* Cambridge.
Brodsky, J. 1996. "Letter to Horace." In *On Grief and Reason: Essays.* New York. 428–58.
Carne-Ross, D., and K. Haynes, eds. 1996. *Horace in English*. Harmondsworth.
Carrington, C. 1978. *Kipling's Horace: Carminibus nonnullis Q. Horatii Flacci nonnulla adiunximus quae ad illius exemplar poeta nostras [sic] Rudyard Kipling anglice vel convertit vel imitatus est*. London.
Clancy, J., trans. 1960. *The Odes and Epodes of Horace*. Chicago.
Commager, S. 1962. *The Odes of Horace: A Critical Study*. New Haven.
Davis, G. 1991. *Polyhymnia: The Rhetoric of Horatian Lyric Discourse*. Berkeley.
Davis, G., ed. 2010. *A Companion to Horace*. Chichester.
Dow, S. 1968. "Latin Calligraphy at Hawara: P. Hawara 24." *Journal of Roman Studies* 58: 50–60.

Edmunds, L. 2010. "The Reception of Horace's Odes." In Davis 2010: 337–66.

Feldherr, A. 2010. "'Dionysiac Poetics' and the memory of Civil War in Horace's Cleopatra Ode." In B. Breed, C. Damon, and A. Rossi, eds., *Citizens of Discord: Rome and its Civil Wars*. Oxford. 223–32.

Fenton, A. 2008. "The Forest and the Trees. Pattern and Meaning in Horace, 'Odes' 1." *American Journal of Philology* 129: 559–80.

Ferry, D., trans. 1997. *The Odes of Horace*. New York.

Fowler, D. 1993. "Postscript: Images of Horace in Twentieth-Century Scholarship." In Martindale and Hopkins 1993: 268–76.

Fraenkel, E. 1957. *Horace*. Oxford.

Garrison, D. H., ed. 1990. *Horace: Epodes and Odes*. Norman.

Gaskin, R. 2013. *Horace and Housman*. New York.

Goad, C. 1918. *Horace in the English Literature of the Eighteenth Century*. New Haven.

Griffin, J. 1997. "Cult and Personality in Horace." *Journal of Roman Studies* 87: 54–69.

Griffin, J. 2002. "Look Your Last on Lyric." In T. P. Wiseman, ed., *Classics in Progress*. London. 311–32.

Griffiths, A. "The Odes: Just Where Do You Draw the Line?" In Woodman and Feeney 2002: 65–79.

Günther, H.-C., ed. 2013. *Brill's Companion to Horace*. Leiden.

Hall, D. 1993. *Museum of Clear Ideas*. New York.

Harrison, S. J., ed. 1995. *Homage to Horace: A Bimillenary Celebration*. Oxford.

Harrison, S. J., ed. 2007a. *The Cambridge Companion to Horace*. Cambridge.

Harrison, S. J. 2007b. "Horace and the Construction of the English Victorian Gentleman." *Helios* 34: 207–22.

Harrison, S. J. 2008. "Horace Epistles 2: The Last Horatian Book of *Sermones?*" *Papers of the Langford Latin Seminar* 13: 173–86.

Harrison, S. J. (ed.) 2017a. *Horace Odes: Book II*. Cambridge.

Harrison, S. J. 2017b. *Victorian Horace: Classics and Class*. London.

Heaney, S. 2006. *District and Circle*. New York.

Hecht, A. 1990. *Collected Earlier Poems*. New York.

Heyworth, S. J. 1995. "Dividing Poems." In O. Pecere and M. D. Reeve, eds., *Formative Stages of Classical Traditions: Latin Texts from Antiquity to the Renaissance*. Spoleto. 117–48.

Hills, P. 2004. *Horace*. London.

Houghton, L. B. T., and M. Wyke, eds. 2009. *Perceptions of Horace: A Roman Poet and His Readers*. Cambridge.

Hutchinson, G. 2008. *Talking Books: Readings in Hellenistic and Roman Books of Poetry.* Oxford.

Johnson, T. 2004. *A Symposion of Praise: Horace Returns to Lyric in Odes IV.* Madison.

Kenney, E. J. 2005. "'A Little of It Sticks': The Englishman's Horace." In C. Burnett and N. Mann, eds., *Britannia Latina: Latin in the Culture of Great Britain from the Middle Ages to the Twentieth Century.* London. 178–93.

Kipling, R. 1917. *A Diversity of Creatures.* London.

Kipling, R. 1937. *Something of Myself: For My Friends Known and Unknown.* London.

Lee, G., trans. 1998. *Horace: Odes and Carmen Saeculare.* Leeds.

Leigh Fermor, P. 1977. *A Time of Gifts.* London.

Lombardo, S., trans. 2018. *Horace Odes with Carmen Saeculare.* Indianapolis.

Lowrie, M. 1995. "A Parade of Lyric Predecessors: Horace C. 1.12–1.18." *Phoenix* 49: 33–48.

Lowrie, M. 1997. *Horace's Narrative Odes.* Oxford.

Lowrie, M., ed. 2009a. *Horace: Odes and Epodes.* Oxford Readings in Classical Studies. Oxford.

Lowrie, M. 2009b. *Writing, Performance, and Authority in Augustan Rome.* Oxford.

Lyne, O. 1995. *Horace: Behind the Public Poetry.* New Haven.

Lyne, O. 2005. "Horace *Odes* Book I and the Alexandrian Edition of Alcaeus." *Classical Quarterly* 55: 542–58.

Mackail, J. W. 1899. *Latin Literature.* London.

Mariotti, S., ed. 1996–98. *Orazio: Enciclopedia oraziana.* Rome.

Martindale, C., and D. Hopkins, eds. 1993. *Horace Made New: Horatian Influences on British Writing from the Renaissance to the Twentieth Century.* Cambridge.

Mayer, R., ed. 2012. *Horace Odes: Book I.* Cambridge.

Maynard, J. 1977. *Browning's Youth.* Cambridge, Mass.

McClatchy, J. D., ed. 2002. *Horace: The Odes; New Translations by Contemporary Poets.* Princeton.

Mendelson, E. 1999. *Later Auden.* New York.

Michie, J., trans. 2002. *Horace: Odes.* New York.

Money, D. K. 1998. *The English Horace: Anthony Alsop and the Tradition of British Latin Verse.* Oxford.

Moul, V. 2010. *Jonson, Horace and the Classical Tradition.* Cambridge.

Nisbet, R. G. M. 1962. "Romanae Fidicen Lyrae: The Odes of Horace." In J. P. Sullivan, ed., *Critical Essays on Roman Literature: Elegy and Lyric.* London. 181–218.

Nisbet, R. G. M., and M. Hubbard, eds. 1970. *A Commentary on Horace: Odes Book I*. Oxford.

Nisbet, R. G. M., and M. Hubbard, eds. 1978. *A Commentary on Horace: Odes Book II*. Oxford.

Nisbet, R. G. M., and N. Rudd, eds. 2004. *A Commentary on Horace: Odes Book III*. Oxford.

Obbink, D. 2014. "Two New Poems by Sappho." *Zeitschrift für Papyrologie und Epigraphik* 189: 32–49.

Ogilvie, R. M. 1964. *Latin and Greek: A History of the Influence of the Classics on English Life from 1600 to 1918*. London.

Oliensis, E. 1998. *Horace and the Rhetoric of Authority*. Cambridge.

O'Neill, J. N. (= Neumann, J.) 1994. *Place in Horace: An Examination of Social Hierarchies in* Epistles *I*. Cambridge, Mass.

Overton, J. H., and E. Wordsworth. 1888. *Christopher Wordsworth, Bishop of Lincoln, 1807–1885*. London.

Pasquali, G. 1920. *Orazio lirico*. Florence.

Pound, E. 1929–30. "Horace." *Criterion* 9: 217–27.

Putnam, M. C. J. 1986. *Artifices of Eternity: Horace's Fourth Book of Odes*. Ithaca.

Putnam, M. C. J. 1996. "Horace C. 3.14 and the Designing of Augustus." In H. Krasser and E. A. Schmidt, eds., *Zeitgenosse Horaz: Der Dichter und seine Leser seit zwei Jahrtausenden*, 442–63. Tübingen.

Putnam, M. C. J. 2000. *Horace's Carmen Saeculare*. New Haven.

Putnam, M. C. J. 2006. *Poetic Interplay: Catullus and Horace*. Princeton.

Putnam, M. C. J. 2009. "The Languages of Horace *Odes* 1.24." In Lowrie 2009: 188–201.

Quinn, K. F. 1963. *Latin Explorations: Critical Studies in Roman Literature*. London.

Quinn, K. F., ed. 1980. *Horace: Odes*. London.

Renehan, R. 1988. "Shackleton Bailey and the Editing of Latin Poetry: A Latin Classic." *Classical Philology* 83: 311–28.

Rudd, N., ed. 1989. *Horace: Epistles Book II and Epistle to the Pisones ('Ars Poetica')*. Cambridge.

Rudd, N., ed. 1993. *Horace 2000: A Celebration. Essays for the Bimillennium*. London.

Rudd, N., ed. and trans. 2004. *Horace Odes and Epodes*. Cambridge, Mass.

Santirocco, M. 1986. *Unity and Design in Horace's Odes*. Chapel Hill.

Shackleton Bailey, D. R. 1982. *Profile of Horace*. London.

Syme, R. 1939. *The Roman Revolution*. Oxford.

Syndikus, H. P. 1972. *Die Lyrik des Horaz*. Darmstadt.

Talbot, J. 2009. "A Late Flowering of English Alcaics." In Houghton and Wyke 2009: 305–23.

Tarrant, R. J. 1995. "*Da Capo* Structure in some *Odes* of Horace." In Harrison 1995: 32–49.

Tarrant, R. J. 1996. Review of Lyne 1995. *Bryn Mawr Classical Review* 96.9.15.

Tarrant, R. J. 2007. "Ancient Receptions of Horace." In Harrison 2007a: 277–90.

Tarrant, R. J. 2015. "Virgil and Vergilius in Horace *Odes* 4.12." In H.-C. Günther, ed., *Virgilian Studies. A Miscellany Dedicated to the Memory of Mario Geymonat*. Nordhausen. 429–52.

Tennyson, H. 1899. *Alfred Lord Tennyson: A Memoir*. 4 vols. New York.

Thayer, M. R. 1916. *The Influence of Horace on the Chief English Poets of the Nineteenth Century*. New Haven.

Thomas, R. F., ed. 2011. *Horace Odes Book IV and Carmen Saeculare*. Cambridge.

Vance, N. 1993. "Horace and the Nineteenth Century." In Martindale and Hopkins 1993: 199–216.

Vasunia, P. 2013. *The Classics and Colonial India*. Oxford.

Wälli, S. 2002. *Melodien aus mittelalterlichen Horaz-Handschriften: Edition und Interpretation der Quellen*. Kassel.

Wardle, D., ed. 2014. *Suetonius: Life of Augustus*. Oxford.

Watson, L., ed. 2007. *A Commentary on Horace's* Epodes. Oxford.

West, D. 1995. *Horace Odes Book I: Carpe Diem*. Oxford.

West, D. 1998. *Horace Odes Book II: Vatis Amici*. Oxford.

West, D. 2002. *Horace Odes Book III: Aere Perennius*. Oxford.

Wilkinson, L. P. 1945. *Horace and His Lyric Poetry*. Cambridge.

Wilkinson, L. P. 1959. "The Language of Virgil and Horace." *Classical Quarterly* 9: 181–92.

Williams, G. 1962. "Poetry in the Moral Climate of Augustan Rome." *Journal of Roman Studies* 52: 28–46.

Williams, G. 1969. *The Third Book of Horace's Odes*. Oxford.

Woodman, A. J., and D. Feeney, eds. 2002. *Traditions and Contexts in the Poetry of Horace*. Cambridge.

Yatromanolakis, D. 2007. *Sappho in the Making: The Early Reception*. Cambridge, Mass.

Ziolkowski, J. M. 2007. *Nota Bene: Reading Classics and Writing Melodies in the Early Middle Ages*. Turnhout.

General Index

ABA' structure, 51, 55, 70–71. See also *da capo* structure
ABC structure, 70–71, 72
ablative absolute, 180–81
Accius, 7, 12
Acro, Helenius. *See* pseudo-Acro
Actium, 22, 22–23, 23, 43, 54, 84, 121–22, 125, 151
Aelius Lamia, 30
Aeneas, 152, 164–65
Aeschylus, 63
Agrippa, Marcus Vipsanius, 22, 30, 36, 84, 150
Alcaeus, 26, 27, 28, 37, 38, 41, 56, 63–64, 74, 81, 102, 117, 121, 147, 156, 213
Alcaic stanza, 39, 127, 192, 199, 212, 213
Alcman, 27
Alcuin, 195
Alexander the Great, 186
Alfius, 21
Alsop, Anthony, 199
amatory poems, 90–116
Anacreon, 26, 27, 37, 93, 94, 102, 117, 201
Anderson, William, 15
Antimachus, 9

Antony. *See* Mark Antony
Apollo, 151
Archilochus, 19–21, 23, 56, 146–47
Aristarchus, 27, 37
Aristippus, 143
Aristophanes, 63
Aristotle, 142, 184
Armstrong, David, 90–91, 173–74
arrangement, principles of in *Odes*, 1–3, 35–46
Ars poetica. See *Letter to the Pisos*
Asclepiad meter, 194, 213
Auden, W. H., xvii, 30–31, 211–13
Augustus, 4–5, 28, 36, 43, 44, 45, 54–55, 78, 83, 84, 87, 94, 117–18, 129, 130, 132, 133, 134–40, 145–46, 147, 149, 150–53, 161, 171–82. *See also* Octavian
Avitus, 195

Bacchylides, 27, 37
Bach, J. S., 28
Bandusian spring, 30, 42
barbitos, 26
Beethoven, L. v., 189
Behn, Aphra, 199n5

Bernard, Francis, 199
Bly, Robert, 211
Boethius, 128
Boswell, James, 202
Bourdieu, Pierre, 205
Brink, Charles, 188
Brodsky, Joseph, 213
Browning, Robert, 128
Brundisium, 14, 15, 22
Brutus, Marcus, 2, 55, 57, 118
Bulwer-Lytton, Edward, 206–7
Byron (George Gordon, Lord Byron), xx

Caesar (i.e., Augustus), 180–81
Caesar (i.e., Octavian), 122
Caesar, Gaius Julius, 118
Callimachean poetics, 13, 15–16, 27, 28, 41, 63–64, 189
Callimachus, 7–10, 21, 22, 138
Calverley, C. S., 199
Campbell, A. Y., 73
Canidia, 20, 24
Carmen saeculare, 149, 150–53, 155, 163, 186, 197–98, 206
carpe diem, xix, 51–52, 80, 87, 144, 169, 185
Carrhae, 130
Catius, 18
Catullus, Gaius Valerius, 7–9, 20, 27, 29, 38, 91, 94, 95, 95–96, 97, 104–5, 108, 109, 115, 124, 142, 160, 162
Celsus, Albinovanus, 143, 146
Censorinus, 171
Channing School for Select Young Ladies, xix
Charles I, 200, 201–2
Choerilus, 186
Christ, Karl, 37
Cicero, Marcus Tullius, 6–7, 9, 27, 187, 198
Cinna, Gaius Helvius, 8–9
Cinyra, 93, 144, 159, 160, 161–63
civil wars, 2, 22–23, 39, 43–44, 77–78, 119–26, 139

Clancy, Joseph, 67, 68, 84, 89, 103, 110, 130, 158, 159, 160, 177
Cleopatra, 119, 120–23, 129
Coleridge, Samuel Taylor, 199
Commager, Steele, xix, 41, 95, 102, 115
Coubertin, Pierre de, 25
Crassus, Marcus, 130
Creeley, Robert, 106–7, 211
Crofts, William, 207
Cromwell, Oliver, 201–2
Cyrus, 102–3

da capo structure, 51, 55
Damasippus, 18
Danaids, 113–14
Dante, 197
Davie, Donald, 211
Davison, Archibald T., 217
Davus, 18, 18–19
Dellius, Quintus, 44, 76–78
Diana, 151
Dracontius, 195
Drusus (stepson of Augustus), 5, 139, 153, 171, 177
Dryden, John, 198, 202

elegy, 94–111, 115, 160
Eliot, George, 128
Eliot, T. S., 31
Elizabeth, Countess of Rutland, 200
Ennius, Quintus, 7, 8, 11, 129
Epicureanism, 111–12, 143
Epicurus, 66, 142
Epistles I, 141–49
Epodes, 19–24, 100
Euripides, 63, 189
expurgated editions of Horace, 203–4

Faunus, 100, 102
Fenton, Andrew, 37
Ferry, David, 106, 211
Florilegium Gallicum, 216
Florus, Julius, 143, 146, 149, 183
Fraenkel, Eduard, 84, 90, 115, 169, 173
friendship and advice, 66–89
Fundanius, 11

Gallus, Cornelius, 95, 162
Gerbert of Aurillac, 195
Gesualdo, Carlo, 1
Glycera, 106
Goad, Caroline, 203
Godley, A. D., 208
Graves, C. L., 208
Greater Asclepiad, 50
Griffin, Jasper, xx, 181
Guido of Arezzo, 196
Hannibal, 178
Hadas, Rachel, 211
Hall, Donald, 214
Hardy, Thomas, 206
Harrison, Stephen, 205
"Harvard Horace," 204
Harvard Yard, 217
Hasdrubal, 178
Heaney, Seamus, 214–16
Hecht, Anthony, 213–14
Heiric of Auxerre, 195
Hellenistic poetry, 7, 24
Henrichs, Albert, 216n36
Herrick, Robert, 198
Hesiod, 19, 63
Heyworth, Stephen, 127
Hine, Daryl, 211
Hollander, John, 211
Homer, 19, 63, 64, 195
  Odyssey, 103
homosexual relationships, 73–74, 94
Horace's father, 1–2
Hortensius, 8
Housman, A. E., 165, 181, 209–11
Hutchinson, Gregory, 35
Hypermestra, 113–15

Ibycus, 27, 93
irony, xxi, 24, 60, 61, 93, 99, 106, 108, 115, 160, 188–89, 213
Iullus Antonius, 172

Jackson, Gabriel, 216–17
Jackson, Moses, 210
Jefferson, Thomas, 21
Jesuits, 203–4

Johnson, Samuel, 198, 202–3
Johnson, Timothy, 154
Jonson, Ben, 42, 198, 199, 200–201
Julia (daughter of Augustus), 182
Juvenal, 193–94, 196
juxtaposed poems, 39–41

Kenney, E. J., 90
Kilvert, Francis, 207
Kipling, Rudyard, xx, 73, 207–9
Knox, Ronald, 205, 208
Kreipe, Heinrich, 206

Larkin, Philip, 29, 35
laudandus, 172
laudator, 172
Leigh Fermor, Patrick, 205–6
Letter to Augustus (= *Epistles* 2.1), 183–86
Letter to Florus (= *Epistles* 2.2), 183–86
Letter to the Pisos (= *Ars Poetica*), 184–89
Leuconoe, 48–52
Licymnia, 83–86
life of Horace, 1–5
lifelong love, 109–11
Ligurinus, 157, 160, 161
literary epistles, 183–89
Livia, 137, 139–40, 178
Lollius, 171, 172
Lombardo, Stanley, 43, 137, 138, 139
love poetry. *See* amatory poems
Lowell, Robert, 47, 211
Lowrie, Michèle, 37, 115, 181
Lucan, 196
Lucilius, Gaius, 7, 11–15, 16, 23, 142, 172, 185
Lucretius (Titus Lucretius Carus), 7
Ludi saeculares, 150–51
Lycambes, 19
Lyce, 161, 164
Lycidas, 170
Lyde (in *Odes* 2.11), 138
Lyde (in *Odes* 3.11), 113–15
Lyde (in *Odes* 3.28), 103, 163
Lydia, 111
Lyne, Oliver, 37, 38, 87, 174

Mackail, J. W., 211
MacNeice, Louis, 211
Maecenas, Gaius Cilnius, 3–5, 16–17, 18–19, 20, 22, 22–23, 28, 36, 38, 42, 44–45, 81–89, 112, 117, 118, 119, 141–42, 143, 144–45, 146, 155, 158, 163
Manchester Grammar School, xix
manuscripts of Horace's works, 195–96, 196–97
Mark Antony, 3, 9, 22, 54, 118–19, 121, 124, 130
Martial, 31
Martianus Capella, 196
Martindale, Charles, 190
Marvell, Andrew, 48, 192, 201–2
Massachusetts Institute of Technology, xix
Massey College, Toronto, xix
Maximian, 195
McClatchy, J. D., xvii–xviii, 211
Mercury, 56
Merwin, W. S., 211
Messalla Corvinus, 77–78
Metellus of Tegernsee, 196–97
meter, 26, 27, 37, 50–51
Michie, James, 59, 61, 62, 81–82, 86, 99, 100, 162, 211
Milosz, Czeslaw, 25
Milton, John, 198
Montague, Lady Mary Wortley, 198–99
mottos, xix
Moul, Victoria, 200
Mozart, W. A., 111, 189
Muldoon, Paul, 211
Munatius, 143
Muse *or* Muses, 30, 32–34
music, 25–27, 156–57, 196
Mussolini, Benito, 198

Nasidienus, 18
Naulochus, 125
Neaera, 138
Neobule, 19
Nero, Gaius Claudius, 178
Nero, Tiberius Claudius (father of Drusus), 139, 178
Neruda, Pablo, 60

Nisbet, Robin, v, xxi–xxii, 90, 95
Nisbet, Robin and Hubbard, Margaret, xxii, 51, 52, 57, 64
Nisbet, Robin and Rudd, Niall, 114–15
number of poems in *Odes* 1, 38–39

Octavia, 137
Octavian (Gaius Octavianus), 2, 3, 9, 22, 43, 54, 55, 57, 58, 118–19, 124, 129. *See also* Augustus
Ode, meaning of, 25–26, 29
Ofellus, 18
O'Hara, Edward, xviii
Oliensis, Ellen, 188–89
O'Neill (= Neumann), Jeanne, 148n1
Orbilius (L. Orbilius Pupillus), 2
Orion, 64
Orpheus, 64, 68–69
Ovid (Publius Ovidius Naso), 8, 32, 38, 115, 142, 159, 180, 191–92
Owen, Wilfred, 128

Pacuvius, 12
panegyric, 30, 154, 174, 178. *See also* praise poetry
"Parade Odes," 37, 197
Pasquali, Giorgio, 114, 134
Paul the Deacon, 195, 196
Paulinus of Nola, 142
Paullus Fabius Maximus, 157, 159, 160
Pelagian heresy, 195
Petrarch, 197
Petronius, 193
Philippi, 2, 54, 55–57, 139
Phyllis, 155, 163–64
Pindar, 27, 30, 37, 41, 128, 129, 156, 172, 177, 201
Pinsky, Robert, 211
Pirithous, 170–71
Plancus, Munatius, 36, 139
Plato, 142
Plautus, 6, 7
Pollio, Asinius, 11, 43, 78, 123–26, 142, 143
Pompeius, 54–58
Porphyrio, Pomponius, 127, 194
Postumus, 79–80

Pound, Ezra, 165, 190, 211
praise poetry, 29–30, 156, 172–73. See also panegyric
Prometheus, 64
Propertius, Sextus, 32, 36, 38, 38–39, 41, 85, 91, 95, 97, 104, 109, 125, 142, 162, 191
Prudentius (Aurelius Prudentius Clemens), 128, 194–95
pseudo-Acro, 85, 161, 194
Pulteney, William, xviii
Putnam, Michael, 69, 139, 154
Pym, Mrs. T. W., 210
Pyrrha, 95–98, 161

Quinctius, 143
Quinn, Kenneth, xxii, 52, 139, 154, 169
Quintilian, 184, 191, 193
Quintilius, 66–69, 209

Rayor, Diane, 105, 108
recusatio, 83–84
Regulus, Marcus Atilius, 130
Remus, 23
Res Gestae, 132, 153
Rist, John, xxn9
"Roman Odes," 127
Romulus, 23
Rossini, Gioachino, 141
Rostagno, Enrico, 197–98
Rudd, Niall, xxn9, 16, 17, 28, 187

Sabine estate, 3, 82, 100–102, 155, 162
Sallustius Crispus, 44, 78
Sapphic stanza, 27, 37, 39, 151, 192, 196, 199
Sappho, 27, 28, 30, 37, 41, 63–64, 74, 81, 93, 102, 104–5, 108, 117, 146–47, 156, 160
Satires, 3, 12–19, 38
Scaeva, 146
seasonal poems, 73, 164–71
Secular Games, 5. See also *Ludi saeculares*
Seneca the Younger, 4, 27, 85, 128, 192
Septimius, 155–56

Sestius, Lucius, 36, 169, 170
Sextus Pompey, 54, 125
Shakespeare, William, 42, 145
Simonides, 27
Sisson, C. H., 211
Smart, Christopher, 198
Sophocles, 189
Spartacus, 138
Statius, Publius Papinius, 192–93
Stesichorus, 27, 37
Stoicism, 143, 144
Stoppard, Tom, 210
Storrs, Sir Ronald, 198–99
Suetonius (Gaius Suetonius Tranquillus), xx, 1, 2, 4, 5, 140, 153, 161
Syme, Ronald, 12, 123

Tantalus, 64
Telephus, 163
temporality, 112–13, 161, 182
Tennyson, Alfred, xx, 199
Tennyson, Charles, 198
Terence, 2, 7, 196
Teutoburg Forest, 182
Thaliarchus, 73–74
Theseus, 170–71
Thomas, Richard, 154, 174
Thompson, Randall, 217
Tiberius (stepson of Augustus), 5, 139, 146, 153
Tiberius Claudius Nero. See Nero, Tiberius Claudius
Tibullus, 36, 38, 95, 98, 100, 160, 162
Tiresias, 18
titles of poems, 47, 194
Torquatus, Manlius, 144, 146, 170
Trollope, Anthony, 205
Tyndaris, 100–103, 163

unicus, meaning of, 139–40
University College, Toronto, xix
University of Toronto, xix

Varius (L. Varius Rufus), 3, 9, 11, 42, 142, 186
Venosa, 1–2

Venus, 106, 157
Verdi, Giuseppe, 189
Vergilius, 171
Virgil (Publius Vergilius Maro), 3, 8, 9,
    11, 22, 38, 64, 66–69, 112, 118, 143,
    186, 193–94, 195, 197
  Aeneid, 36, 62, 129, 142, 152, 165, 170, 178
  Eclogues, 11, 23, 38, 125
  Georgics, 11, 68–69, 142
Volusius, 8

Walpole, Sir Robert, xviii
Walter, Johann, 216
Warren, Rosanna, 211
wealth, denunciations of, xxii, 126, 134,
    144, 155

West, David, xxii, 33, 42, 49, 61, 80,
    88, 90, 104, 105, 109, 114, 128,
    163, 177
Wickham, E. C., 208
Widener Library, 217
Wilbur, Richard, 70, 211
Williams, Gordon, 110–11
wine, 45, 49–50, 52, 57, 80, 86,
    103, 144
  Caecuban, 121
  Lesbian, 102
  Mareotic, 121
  Massic, 57
  Sabine, 82
  semiotics of, 82
Wordsworth, Christopher, 207

Index of Passages

Avitus
1.228–29, 195
Catullus
34, 38
51.3–5, 108
51.6–12, 105
95, 8–9
Cicero
In Defense of Archias 23, 6
Dante
Inferno 4.86, 197
Heiric of Auxerre
Vita Sancti Germani 4.378–82, 195
5.369, 195

Homer
Odyssey 11.572–74, 64
Horace
Ars Poetica (= *Letter to the Pisos*)
47–48, 185
78, 194
128, 185
343, 187
348, xix
388, 186

438–44, 66
445–50, 186
448, xix
470–76, 188–89
Carmen saeculare
11–12, 197–98
Epistles
1.1.4, 143
1.1.10–11, 142
1.1.61, xviii
1.1.107–8, 143
1.2.40, xix
1.3, 146
    1.3.15–20, 143
    1.3.30–34, 143
1.4.16, 143
1.5.9–11, 146
1.5.16–20, 144
1.7.11–12, 145
1.7.25–28, 145
1.7.28–29, 93
1.7.28, 144, 158
1.7.34, 89, 145
1.8, 146
    1.8.17, 143

Horace (*Cont.*)
1.9, 146
1.10.12–14, 144
1.10.39–41, 144
1.11.9, 147
1.11.25–26, 144
1.13.17–18, 145
1.14.1, 144
1.14.33, 93, 144, 158
1.15.20–21, 93, 144
1.16.17–23, 143
1.17.23–32, 143
1.17.35, 146
1.18.107–10, 148
1.19.19–20, 146
1.19.21–34, 146–47
1.19.21–22, 28
1.19.23–25, 20
1.19.32–33, 191
1.20, 148–49
   1.20.11, 148
   1.20.17–18, 193
   1.20–28, 148–49
   1.20.24–25, xx
2.1.70, 2
2.1.132–38, 186
2.1.229–50, 186
2.1.248–50, 187
2.1.250–59, 186–87
2.2.45, 2
2.2.46, 56
2.2.49–52, 2
2.2.109–21, 185
2.2.122–23, 186
Epodes
1, 22, 119
2, 21
7, 23, 119
8, 21, 204
9, 22–23, 119
11, 93
   11.2, 93
12, 21, 204
   12.1, 20
13, 21
14, 31, 93
   14.1, 24

15, 93
16, 23, 119
Odes
1.1, 30, 36, 41, 42, 44, 45, 133, 200, 208, 213–14
   1.1.1–2, 29
   1.1.2, 89
   1.1.29–36, 28
   1.1.30–32, 191
   1.1.30, 38
   1.1.32–34, 32
   1.1.34, 26
   1.1.35–36, 201
1.2, 37, 41, 43, 119, 135
   1.2.21–24, 202
1.3, xxii
   1.3.8, 112, 210
1.4, 36, 113, 164–71
   1.4.1–2, 195
   1.4.1, 197
   1.4.15, 40
   1.4.17, 170
1.5, xviii, xxii, 36, 95–98, 113, 198–99, 213
   1.5.5, 185
   1.5.11, 40
   1.5.14, 36
1.6, 22, 30, 84
1.7.32, xix
1.9, xviii, 49, 71–74, 94, 113, 199
   1.9.1–4, 209
   1.9.1, 206
   1.9.15, 204
   1.9.16, 204
   1.9.21–24, 204
1.10, 37
1.11, 37, 41, 48–52, 201, 208–9
   1.11.7–8, 193
   1.11.8, 185
1.12 *to* 1.18, 37
1.12, xix, 30, 156
   1.12.45, xix
   1.12.49–52, 135
1.13, 41, 160
   1.13.1–4, 104
   1.13.17–20, 109, 216–17
1.17, 100–103, 163, 163–64

1.19, 105–7, 113, 119
   1.19.1, 157
1.20, 38, 45, 81–82, 86, 202
1.21 *and* 1.22, 38
1.22 *and* 1.23, 92
1.22, 107–8, 202
   1.22.10, 204
1.23, 113
   1.23.11, 159
1.24, 38, 66–69, 209
1.25, 113
1.26, 30
1.31.2, 145
1.32, 117
1.33, 30, 92, 98–100
1.34, 214–16
1.35, 119
1.37, xviii, 39, 43, 119–20, 120–23, 125, 201–2, 207, 214
1.38, 39, 42, 119
2.1, 39, 42, 43, 119–20, 123–26
   2.1.37, 32
2.3, 75–78
   2.3.25–26, 193
2.5, xxii, 112
2.6 *and* 2.7, 39–40
2.6.24, 155–56
2.7, 44, 53–58, 121, 126
   2.7.21, 44
2.9, 30, 135
2.10, 69–71, 86
   2.10.5, 36
2.11.21–24, 138
2.12, 44, 45, 82–86
2.13, 40, 58–65, 81, 213
   2.13.22, 193
2.14, 40, 78–81, 126
   2.14.25–28, 169
2.15, 126
2.16, 126
2.17, 44
   2.17.5–12, 112
   2.17.5, 210
   2.17.6–8, 210–11
   2.17.10, 79, 193
   2.17.27–30, 60
2.18, 126

2.19, 39
2.20, 39, 42, 44
3.1–3.6, 127–34
3.1, 39, 42, 128
   3.1.1–4, 127
   3.1.2–4, 186
   3.1.3, 33, 191
   3.1.48, 127, 134
3.2, 128
3.3, 42, 128–29
   3.3.18, 79
3.4.20, 33, 129–30
   3.4.27, 60
3.5, 130, 207
   3.5.34, 168
3.6, 40, 131–34, 173
   3.6.45–48, 80–81
   3.6.48, 127, 134
3.7, 40
3.8 *and* 3.9, 40
3.8, 44, 45
   3.8.6–8, 60
3.9–3.11, 92
3.9, 109–11
   3.9.15, 195
3.10, 104
3.11, 40, 113–15
3.12, 40
3.13, xviii, 30, 42–43
   3.13.13–16, 43
3.14, 136–40
   3.14.14–16, 44, 180
3.15, 113
   3.15.4, 159
3.16, 44, 45
3.25.3–6, 136
3.26–3.28, 92
3.26, 36, 100, 113
   3.26.4, 36
3.27, 115
3.28, 103–4, 163, 163–64
3.29, 44, 45, 86–89, 212
   3.29.49–50, 193
   3.29.54, 145
3.30, 36, 42, 45, 200
   3.30.1–5, 192
   3.30.13–14, 27, 102, 157

Horace (*Cont.*)
  3.30.14–16, 33
  4.1, 157–58, 158–61, 210
    4.1.1–8, 158
    4.1.1–2, 195
    4.1.3–4, 162–63
    4.1.3, 195
    4.1.5, 157
    4.1.21–24, 157
    4.1.29–32, 159–60
    4.1.33–40, 160
  4.2, 156, 213
    4.2.1–4, 172
    4.2.5–8, 177
    4.2.33–44, 172
    4.2.45–48, 173
  4.3.17–24, 34
  4.3.22–23, 155
  4.3.23, 26
  4.4, 5, 172, 174–78
    4.4.70, 79
  4.5, 172, 173, 174
    4.5.5 *and* 37, 195
    4.5.17–28, 155
    4.5.17–24, 173
    4.5.25–28, 180
    4.5.26–27, 182
  4.6, 163
    4.6.44, 156
  4.7, 154, 164–71, 198, 202, 209, 209–10
  4.8, 171, 187, 199
  4.9, 171, 199
    4.9.25–28, 171–72
  4.10, 154
  4.11, 155, 163–64
    4.11.13–20, 4
    4.11.31–36, 163–64
    4.11.35–36, xxi
  4.12, 155, 171
  4.13, 164
    4.13.17–28, 161–62
    4.13.18–20, 203
    4.13.18, 79
  4.14, 5, 164, 172
  4.15, 157, 164, 172, 173, 178–82
    4.15.4–24, 155
    4.15.30–32, 157

Satires
  1.1.1, 13, 29
  1.1.23–24, 13
  1.1.49–60, 16
  1.2, 204
    1.2.119–27, 92
  1.3.4, 119
  1.4.17–18, 16
  1.4.42, 14
  1.4.73–74, 188
  1.5, 29, 22
    1.5.82–85, 15, 93
    1.5.104, 14
  1.6.45–48, 2
  1.6.56–62, 3
  1.9.23–28, 17
  1.9.44–53, 17
  1.9.44, 16
  1.10.31–35, 9–10
  1.10.40–49, 10–11
  1.10.48–49, 13
  1.10.50–51, 13
  1.10.67–71, 14, 31
  1.10.73–74, 3, 16
  1.10.81–90, 3
  2.1.5, 18
  2.1.12–13, 119
  2.1.18–20, 22
  2.1.28–29, 18
  2.1.32–34, 15
  2.3.325, 92
  2.6.29–32, 18
  2.7.46, 93
  2.7.81–82, 18
  2.7.83, 19
  2.7.89–94, 19
Juvenal
  Satires 7.225–27, 193–94
Martial
  Epigr. 1.16, 31
  1.57, 193
Metellus of Tegernsee
  Quirinalia 4, 197
Ovid
  Amores 1.9.4, 159
  Metamorphoses 15.871–72, 191–92
  Tristia 4.10.49, 191

Petrarch
Epistulae familiares 24.10, 197
Petronius
Satyricon 118.5, 193
Propertius
1.1.2, 97
2.1.55–56, 109
2.15.17–18, 102
2.15.36, 109
2.15.44, 125
3.1.1–4, 191
3.10.29–32, 104
4.11, 115n19
Prudentius
Peristephanon 1.25 and 51, 195
3.87, 195
Quintilian
Inst. or. 10.1.96, 193
Sappho
31.2–5, 108
31.5–14, 105

"Brothers Poem," 74
Seneca
Epist. 58.22–23, 193
Epist. 114.4–8, 4
Epist. 114.4, 85
Thyestes 393–400, 192
Statius
Silvae 2.1.218–19, 192–93
Tibullus
1.1.55, 100
1.3.5, 160
1.3.51, 160
1.8.51, 160
Virgil
Aeneid 2.601, 194
6.851–53, 152
6.852, 178
12.330, 168
Eclogues 6.1–5, 10
Georgics 4.481–84, 64